Victoria's Victories

Victoria's Victories

by

Peter C. Smith

**Foreword by
David Chandler
Head, Department of War Studies, RMA Sandhurst**

**Seven Classic Battles of the British Army
1849-1884**

HIPPOCRENE BOOKS INC
New York

SPELLMOUNT LTD
Tunbridge Wells, Kent

In the Spellmount Military list:

The Uniforms of the British Yeomanry Forces
1794-1914 Series:
The Sussex Yeomanry
The North Somerset Yeomanry
The Yorkshire Hussars
Westmorland and Cumberland Yeomanry
3rd County of London (Sharpshooters)
Duke of Lancasters Own Yeomanry
Yorkshire Dragoons
Lovat Scouts

The Yeomanry Regiments—A pictorial history
Over the Rhine—The Last Days of War in Europe
Riflemen Form
History of the Cambridge University OTC
Yeoman Service
British Sieges of the Peninsular War
The Territorial Battalions—A pictorial history
The Scottish Regiments—A pictorial history
Intelligence Officer in the Peninsula
The Fighting Troops of the Austro-Hungarian Army

In the Nautical list:

Sea of Memories
*Evolution of Engineering in the Royal Navy Vol 1
1827-1939*

In the Aviation List:

Diary of a Bomb Aimer

First published in the UK in 1987 by
Spellmount Ltd,
12 Dene Way, Speldhurst,
Tunbridge Wells, Kent TN3 0NX
ISBN 0-946771-17-0 (UK)

First published in the USA in 1987 by
Hippocrene Books Inc,
171 Madison Avenue,
New York, NY10016
ISBN 0-87052-443-7 (USA)

British Library Cataloguing in Publication Data
Smith, Peter C. (Peter Charles), 1940-
Victoria's Victories: seven classic battles of the
British army 1849-1884.
1. Battles—History—19th century
2. Great Britain—History, Military—
19th century
I. Title
909.81   DA68

Designed by Military Archive & Research Services/G. Beehag
Figure artworks by Richard Scollins
Typeset by Staples Printers Rochester Limited, Love Lane, Rochester, Kent.
Printed and bound in Great Britain by Robert Hartnoll (1985) Limited, Bodmin, Cornwall.

Foreword

The final defeat of Napoleon at Waterloo on 18 June 1815 ushered in a 30 year period of comparative peace for the European powers. The position of Great Britain was particularly strong: her traditional foe, France, was humbled; Germany still disunited; Tsarist Russia internally troubled; the emerging United States in no way a rival. Furthermore, the economic benefits of the Industrial Revolution soon began to be felt once the post-war slump and period of unemployment and social unrest had been weathered. The Royal Navy hunted down slavers and protected Britain's wealth-earning commerce over the oceans of the world, and in particular the route around the Cape to India; while in the British Isles—although much poverty still remained and public health measures, factory and educational regulations were only slow in appearing—there was much pride amongst all classes of a deeply-riven society in what was dubbed the *Pax Britannica* overseas, and in the rapid developments in shipping and railways directed by the genius of men such as Kingdom Isambard Brunel at home. Britain's self-confidence grew apace throughout the reigns of George IV, William IV and then Queen Victoria. *The Times* said it all in the late 1860s when a bad gale forced the cross-Channel ferries to keep harbour: 'Continent Isolated'. How right, it must have seemed, to be born British.

But periods of so-called 'peace' can be deceptive. Perhaps the major powers avoided direct major confrontations with one another, but around the periphery of the globe the story was different. Just as there have been at least 210 classifiable wars in the Second and Third Worlds during the '42 year peace' since 1945 despite the pacific efforts of the United Nations, so there were no insignificant numbers of struggles and 'little wars' in the 1816-1914 period despite the well-intentioned efforts of the Congress System. There were colonial wars of liberation against Spain and Portugal in Central and South America; there were internal struggles of considerable seriousness within Spain (the Carlist Wars), within Italy (the *Risorgimento*), within Prussia, Austria and France (the Revolution of 1848—which almost spilt over into insular Britain in the form of the Chartist Movement), whilst Tsarist Russia had endemic problems with its serfs within and its neighbour Poland without.

Although there was no systematic attempt within Great Britain to study colonial warfare until as late as 1896—when Capt Charles Callwell RA, published his book: *Small Wars: Their Principles and Practice*—there was no shortage of 'little wars' to employ the services of the Victorian Army, and to provide the *mobile* with yellow-press distractions and rousing music-hall patriotic ditties. First, there were problems within the huge Indian sub-continent, reaching a terrible peak in the Indian Mutiny (1857-59), but preceded by no fewer than fourteen separate wars of conquest and pacification, of which the battle of Goojerat—sometimes spelt 'Gujrat'—in 1849 (during the second of three Sikh wars) stands as a representative example in this volume.

The Crimean War (1854-55) was a confused struggle fought out along the shores of the Black Sea and on the waters of the Baltic, involving Britain, France, Turkey and Piedmont against Russian ambitions, real and imagined, in the Balkans, the eastern Mediterranean and Afghanistan.

'We don't want to fight, but by jingo if we do,
We've got the men, we've got the ships, we've got the money too . . .'

sang the Victorian lower classes, reflecting Palmerston's stand, concluding:

'But Russia shall not have Constantino-o-ple.'

Neither did she then, nor to the present day. The storming of the Alma Heights by Lord Raglan and St Arnauld in September 1854 was the British Army's first major engagement since Waterloo 29 years before, and somehow it 'muddled through' to a moderate victory.

The Crimea, however, showed up the weaknesses of the Victorian Army's capacity to fight a large-scale war, and it was with relief that soldiers returned to colonial warfare once it was over. The Indian Mutiny apart, these proved relatively small in scale and successful in outcome—on the whole. In 1860 the so-called 'Opium War' was fought to compel China to grant advantageous trading terms to Britain in that, and other, valuable commodities, and the storming of the Taku Forts at the mouth of the Pei-Ho River was followed by a march to Peking, the plundering and burning of the Summer Palace, and the negotiation of a favourable peace that remained unbroken for 40 years.

Not all Queen Victoria's 'little wars' were dictated by considerations of commercial or territorial advantage. In 1868 General Napier's daunting march deep into Abyssinia to storm the mad, self-styled Emperor Theodore's fortress-sanctuary of Magdala on Easter Monday was inspired 'by no thirst for glory, by no lust of conquest' but for 'the sake of humanity' as Capt Hozier, a participant and writer of the first true British campaign history, described it. The rescue of some 60 European missionaries and their families, held hostage by Theodore, for minimal loss (except to the Indian Labour Force and the huge animal component) resulted in their safe rescue, the death of the tyrant by his own hand, and the destruction of Magdala. The British Army's post-Mutiny reputation was bolstered by this display of controlled force—which faced natural hazards as daunting as human ones—but it also led to an increase in income tax by one penny (to a terrible total of five pence in the pound) to meet the cost of the operation.

After Abyssinia there was much talk of avoiding any more such costly ventures, but it proved at best a pious hope. If the acquisition of the Second British Empire up to 1870 had been a somewhat haphazard and unwilling affair, once Victoria had been proclaimed Empress of India and the all-important Suez Canal had been opened, halving the journey-time by steamship between Southampton and Bombay, new colonial wars were not long in appearing. As the 'Race for Africa' developed (Germany and Belgium moving-in on the act) international rivalries began to grow. To safeguard Natal from Cetewayo's depredations, Lord Chelmsford marched via a disaster at Isandhlwana and a heroic episode at Rorke's Drift to seize the Zulu capital of Ulundi. Once again, superior weaponry triumphed over the superb courage and fighting-skills of the Zulu *impis,* and mid-Victorian England settled down to a complacent glow of self-satisfaction.

Not, however, for long. The short, sharp shock of the First Boer War (1880-81) was followed by the need to protect British Suez interests by the rapid and unusually efficient seizure of Egypt in 1882, during which Sir Garnet Wolseley (inspiration for W. S. Gilbert's 'very model of a modern Major-General' in *The Pirates of Penzance*) earned himself his peerage following his victory at Tel-el-Kebir at the culmination of a night-attack. It was all a very clean-cut affair, in marked contrast to Suez in 1956.

Two years later, and it was a *Jehad* or 'Holy War' raised by the fanatical Moslem leader known as the Mahdi deep in the Sudan that tested the martial mettle and political resolve of late-Victorian England. At Tamaii, General Sir Gerald Graham fought some 20,000 Mahdists with barely 4,000 troops—and accounted for over 2,000 of them for a loss of 214 casualties. 'Pity the hapless Hottentot; we have the gatling, he has not.'

Here Peter Smith ends his series of seven glimpses of the Victorian Army in action. Besides being required to provide for home defence, the Army was between 1849 and 1884 continually being called on to safeguard the route to India, beard tyrants in their dens, safeguard the interests (legitimate and occasionally otherwise) of British commercial aspirations, and generally keep (in the words of the Hymnal) '. . . the lesser breeds without the pale' in respectful subservience to the British Lion, the Union Jack, and (from 1871) to the Queen-Empress. Given the small size of the Victorian Army in overall terms, it never proved an easy task to provide the necessary expeditionary forces without risking the compromising of home defence, but it was done.

And, just as in 1982 the British populace turned out to cheer an expeditionary force on its way to the 20th century equivalent of a small colonial war—and even more to welcome back their fighting men from the Falklands as victorious heroes—the people rallied behind their red- and then khaki-coated soldiery as they rose triumphantly to meet each successive challenge. But within a generation of Tamaii, war would become almost unrecognisably different, as with the outbreak of the First World War Armageddon gripped the civilised world. Warfare had never been truly a romantic concept for those called upon to execute it; but peoples at home, insulated by distance and ignorance from reality, had often regarded it as such. But from 1914 that was to become an attitude of the past. The period of 'limited war' had ended. So had that of the *Pax Britannica.*

David G. Chandler
Head, Department of
War Studies,
R.M.A. Sandhurst.

14 February, 1987

Introduction

The 'little wars' of Queen Victoria's long reign are so numerous and diffuse that my sample selection could have been repeated many times over without duplicating any of them. In the end I have tried to draw a measured balance to show the many facets of this fascinating period, blending what I hope is an interesting and lively narrative with research which I hope will throw up a few new highlights. I have therefore made my book a steady progression through the decades and included a representative battle from most of them to reflect changes in thought, fighting equipment, methods and attitudes.

With this in mind I selected my campaigns and tried to spread them around the Empire. One could easily concentrate entirely on India for example, or Africa. Equally one could be diverted to more exotic locations such as South and Central America or Canada, but I felt that such little battles were not significant enough to include in this volume. Restricted by wordage limit to seven battles, they must be well-known but not necessarily world-shaking. Like any such collection therefore, such a selection will invariably please some and annoy others whose own particular favourite campaign or battle has been omitted.

The final key to my choice was that each battle had to be a British victory, be it an easy one such as Tel-el-Kebir, or a hard-won dogfight, like Goojerat. Over the years one has tended to become rather tired of gloating descriptions of British defeats and massacres, thus my choice of Ulundi instead of Isandlwana may come as a refreshing change to those whose admiration of the noble savage leads them into a sneering degradation of the fighting qualities of the British soldier. In this volume therefore the outcome of the fight, while often in doubt during the battle, is never in dispute by the end of it.

Peter C. Smith. Riseley, Bedford.

March, 1987

Chapter One

GOOJERAT

21 February 1849

SIKH POWER AND BRITISH RIPOSTE

It seems strange nowadays to state that the expansion of the British *Raj* throughout the whole of the Indian sub-continent was not always the result of a systematic step-by-step plan of ruthless annexation. And yet, as in other parts of the old Empire, British rule often took place *against* the wishes of the Government of the day and wars were fought with reluctance rather than eagerness. Most conflicts were not sought. Some were the result of a deliberate policy of aggression against British possessions by neighbouring states.

Today India and Pakistan are two separate nations, but 150 years ago they were a conglomerate of permanently feuding states, feudal in many aspects and fiercely independent. Although it may be argued that this provided an opportunity to 'divide and conquer' that aided the spread of British power, the numerous treaties and attempts to co-exist with the vagaries of the complex plottings of their despotic rulers and the machinations, often religiously inspired, of their politicians, made any consistent overall British policy most difficult to pursue, no matter what party might be in power at home. The defeat of the French at Pondicherry in 1793 and the abolition of the East India Company's monopoly in 1813 were but two steps in the

The closing stages of the battle of Goojerat. The British artillery, having gained the upper hand the infantry went in to finish off matters with the bayonet. They met fierce resistance in places before the Sikhs gave way.

long process of British hegemony, while from the strictly military viewpoint the reforms of the Company and Imperial armies in 1795 and the subsequent wholesale re-organisation in 1824 gave coherence to the Bengal Army and the Royal troops, both European and Native, in India. All these everts were ultimately to lead to the establishment of Queen Victoria as Empress of India. But that was a long way off when in 1847 our story commences and the young Victoria had been enthroned but a decade.

The most fierce and disciplined troops which the British Indian Army ever had to face were the Sikhs of the Punjab. The area they inhabited lay in the north-west of the Indian sub-continent, bordering on Afghanistan. The continual British attempts to thwart Russian dominance of the Afghans had already led to a series of military disasters that had lowered the British troops' hitherto invincible reputation in the eyes of the local population. In the 'Land of Five Rivers', the rivers concerned (the Sutlej, Beas, Ravi, Chenab and Jhelm) all rise in the Himalayas and flow into the Bay of Bengal joining up with each other as the Panjnad and then flowing into the mighty Indus below Multan and Jalapur at Mithenkote. Along the headwaters of these rivers lay the heart of the Sikh state. Its heartland lay in the great cities that centred on the holy shrine of the Golden Temple at Amritsar.

The consolidation of the Lahore state as then known, into a Sikh state, which was itself a religious rather than an ethnic nation, had been largely the work of one man, Ranjit Singh. Three races inhabited the area, the Afghans (or Pathans) being Islamic, while the Jats and Rajputs further south were divided between both the Hindu and the Islamic faiths. Although the majority of the Sikh sect, which was first founded in the late 15th century and revived in the early 19th century, were Jats, they were not universally so. Moreover the empire built up by Ranjit Singh did not tidily follow the pattern of the religious groupings, but took in non-Sikh areas of the Punjab, Kashmir and ever border areas of Afghanistan but excluding predominately Sikh Malwa.

While Sikh power and influence were steadily increasing, the British for their part had smashed the Mahrattas of central India in a series of campaigns, taken over Delhi, and extended their 'protection' over the Sikhs of Malwa. Most of these were not unhappy at this for they did not relish their former subservience, nor did they take kindly to the excesses of Ranjit Singh. Singh, a powerful militarist who exhausted himself by excessive debauchery, was intelligent enough to avoid direct conflict with the growing power of British India and even

Typical of the varied weapons carried by the Sikh infantry. Both in musketry and other small arms it was a mixture of old and new.

co-operated with it on occasions when it suited him. His successors changed that policy, not so much due to stupidity as for their own devious internal political motives, one of the principal of which was their own leaders' fear of the power of the Sikh military machine which Singh had raised to unprecedented heights.

Singh created not an Empire but a formidable fighting machine, and he spent most of his nation's wealth on his creation, building powerful forts, and purchasing the most modern equipment. He also bought in foreign expertise and officers, mainly French Napoleonic veterans such as Allard, Avitablile and Ventura, to train his soldiers to European standards. By the time of his death in 1839 he had succeeded in all these aims, beyond the wildest expectations of many British officials who thought it could not be done. Ever since the days of Clive, the British soldier had been expected to campaign against the most powerful of the Indian princes by fielding vastly inferior numbers in a hostile climate, but to overcome all obstacles by sheer grit. This they had done with remarkable consistency but, because they had achieved everything asked of them, and more, in the past, it was taken as an article of faith that no enemy,

During the battle of Aliwal the charge of the 16th (Queen's Own) Lancers proved decisive.

no matter how powerful or well-equipped, could ever hope to prevail against them in their well regimented formations. When the Sikhs finally crossed the Sutlej river at the start of the First Sikh War in December 1845 and entered British territory it came as a shock, not because the British armies lost any of the four bloody pitched battles fought at Mudki, Ferozeshah, Aliwal and Sobraon, but because of the heavy European casualties taken to obtain a quick ending of the war.

The fierce and bloody battle of Ferozeshah during the 1st Sikh war, one of Gough's 'butcher's bills'.

What was not generally known outside India was the organisation of the 60,000-strong Sikh army and its overwhelming preponderance of artillery, (which had been Ranjit Singh's military passion, both in numbers of pieces and their size). The sinister and cynical behind-the-scenes machinations that worked away to try to ensure that the Sikh army was defeated was of course also unknown but did not detract from the British soldier's magnificent achievement on the field of battle, although it was later said to have influenced the outcome at Ferozeshah.

The victor of this vicious little war had been sixty-five-year-old Sir Hugh Gough, an officer in the grand old style. He was a 'Soldier's General' as much loved by his men as he was criticised by his fellow officers. On the second day of the battle of Ferozeshah he had been so concerned at the terrible casualties being inflicted upon his troops by the heavy Sikh guns that, dressed conspicuously in his white fighting coat and accompanied only by a solitary *aide-de-camp*, he rode out to the flank and remained stock-still attracting shot-and-shell away from his men. After the battle at Chillianwalla when officers approached him for requests to go for water, he replied with some force, ' "I'll be damned if I move till my wounded are all safe!" '. Such a man could do no wrong with the men, no matter what degree of carnage on the battlefield itself.

A recent description of Gough as a leader represents the modern view that he was, '. . . impetuous, hardy and very brave; but his orders were seldom clear and his staff had a genial habit of not only keeping no record of the instructions they were issued, but frequently forgetting what they were. Gough's battles tended to be gallant but somewhat muddled affairs . . .'.

Like many successful British army leaders Gough was an Irishman, brave, but unimaginative and lacking in subtleties of military technique. He had an overwhelming (and, as was demonstrated on numerous occasions) totally justified belief in his men. He led from the front, was honest and straightforward and was totally fearless in combat. 'Get stuck in' would probably be an accurate summary of his philosophy of war and he had the usual British *penchant* for the shock of the charge and close work with butt and bayonet. Typical of this is the following anecdote, probably apocryphal, but widely told and certainly in keeping with the man.

At the battle of Sobraon in 1846, when the British artillery fire was slackening through lack of ammunition and it became clear that the issue must be decided once again by the foot soldiers, the word spread down the British line that, '. . . old Gough had been told that there were only four more rounds left per gun, and says "Thank God! then I'll be at them with the bayonet"'. General Sir Robert Napier described Gough as '. . . a glorious old fellow, brave as *ten* lions, each with two sets of teeth and two tails'. Certainly Gough scorned death and it passed him by, for he lived until he was ninety and died a much decorated Field-Marshal.

Whatever Gough's merits, or failings he won his battles, resolutely beating the most formidable and disciplined native army in India on the battlefield and bringing the First Sikh War to an abrupt conclusion. However Britain won the war but lost the peace. The Sikh army had audaciously taken on the British and had been resoundingly beaten. Why were they able to repeat the process within a few years? The British had quickly broken the power of a dangerous state but had no desire to take it over. Within a short while they were at war with that state once more.

Napier saw the renewed conflict coming even as the celebrations were in hand to mark the victory, writing at that time, 'This tragedy must be re-enacted a year or two hence: we shall have another war'. Others were not so accurate in their deductions, Henry Havelock confidently predicting that: 'It remains to be seen whether the army can be so remodelled as to cease to be dangerous to its own master and mistress. It will hardly attempt anything against us.' But it was Napier who was proved absolutely right. Why was this?

The Governor-General of India, Lord Hardinge, had spelt out the British attitude to the war, and its conclusion, in a speech made at Lahore on the occasion of its occupation in the aftermath of the first conflict.

'The British army, suddenly compelled to assume the defensive by the unprovoked invasion of its territory, has in sixty days defeated the Sikh forces in four general actions, captured 220 pieces of field artillery, and is now in the capital dictating terms of a treaty which shall

The 'Soldier's General', Sir Hugh Gough, GCB, C-in-C of Her Majesty's army in India. Brave and dogged, he trusted his men to do anything he asked of them.

secure the British provinces from a repetition of similar outrage.' Hardinge also announced that the Punjab would not be relinquished until 'ample atonement' for the insults offered by the unprovoked invasion had been made. An area between the rivers Beas and Sutlej, the Jullundur Doab, was to be annexed and an indemnity of £1,500,000 exacted. The Treaty of Lahore was signed on 8 March by the Maharajah Gholab Singh, Lal Singh, Ram Singh, Tej Singh, and the keeper of the purse strings, Dina Nath. The vicious and spiteful Rani Jinda kept her hatred of the British festering in the background, while the boy Maharajah, Dhulip Singh, who had been educated in England, was presented to the victors.

However the Maharajah's coffers were empty and only a third of the indemnity could be a paid, so Hardinge took the province of Kashmir in lieu of the money. The British found Kashmir indefensible so they sold it to the wily Ghulab Singh for £1,000,000 but retained suzerainty. The army of the Khalsa was ordered to be reduced to 20,000 infantry and 12,000 cavalry and the surrender of the all-important artillery, some 250 guns, was also insisted upon. A Council of Regency was set up, composed of a few of the leading Sirdars and a British agent, Major Henry Lawrence, was appointed. Because the council announced it could not control the Khalsa without help it was agreed that a British force should remain until the end of the year only.

Hardinge impressed on Lawrence the fact that plotting would commence among those at the Durbar and that he must maintain military vigilance. Nonetheless he insisted that Lawrence do everything possible, '. . . to ensure the success of this trial of re-establishing a Sikh Government, which may eventually carry on its functions without British aid or British interference'. He added, '. . . the Government is determined not to lend itself to any subsidiary system, and as soon as its troops are withdrawn will decline to interfere in the internal affairs of the Sikh State'.

Despite these avowed intentions, the Sirdars refused to allow the British to leave when the deadline came, asking for the garrison to remain. The discharged troops of the Khasla maintained they had not been beaten 'fairly', that they were still a match for the British and that the first war would not be the last. Many had realised their limitations but in such a well-drilled and proud force the bitter taste of defeat quickly turned to thoughts of revenge and many only awaited the opportunity to take up arms again. Nor was the rump Khasla inclined to view diminished influence with much favour, especially as it knew the Regency was both scared of it and divided among itself

Hardinge agreed to leave a 10,000 man garrison at Lahore for a further year which Gough, among others, viewed with dismay, predicting another Kabul massacre. Meanwhile Lal Singh's part in plotting of the war had been unmasked and he was banished, which met with the approval of the Sirdars but not the Rani, whose favourite he was. She made vain attempts to have herself proclaimed Regent until the young Maharajah came of age but the fifty-two Sirdars unanimously requested that a British Protectorate be established until the boy reached maturity. Eventually this was agreed and in December, 1846, the Treaty of Bhyrowal confirmed it.

In the so-called Preyma plot the Rani was soon discovered scheming the assassination of Tej Singh and Lawrence. Correspondence linking the plot with the Governor of Mooltan, Dewan Moolraj was also discovered. As a result, in August 1847, the Rani was exiled to Sheikapore, only twenty miles from the young Maharajah. Lawrence wanted her removed from the Punjab altogether, which, as events turned out, would have been wise. As it was she continued to scheme until the unearthing, in May 1848 of yet another intrigue, this time involving Sepoys at Lahore and this finally saw her kicked out, first to Ferozepore and then Benares.

Gholab Singh and his son inspect their personal bodyguard. The rulers of the Sikh state were as much the victims of the army they had created as its controllers.

Goojerat

But though she had gone her maleficent influence lived on and the seeds of discord she had diligently been sowing eventually bore fruit.

Meanwhle both Lawrence and the Governor-General were replaced by new men, Sir Frederick Currie and Lord Dalhousie. Their predecessors had wide knowledge of the Sikhs together with the many complexities involved and both had established sympathetic relationships which had smoothed over numerous problems during a difficult period. Their successors, no matter how well-meaning, could not establish the same rapport quickly and meantime the cauldron was simmering. Lawrence himself recalled that, '. . . the people had not lost their spirit; and so fickle were they, so easily led by their party, so filled with pride of race and of their old triumphs, that it would be the extreme of infatuation to believe in their satisfaction with their present state, or in their not chaffing at our victory and their own loss of power'.

In other words the Khalsa needed close watching even though, as the Queen had acknowledged in a speech to Parliament, only 'perfect tranquility' was apparent on the surface in India. Sir George McMunn described this experiment as an '. . . attempt to bolster up the Sikh State' which was '. . . doomed to failure. The Sikhs had not yet made up their minds to accept even British domination'. It needed a malcontent to provide the spark and the rallying point, and, thanks to the Rani's long plotting, that person soon revealed himself in the form of Dewan Moolraj.

Early in 1848 he announced his wish to retire from public life as he was tired of attempting to raise taxes for the Lahore government. After considerable negotiations his resignation was accepted and he was asked to prepare a statement of accounts for his successor, Khan Singh. The latter was sent to Mooltan with an escort of 1,400 Sikhs, a regiment of Gurkhas, 700 cavalry and six guns. He was also accompanied by two English *aides*, Vans Agnew, a civil servant, and Lt Anderson. The whole party arrived at Mooltan on 18 April and were received by the Moolraj, but, after talks he revealed the whole episode as an elaborate trap. His soldiers attacked and wounded Vans Agnew and Anderson and they and Khan Singh only owed their salvation to the Gurkhas. Agnew sent off an urgent despatch describing the treacherous attack. Meanwhile the Moolraj, having persuaded the Sikhs from the British force to desert to him, raised the flag of revolt over the fortress and had Khan Singh seized and the two Englishmen murdered by the mob. Defiantly the Moolraj also despatched riders to instigate a general Sikh

Lord Dalhousie took over the task of overseeing the transition from peace to war with the Sikh nation, but did not fully understand the complexities below the surface.

uprising against the British. In most areas the festering resentment needed no second bidding and soon the general revolt was in progress.

However in May, before the rising became fully apparent, General Gough, still Commander-in-Chief, counselled caution in any precipitate action by British troops in conjunction with Sikh forces, who might at any time go over to the enemy. The appearance of a British force might also help spread the revolt rather than quell it. Finally it was also the hottest part of the year and not suitable for European troops to go on campaign. Both Lord Dalhousie and Sir Frederick Currie agreed. The Governor-General announced on 11 May that:

' "However imminent may be the risk, that, if the British troops do not now move, insurrection, apparently successful for a time at Multan, may extend its influence over the Punjab, and may cause disturbance and revolt throughout its bounds, we yet think that the dangers which would thence arise to British interests in India, are far less than those which would be created by our being compelled to discontinue operations, once begun, before they had been brought to a satisfactory termination; and by the fearful loss among the troops which is anticipated as the consequence of entering on military operations on the scale required in such a district as Multan, at such a season of the year as this." '

Meanwhile a small force under Lt (later Sir Herbert) Edwardes fought two containment battles to keep the

Moolraj bottled up in the fort, which was being strengthened against the anticipated forces of retribution. On 5 September Edwardes's force was joined by General Whish (with Major Charles Napier as his engineering officer) and the siege began in earnest but before it was many days old there was further treachery when Shere Singh deserted, taking with him his force of almost one thousand infantry and 3,400 cavalry. This followed abortive plans to fall on the rear of the British force while pretending to co-operate in the attack which fell through, as did an attempt to seize the British officers by *coup de main* during an evening dinner.

Whish, with a quarter of his force gone and his opponent thereby reinforced, had little option but to fall back on prepared defensive positions at Ram Teerut, Sooruj Khoond and Tibbee and await further reinforcements before resuming the siege. On his part Shere Singh remained only a short time at Mooltan, his relations with the Moolraj not being the most cordial. Instead, on 9 October, he took his force north, gathering ex-soldiers in his wake, to where his father Chutter Singh was already raising the whole Sikh nation under the banner of the regenerated Khalsa. The war had now become widespread and the Governor-General acknowledged this fact with a stern warning of the consequences:

'Unwarned by precedents, uninfluenced by example, the Sikh nation has called for war, and on my word, sirs, they shall have it with a vengeance.'

THE WAR

The flame of war was soon spreading. The most exposed positions were near the Afghan foothills, at Peshawar on the North-West Frontier, which contained a large number of Sikh soldiers under the old Governor, another Gholab Singh. Also there was Major George Lawrence, the British representative. At Kohat, to the south of Peshawar, lay yet more Sikhs led by the Mussulman Governor Sultan Dost Mohammed. He was not to be trusted, despite loud protestations of loyalty and there was no British representative there to watch him.

Across the Indus in the Hazara district the Governor was Chutter Singh and in August he ordered out the troops at Hurripore, and when their American commander, Colonel Canora, tried to prevent this without orders from the British representative, Major James Abbott, the Colonel was murdered. Abbott however rallied the local troops with whom he had good relations. Meanwhile a force under John Nicholson was despatched by Lawrence to secure Attok to their rear

on the route to Rawalpindi. Both men repeatedly called for reinforcements from Lahore but none were forthcoming. Nicholson was soon replaced by Lt Herbert with a garrison of Mussulmen and reinforced by Major Abbott's Hazara tribesmen.

For a short time the local British initiative seemed outwardly to have checked Chutter Singh's ambitions, but though he continued to protest his loyalty, at the same time he was secretly urging his son at Mooltan, the new ruler of Kashmir, together with the Governor at Kohat, the troops at Peshawar and the Afghan Amir in Kabul to join the revolt against the British. His conspiracy with his son with the troops at Peshawar and also with the crafty and influential Mohammed had the desired effect and when, in October, the British officers at Peshawar had to leave hastily with news that the troops were going over, and sought refuge in Kohat, Mohammed too showed his true colours and handed them over as prisoners to Chutter Singh.

Yet further reverses took place as the months passed. During November the revolt spread further with Shere Singh gathering Khalsa soldiers to his banner. Futteh Khan was killed when the Bunnoo regiments went over and most of north-west Punjab followed. Ram Singh in Nurpur also rose but John Lawrence somehow persuaded Sikh troops still loyal to nip this rising in the bud. But Attok was placed under siege by the Sikhs, now reinforced by Dost Mohammed's forces, and the garrison urged Herbert to surrender, which was finally done on 3 January 1849, when Herbert himself was taken prisoner.

In Lahore and neighbouring Amritsar tension was also high. Despite repeated warnings Sir Frederick Currie was reluctant to believe in the treachery of Chutter Singh but by October proof had been found of widespread plotting and several leading members of the Durbar were arrested. At the fort of Govindguhr the Sikh garrison was mounting eighteen heavy guns and burying thirty more in readiness for the right time to join in the rising, but a ploy enabled them to be evicted by loyal Sepoys before their plotting came to fruition.

Only Lehna Singh of the Sirdars at Manjha, could be relied upon. Lahore itself was soon threatened by Shere Singh's growing horde marching up the Chenab, his scouting cavalry reaching the river Ravi by the end of October. The whole force joined with the Bunnoos before falling back on Ramnuggur as news of the advance of the main British force became known.

At Mooltan things remained in stalemate with the Moolraj reiterating his loyalty while at the same time trying to enlist the support of the Afghans and Pathans

Goojerat

and all the time refusing to obey the commands and orders of the Durbar. The British slowly drew up their plans. Lord Gough wished to crush the main Sikh armies in the north with an overwhelming force but Mooltan could not be ignored. To enable this to be done it was left to the Bombay Brigade to come up as reinforcements for Whish's little army while the Commander-in-Chief himself concentrated on assembling his forces in readiness to cross the Sutlej and starve out Lahore. Between 16 September, when Whish had withdrawn, and 16 November when Gough's force reached the Ravi from Ferozepore, what little fighting there was was concentrated on the siege in the south.

Whish and Edwardes were on the defensive, throwing up earthworks to defend the vital lines of communication from Bhawalore in the south and from the Rajghat ferry in the west. The aggressive stance of the Moolraj's forces and the slow advance of the Bombay column (two British and five native infantry regiments, three cavalry regiments plus artillery under the command of Brigadier Dundas) caused concern. This was further compounded by desertions from his force, such as that of the Hindustani regiment Katar Mukhi on 6 November

The great bulk of the British army was made up of Sepoy regiments, trained, armed and uniformed in their own image by the British.

Once the Sikh's declared themselves eager for another trial of strength, General Gough quickly marched north to give them 'war with a vengeance!'

which forced him to fight some short sharp actions.

On the 7th, bolstered by this fresh defection to their cause the Sikh garrison made a probe in force against the left flank of the British defence, held by Edwardes. The attackers were held and driven back with some loss and Whish completed their discomforture by outflanking them on the right and capturing three guns in the process.

Meanwhile Gough's main force was advancing on Shere Singh's army positioned on the west bank of the Chenab. Here the Sikh had Goojerat to his right flank. He protected his line of retreat northward toward the Jhelum River by covering the ford at Ramnugger. To his front the way lay open to Lahore if the British could be defeated. It was a strong position.

On 22 November Gough made a reconnaissance in force to probe the enemy's outposts on the southern side of the river and gauge their strength. His probe by light artillery and the 1st Light Dragoons was met by intense and prolonged artillery fire from the excited Sikhs and by the deployment across the river of large bands of their own cavalry. They expected a major attack and were obviously eager to become engaged but Gough stuck to his plan. The Sikh mounted men continued to flood across the river in large numbers and Brigadier White, in order to prevent his own advance cavalry being cut off, was forced to commit more and more aggressive

tactics resulting in a charge. Further confusion followed, which led to a second cavalry charge by the 14th Light Dragoons and the 5th Light Cavalry which resulted in Lt-Col Havelock and fifty troopers being cut down when they became enmeshed in sandy soil of the river bed which was unsuitable for horses. Brigadier Cureton himself was killed trying to prevent the charge from taking place.

It was obvious that the army could not attack across the river at this place against such a powerful and well-entrenched position so while the artillery kept up a constant bombardment during 1 and 2 December, a powerful detachment was despatched under Sir Joseph Thackwell of the 3rd Division. It consisted of two British and five Native Infantry regiments, a mixed Cavalry Brigade, two heavy and thirty field guns. It made a night march up the right bank of the Chenab to seek an alternative crossing and take Shere Singh on the flank. Fords at Hence Runniki and Ali-Sher-ki-Chuk were found unsuitable but the whole force eventually crossed at Wazirabad on the night of the 1/2 December.

The expected battle hardly took place as Thackwell, instead of using his own initiative as ordered, contented himself with merely holding forward positions at Sadulapore to cover the Ghurriki ford where further reinforcements were expected to cross. Shere Singh discovered the British force had crossed and immediately marched out of his defensive positions with the bulk of his troops in the hope he could wipe out the British piecemeal. Unfortunately for him and luckily for the British his troops, once they had left the shelter of the sugar cane fields, showed considerable reluctance to advance across open country and contented themselves with a long bombardment, which caused only light casualties and achieved nothing.

However during the hours of darkness the Sikh army took the opportunity to slip away and by the time it was discovered that the strong entrenchments had been abandoned it was too late to follow up with any hope of catching them. Early in December Shere Singh fell back to the Jhelum River where he had very strong defensive positions awaiting him between the jungle around Chillianwalla in the west, the hills at Rusool in the north and with the river at his back. Here he entrenched himself in an arc of defences that ran in a crescent through a series of villages on the Jhelum's right bank, from Lucpnewalla in the south through to Rusool itself. However in abandoning the fertile lands on the Chenab for the jungles of Chillianwalla he had created a foraging problem for his army and in permitting the easy crossing of the Chenab he had forfeited the potential

The Sikh army held a strong position at Ramnugger but failed to take advantage of British errors. Here General Cureton is killed trying to stop a cavalry charge.

to inflict considerable casualties on the British. This force now advanced east from Dinghi on 13 January and arrived before the Sikh positions after an exhausting march through the jungle at midday.

There was considerable speculation as to why Gough chose to press his attack against such a strong position, or even to approach it, when his declared intention and the reason for so much delay had been to wait until he had been reinforced and was able to deliver a decisive blow. A note in the General's diary for 9 January read: ' "Heard from G.G. that he would be glad if I gained a victory" '. Being a politician the Governor-General (what else would GG stand for?) was probably influenced by the steadily deteriorating position elsewhere. He put pressure on Gough to press his attack.

The old General himself, never really doubting his beloved troops could do *anything* , and bolstered by the fact that he had lost very few men crossing the Chenab when he expected to lose many, may have become over-confident. His enemy had his back to the river. Gough had him cornered and did not wish to let him slip away again. The sound of the enemy guns, many believed, proved irresistible to the old warhorse and he could not help but attack. Mrs. Armytage gave the polite contemporary assessment thus:

' "He had been led to fight the battle of Chillianwalla by the attacks of the Sikhs on his camp. The battle of Chillianwalla was fought under disadvantageous circumstances, for Lord Gough had no intention of risking a general engagement late in the afternoon with troops weary after a long march, but Shere Singh opened fire and thus began the action." '

But of course that will not do. If Shere Singh did open fire, was there any need for the engagement to become general at that time? Initially, it appears, Gough fully intended to camp and take up the battle in the morning after probing the defences. However the Sikh guns commenced firing, thus giving away their positions early. Moreover by moving out from the strongly fortified villages the impulsive enemy were again seemingly throwing away a trump card and not many generals, of Gough's temperament or not, would have cared to refuse such a temptation to crack so powerful an enemy force while they were out in the open. Criticism later would have been far more harsh had he *refused* battle in such circumstances.

British and Sikh guns exchanged fierce cannonades for about an hour, with the former, for once outnumbering the latter, which however were well placed and concealed. Then, at 15:00 a general advance by the British against the six-mile wide Sikh front began with cavalry on both flanks. The field artillery also advanced in line but due to confusing orders their fire, although deadly and valuable, was not directed in support of the infantry to which they had been assigned.

Moreover Sir Colin Campbell, who had taken over command of the infantry had split the command of the two brigades between Brigadiers Hoggan and Pennycuick. After the initial open area the advance continued through thick bush and trees and the two brigades lost touch with each other. Pennycuick's force was met by both round and grape shot at close range from an unseen enemy whose raking fire decimated regiments such as the 24th in the centre of the attack. Worse, once clear of the trees, the survivors were brought to a halt under the very muzzles of the Sikh guns by an area of swamp which they could not penetrate. They thus had to be turned and redirected and while this was happening were swept by grape again and again. The survivors then gallantly charged the guns which they took but losses were fearsome, including Colonel Brookes, Major Harris, Capt Trevers, two colour bearers, Lts Colis and Phillips, three other lieutenants and 231 troopers with 266 more wounded. Cut to ribbons as they were they could not hold the

Like the Sepoy infantry, most of the British cavalry comprised regiments of Indian irregular units. Note the inclusion of some camels.

positions they had so bravely taken and withdrew, causing their flanking regiments, the 25th and 45th Native Infantry to fall back also. The former lost 6 officers and 105 men killed and the latter 20 men killed alone.

On the left Hoggan's Brigade, with Campbell himself leading, and very well supported by Major Mowatt's No5 Battery, broke clear and smashed into the Sikh cavalry with the 61st doing great execution among them and capturing two guns in the process. The 46th also repulsed heavy Sikh cavalry attacks on the left of the line and withstood artillery and infantry assaults while rolling up the enemy line with some aplomb in a hot, close-range action.

Meanwhile the various cavalry formations had come to grief in the totally unsuitable jungle conditions and were unable to make any headway save for the 3rd Light Dragoons which broke through the enemy line and vanished from sight. Cavalry losses were severe and by the time they had fought their way out again the battle was for all intents and purposes over. Worse still, over on the right flank a misdirected 'canter' by Brigadier Pope's nine squadrons of Dragoons, advancing without support and across the muzzles of their own guns, was turned into a shameful, panic-stricken rout. The Sikhs

followed this up with *élan*, overrunning the exposed guns of Major Christie's batteries and capturing four of them.

The 2nd Brigade under Brigadier Godby had charged to their front with success but were then surrounded by the enemy in front of Lullianee village and had to cut their way out of the trap. The same fate befell Brigadier Penny's 3rd Brigade. At the end of a hard day's fighting the Sikhs had been forced back to the river at Tupai but the exhausted British were unable to follow up in the darkness and themselves withdrew back to Chillianwalla. In all the British casualties amounted to 2,338 killed and wounded. Three regimental colours, four guns and many horses and waggons were lost, leaving aside the shame of the panic in the face of the enemy.

Gough had pinned down his enemy on the river as planned but darkness prevented the killer blow. Three days of torrential rain followed which denied him his last chance to finish the job there and then. In the fortunate breathing space thus afforded to it, the Sikh army was able to reposition itself on the much stronger position of Russool and there it was joined by powerful reinforcements with the arrival of Chutter Singh. Their initial demoralisation was thus quickly turned into relative euphoria and their spirit was unbroken. The chance of a quick victory had gone for Gough who was left to face the music for the resultant butcher's bill, which horrified Queen Victoria when the news reached London, as it did Parliament and the nation. At home they naturally lacked all the facts and merely saw it as another example of Gough's misuse of men. Nor was it encouraging (nor fair) that the immediate response at home was to appoint Sir Charles Napier as the new Commander-in-Chief to supersede him.

It is little wonder then that Gough now reverted to his old strategy of sitting tight and awaiting his reinforcements from Mooltan before finally making a conclusion with the enemy. Despite lures to attack the strong positions at Russool and elsewhere he contented himself with a waiting game and eventually it was Shere Singh who tired first and moved back to Goojerat on 14 February where he prepared new defences. Gough followed him in a series of quick short marches in battle order until he reached Shadjwal where, on 20 February, he was at last joined by the Mooltan column.

As Mooltan was considered a very powerful fortress most of Napier's engineering officers were concentrated

Treachery at Mooltan led to the defection of a large part of the British army over to the enemy. The siege delayed Gough's final meeting with the main Sikh force.

there and during December Colonel Cheape, Chief Engineer, carried out detailed reconnaissance missions which resulted in the scrapping of plans to attack the north-east angle of the fort and instead to start with the southern end at the Khoonee Boorj. But the attack itself had to be postponed until the Bombay Garrison joined them, which it finally did between 10 and 21 December.

The besiegers now had a total of 67 siege guns and thirty field pieces with which to reduce the fortress but there followed further consultations on how to go about it. After much discussion, by Dundas and Major Scott on one hand, and Whish and Cheape on the other, Colonel Cheape's plans were abandoned. Napier's plan to assault the north-eastern angle of the fort was finally put into effect from the 27th onward. On 28 December a strong sortie by the Sikhs was repulsed and the batteries continued to pound away. On the 30th the main magazine was penetrated and exploded and breaches appeared in the walls. Attacks were launched on 2 January and the city taken.

There remained only the citadel itself, containing the Moolraj and 4,000 picked men. The rest of his force he callously discarded outside the gates and left them to their fate. Slow, sapping work continued, despite a sortie by the Sikh garrison to prevent it, and by the 21 January all was ready for the final assault. But already the battered and worn defenders had had enough and gave their leader the choice of leading them in a final desperate sortie to gain freedom or surrender. The Moolraj chose

It took some time before a sufficient force was assembled, and the diverse schemes agreed upon, before Mooltan was finally stormed and taken by the British.

the latter and emerged with the countenance of the victor not the defeated. He was put on trial, found guilty of the murder of the two British officials, and imprisoned.

The two British columns then began their march north to join Gough the Bengal troops departing Mooltan on the 27 January and the Bombay troops following four days after. A month later they stood with the Commander-in-Chief before Goojerat city ready for the final battle.

THE ARMIES

As related earlier the Sikh army relied heavily on foreign officers, mainly French, for its training, so much so that orders in French were still being given long after this *émeute* had become distant history. The two Frenchmen who exerted the greatest influence were Jean Baptiste Ventura and Jean François Allard experienced colonels in Napoleon's army who had arrived in Lahore in 1822. They laid out drill books translated from the original French for both infantry and cavalry formations and applied them with great severity. A Hungarian, Dr Martin Honigberger, was placed in charge of the gun foundry and powder mills at Lahore and another Frenchman, Henri Court, trained the Sikh gunners to be highly skilful. Again all orders were given in French. The particular passion of Ranjit Singh for guns was reflected in his army and although many of their best weapons had been confiscated after the first war, enough large cannon and field pieces could still be found to outgun the British at the start of the second. Moreover many of the veteran gunners and gunlayers re-enlisted. The French origins reflected the size of the guns, mainly 12pdrs and 18pdrs in the Continental style, and gun-for-gun they had a better range and were heavier than their British counterparts. There were also a number of exceptionally large pieces and conversely many camel-mounted swivels or *zamburuks*. Artillerymen wore black coats and white trousers with black leather crossbelts and powder pouches. Hew Strachan concludes that, '. . . the weight and disposition of the Sikh guns was a powerful incentive in British reform of her own artillery'. However at Goojerat for perhaps the first time, Gough assembled enough guns to outclass his opponent's principal arm.

'The infantry were well equipped with standard flint-lock muskets, similar in most respects to the British 'Brown Bess' having replaced the earlier matchlocks. Extensive copying of British designs extended right across the spectrum from pistols to artillery carriages and were made in specially built arsenals, often by workers hired from British depots in Delhi. They wore

The pride of the Sikh army was her guns and gunners. In fact they were superior to the British in size and numbers. Here are two captured field pieces on exhibition at Windsor after the war.

uniforms of scarlet *kurtis* or jackets with white crossbands with distinctive facings and blue trousers. Some wore turbans but Gurkha regiments of which there were several, featured the standard European Shako and the now-famous green tunics. The foot soldiers were organised in the French style of brigades of three or four battalions with accompanying artillery and cavalry.

Their drill was pure Napoleonic, using the standard forms of column formation, deployed order and skirmishers, with the time beaten out on the drum and moves signalled by trumpets as in Europe. Although few of these foreign officers (*feringhees*) were still serving by the time of Goojerat, their influence lived on. But much of the strict discipline they had originally imposed had been watered down due to the natives' natural disinclination for regimentation. As with the artillery, although a fearful slaughter had reduced their numbers in the four battles of the first war, tens of thousands of veterans joined the revolt and brought their skills back into the army of the Khalsa.

In addition to these regular formations there were, as is usual in Eastern armies, a large number of irregular troops equipped with everything from scimitars and shields to matchlocks and daggers and dressed in both rags or armour. Outstanding among these, because of their fanaticism, were the *Akalis*, a few thousand strong, wild and headstrong and totally fearless. Their dress was merely a turban, loin-cloth or shorts and long blue shirt, while the two-handed sword, wielded at close range, was their principal weapon.

The most famous of the irregular cavalry were the proud and independent *Shorchurra*. They supplied their

Ranjit Singh had worshipped the heavy gun and lavished much wealth and attention upon this arm. Some of the super-heavy pieces required specially trained elephants to move them into battle.

own horses and uniforms, which were lavish. They were a useful force but they could never be persuaded as to the merits, or rigours, of conventional tactics. Regular cavalry were also raised, once more in the French style. They were dressed dragoon fashion, save for their crimson turbans, with crimson jackets and dark blue, red-striped trousers. They were equipped with carbines and pistols in addition to their sabres. By the time of Goojerat however the bulk of the Sikh horsemen were mounted Afghans from the foothills beyond Pershawar.

The movement away from the European regime of tight control to the more normal relaxed eastern attitude was aided by a peculiar feature of the Sikh army. This was its very special constitution, a democracy inside an autocracy in fact. For in addition to the normal military organisation of officers, non-commissioned officers and men, there was another system, the *Panchayet*. These were cadres of five men who represented their battalions or regiments and who were chosen by the free expression of the soldiers themselves. These groups would consult freely on the men's needs, troubles or requirements. But more, the *Panchayets* could openly, and quite legally, make the men's views known to their officers. Indeed, in time, they began to dictate to their own officers and this later was to extend to their taking on the mantle of the voice of the Khalsa in arms and giving orders to the very Durbar itself! Thus the army became more identified with the Khalsa or state than did the actual

rulers and, although they did not initially flex their muscles, no Sikh Sirdar ever discounted the army in any of his calculations. With its backing success was assured, without it, doubtful indeed.

Both these extensions of the army's power had grown to extremes by the 1840's. It was the power of the army that had placed Hira Singh in power and then threatened him. It was the manifestation of the *Panchayets'* excesses, with mutiny and the slaughtering of their own officers, which had to some extent led British officers to under-estimate them and their field discipline.

As to their fighting qualities, as revealed in the first war, it was felt that in defence, well entrenched and with good positions, they were steady and reliable soldiers and in no way inferior to European troops. They were adept at entrenching themselves. In attack they were at their weakest. Their skills and leadership always seemed to break down at this point and they much preferred the enemy to come to them, to be broken on prepared positions by their gunners firing from concealed positions over pre-determined fields of fire. Therefore carrying the fight to the British was rarely undertaken with much enthusiasm. This weakness apart, the Sikhs fully justified

25

their inclusion in the top rank of C. E. Callwell's subsequent definition of colonial foes while Gough himself summed up his opponents thus:

> 'Their valour, their numbers, their means and preparations and the desperate energy with which, in error and deceived, the Khalsa and the Sikh nation mustered and rallied for the struggle, have been conspicuously apparent.'

But all their admirable qualities could not in the end make up for the fact that they missed their European officers to give them steadiness and they always tended to fire high. However, until the first war they had never known defeat and still inspired dread among the native troops of the East India Company's army.

What of Attariwallah, Shere Singh, himself? He was the brother-in-law of the Maharajah and the leading member of the Council of Regency. He had led his reluctant, but obedient troops against Sheikh Imam-ub-Din of Kashmir to enforce the unpopular rule of Gholab Singh on that unhappy state. His 10,000 bayonets loyally supported Lawrence in an act that was against their natural instincts. He had joined the others of the Durbar in requesting the British to stay on as guarantors after the first Sikh war rather than leave the Sikhs to their own devices. Before judging him too harshly we must remind ourselves just how opposed to British influence the majority of the Sikh soldiers were. They followed

Shere Singh went over to the rebels at the urging of his father, and under pressure from the Khalsa which he feared, although he nominally led it.

Singh but he in turn feared them and doubted whether he could retain their loyalty. At Mooltan he kept them in check for a while and they made a show of loyalty but he knew better than anyone how fragile his hold on them was. The discovery of a plot by one of his own men to poison him only reinforced his view that he was both a leader, and a prisoner, of the Khalsa. This realisation was not helped by a string of alternate urgings and sarcasm from his father who had already declared himself for revolt. It is little wonder that, subject to so many stresses, Shere Singh finally gave way and went over.

However once he had made his decision, he acted with the vigour of the newly-converted and quickly became the centrepiece of the revolt. Old Sikh soldiers flocked to his banner as he marched north to Lahore and Goojerat to fulfill his much acclaimed vow of raising the Khalsa to destroy forever, '. . . the oppression of the Feringhis'. His intial moves showed both strategic and tactical sagacity but once Gough had closed with him he showed a less sure touch. He did achieve a surprise at Sadulapore although here his subordinates let him down. His defensive strategy was also sound until the final actions.

For the final defence of their headquarters the Sikh army adopted their usual defensive posture taking advantage of what natural features the area in front of the town possessed. It is probable that Shere Singh abandoned his earlier powerful defences at Russool due to problems of feeding and supplying his army. Whatever the case the decision was his but Gough was delighted that his policy of refusing further combat, until he was ready, had paid off so well.

The city of Goojerat itself lay five miles due north of Chenab and was flanked on either side by two *nullahs*, of which the broader western one was a dry water-course which petered out south of the village of Tricca, in the centre of the initial British line. The smaller, and wet, eastern one ran down to the Chenab itself. In the triangle formed by this *nullah* and the river, Shere Singh had placed large bodies of mounted men, *Ghorchurhas* in the main. These horsemen were stationed between the villages of Gutalie, Malkawaa and Raoki to prevent any outflanking of their main line.

The Sikhs' main defence was two miles in advance of the city itself and ran from east to west with their left flank sitting on the western *nullah* at Chota Kalra. From there the defences ran across in front of Burra Kalra

village before bending back along a loop in the dry *nullah* to rest on the village of Jutimukhi. The villages themselves were fortified strong points with loop-holed houses, and entrenchments had been made right across the narrow neck of land between the *nullahs*. Across the dry bed of the stream to the right, further concentrations of cavalry were deployed in a crescent-shaped formation in front of the hamlets of Sanwal, Moraria and Goorica. To their backs lay the distant mountain peaks of the Sulaiman and Salt ranges.

The fifty-nine guns remaining to the Sikh army were distributed along the front, with batteries at the crucial bend where the defensive lines met the the western *nullah* on the right and others placed in well protected positions in among their infantry. The infantry reserves were held in front of a small village on the outskirts of the city about half-a-mile from the narrowest point between the *nullahs*.

It was a strong position and to their front the defenders could look, out under a brilliant blue sky, directly to the south. The British must advance into their sights across the open fields of waving corn studded with trees but devoid of other obstructions save a string of small villages. Shere Singh and his father stood together with their followers to make the final stand for Khasla and the Sikh nation.

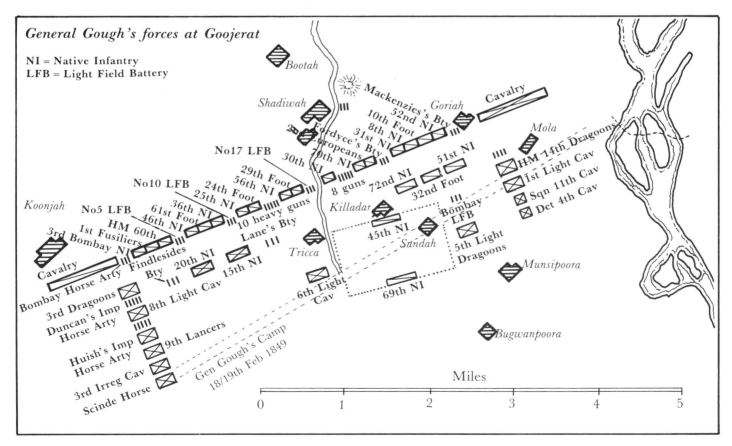

Goojerat

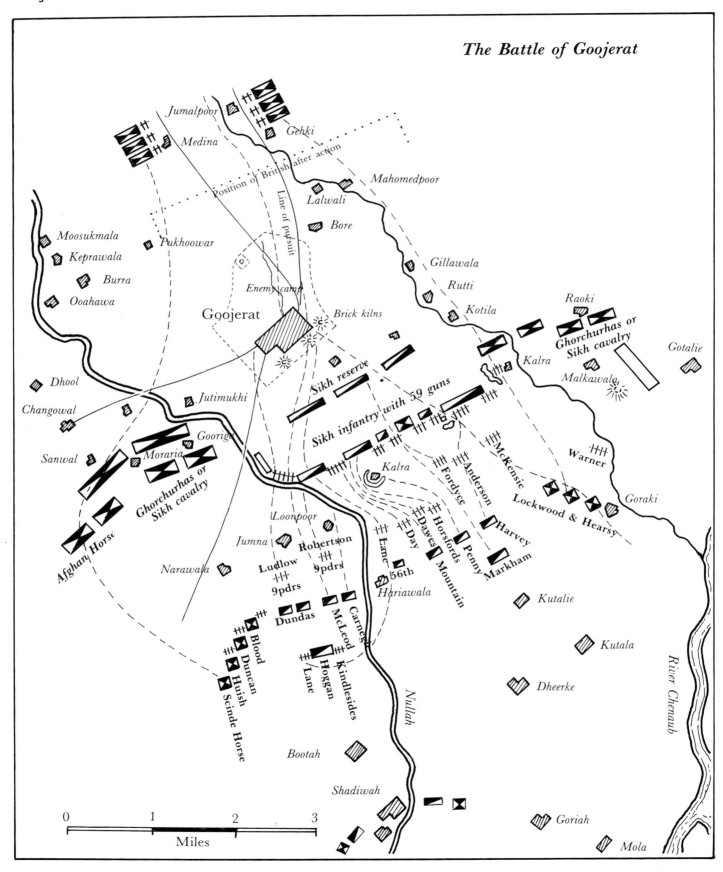

The Battle of Goojerat

28

The British troops were early astir. A corporal in the 32nd Regt recalled:

'A little before four am, on the morning of the 21st, the orderly sergeant came to tell the corporals to go and see the rations drawn, and get them cooked immediately. This order had not been given many minutes before another came, for us to strike our camp and pack out baggage upon the cattle as quickly as possible. This was sufficient to convince us what kind of parade we were going to have, and was a good sign of a general fight, too. Our hungry cattle had cropped off the growing corn close to the ground for a mile or more all round the camp. We had just made fires, and got our frying pans on, and our baggage was not packed, nor the camp struck, when the well-known sound of the bugle was heard, ringing through the camp, for us to stand to arms. All now was confusion: we got a dram of grog served out per man and a pound of bread for every two comrades. Our accoutrements were soon upon us and our muskets in our hands. Some might be seen with a slice of raw meat in their grasp, which they had snatched up as they went by; and others were running with their bread in their hands, eating it as they went. I caught hold of some meat out of the frying pan as it was upon the fire, which had not been on long, so it was raw or nearly so; but I was hungry enough to eat my boot soles if it had been possible. I had often heard talk of a hungry army; but none could be more hungry than this. We were reduced to nothing but skin and bone. My bones were ready to come through my skin; and, as some of the men remarked, their ribs would make gridirons; yet our men were all in high spirits and appeared eager for the battle. As the whole army on both sides was here, we determined to make this a finishing stroke.'

Such was also General Gough's intention. For the final battle there had been some re-organisation of the decimated regiments of the earlier battles and some shifting of units to accommodate the new arrivals from John Company's army from Mooltan. Therefore Penny was replaced by Carnegie, and Pennycuick by M'Leod in Campbell's Division, while in Gilbert's Division, Godby's Brigade was now under the command of Brigadier Penny. Against the reduced number of Sikh guns Gough could now deploy 96 of his own, eighteen of which was of heavy calibre. However it must be remembered that the Skih guns were always capable of firing heavier shot at greater ranges than the British, even if the rounds-per-minute were delivered at a much

---

General Gough's forces at Goojerat

CAVALRY
Cavalry Division: (Sir Joseph Thackwell)

1st Brigade: (Brigadier M. White)
3rd Light Dragoons
14th Light Dragoons
5th Light Cavalry
8th Light Cavalry

2nd Brigade: (Brigadier Lockwood)
9th Lancers
1st Regiment of Light Cavalry
6th Regiment of Light Cavalry

Scinde Horse
3rd Regiment Irregular Cavalry
4th Regiment Irregular Cavalry
9th Regiment Irregular Cavalry
11th Regiment Irregular Cavalry

(European cavalry regiments numbered some 400, native cavalry about 300 effective in the field)

INFANTRY

1st Division (General Whish)

1st Brigade: (Brigadier Harvey)
10th Foot
8th Native Infantry
72nd Native Infantry

2nd Brigade: (Brigadier Markham)
32nd Foot
49th Native Infantry
61st Native Infantry

Bombay Column II (Brigadier Dundas)
60th Rifles
3rd Bombay Native Infantry
Bombay Fusiliers
19th Native Infantry

2nd Division (Maj-Gen Sir Walter Gilbert)

1st Brigade: (Brigadier Mountain)
29th Foot
30th Regiment of Native Infantry
56th Regiment of Native Infantry

2nd Brigade: (Brigadier Carnegie)
2nd European Infantry
31st Regiment of Native Infantry
70th Regiment of Native Infantry

3rd Division (Brig-Gen Sir Colin Campbell)

1st Brigade: (Brigadier M'Leod)
24th Foot
25th Regiment Native Infantry
45th Regiment Native Infantry

2nd Brigade: (Brigadier Hoggan)
61st Foot
36th Regiment Native Infantry
46th Regiment Native Infantry

3rd Brigade: (Brigadier Penny)
15th Regiment Native Infantry
20th Regiment Native Infantry
69th Regiment Native Infantry

European infantry regiments numbered about 900 (1,000 in the 24th), while native infantry numbered about 700 each

ARTILLERY

Artillery Division (Brigadier Tennant)

6 Troops of Horse Artillery (Brigadier Brooke, with Colonels Brind and Grant)
  Troops commanded by Lt-Col Lane, and Majors Christie, Huish, Warner, Duncan and Fordyce
2 Batteries of four 18pdrs and two 8in howitzers each (Major Horsford)
  Batteries commanded by Majors Shakespear and Ludlow
3 Light Field Batteries
  No5 (Lt Walker)
  No10 (Lt Robertson)
  No17 (Major Dawes)
Bombay Light Field Battery
Mackenzie's Battery
Findleside's Battery
Bombay Horse Artillery
Foot Artillery (Brigadier Huthwaite)

slower rate than the British, whose rate of fire was three rounds per minute. Despite this Gough determined that full use should be made of his almost two-to-one advantage in artillery.

The dry *nullah* neatly bisected the final British line which was formed by 7:30. General Sir Walter Gilbert's Division was positioned to the right and Brig-Gen Colin Campbell's Division to the left of this barrier. Gough was up early and eager to get at the enemy after such a long delay. Yet another of the legion of tales that surrounded him owe their origins to this battle. It is said that the only way the old gentleman could be persuaded, by the Deputy Adjutant-General Patrick Grant, from leading the attack personally was to lure him up to a rooftop in the vilage of Tricca and then take the ladder away thus effectively marooning him! Although he certainly did take to the rooftop to scan the enemy lines it is doubtful whether Grant would have taken such a liberty but there is no doubting the eagerness of both General and foot soldier alike in the British force to be at the Sikhs and have done with it!

But as usual the regiments of the Queen were brigaded with, and therefore stiffened, the East India Company's native soldiers. On the British side these troops far outnumbered Europeans. This was always the case and even though the Company's two columns had their own commanders, the commander of the Bengal Army was also C-in-C of all British forces in India responsible and answering to London while the Royal Regiments 'on loan' in India were paid for by the Company.

Their foes were as well-equipped as they. The good old 'Brown Bess' had an effective range of only just under 300 yards, the average foot soldier usually relied on a steady discharge at much closer quarters, this being followed by a bayonet charge. Line or column was the order of the day (the square was not used in this campaign). If the tactics and many of the officers remained almost the same as at Waterloo thirty-odd years before, then so had their uniforms and equipment. Uniform comprised a scarlet shell jacket with stiff upright collar and white crossbelts with black leather pouches, white buttons for fastening and different coloured facing for each regiment. Tight boots and blue cotton trousers finished off their simple dress. The only concession allowed to the Indian climate was the covering of their shakos with white cloth, with an extension down the back to protect their necks from the fierce sun.

There were famous units present this day, the 10th (North Lincolnshire) Regt had a proud history dating back to 1690 and they were known as 'The Springers'. They wore the Sphinx regimental badge to

The Bengal Horse Artillery at the time of the battle of Goojerat. The British artillery, and particularly the fast-moving horse-drawn guns secured the victory.

commemorate their role in Egypt in 1801, as did the equally famed 24th Regt (later to become the South Wales Borderers) whom we shall be meeting again in these pages. They earned themselves the title of the 'Bengal Tigers' for their part in both the Sikh wars and the Indian Mutiny, among other good works on the sub-continent. Like the 10th Regt they had green facings to their tunics. The 29th (Worcestershire) Regt had seen action at Seringapatam and Pondicherry as well as earlier campaigns in India and had taken a French standard at Talavera. The 32nd (Cornwall) Regt was also present together with the 61st (South Gloucester) Regt, known as 'The Whitewashers', who had been present at famous actions from Ramillies to Waterloo.

Apart from the sorry lapse at Chillianwalla, the British cavalry performed well, indeed even Gough, so staunchly for the infantry, highly praised the 3rd Light Dragoons of whom he declared, '. . . no obstacle usually held formidable by horse appears to check'. The 9th (Queen's) Royal Lancers earned themselves the Indian sobriquet of 'The Delhi Spearmen' and wore blue uniform with scarlet facings and had black and white plumed lancer-caps for headgear.

The mounted batteries in this battle were well to the fore, riding to within a few hundred yards of the massed ranks of the Sikhs, unlimbering and delivering their salvoes of roundshot and case at close quarters. The 6pdrs and 9pdrs were most favoured for such actions, but on this occasion the British had some of the heavier pieces from Mooltan in action.

THE RECKONING

Gough certainly made ample use of his guns in the front line. From a gunners' point of view they won the battle on their own. It was their heavy and overwhelming fire that reduced the Sikh counter-battery fire and silenced their batteries. One young officer's view was described thus:

'He says he was ordered with two guns to the front by way of drawing the enemy's fire on them, and before a gun was fired, I suppose returned, seven of their men were knocked over. Immediately however that the enemy's positions was thus shown, the whole of the artillery was ordered to the front and a tremendous cannonade commenced on both sides; our army advancing throwing forward the shoulder, so as to draw round the Sikhs in a semi-circle merely keeping up the fire from the artillery. It would appear that the infantry did little but advance in support of the guns and to complete the rout the battle was decided by the artillery which appears to have been most admirably served.'

Brig-Gen Campbell's Division held the left of the British front line which straddled the dry *nullah* and was drawn up facing the enemy. On the extreme left White's cavalry protected that flank with Sir John Thackwell and Colonel Blood's Bombay Horse Artillery. To their right stood the 3rd Bombay Native Infantry, the 1st Fusiliers and HM 60th Foot of Dundas's Brigade. No5 field battery filled the gap between these. Next right was M'Leods's Brigade with the 36th and 46th Native Infantry, with the 61st between them. Then came No10 battery, the 25th Native Infantry and HM 24th Foot under Carnegie. Campbell had ten heavy guns filling the next part of the line, and filling the gap between these and the 17 Light Field Battery which rimmed the watercourse. Behind Shadiwah village, were the 56th Native Light Infantry and the 29th Foot of Mountain's Brigade.

Hoggan's Brigade comprised the second line on the left with Findleside's battery and the 29th and 15th Native Infantry and further squadrons of the 6th Light

General Gough and his staff assemble under a tree as the battle gets underway. At one time this exposed group was threatened by Sikh cavalry.

Cavalry. In line on the extreme left were the 3rd Dragoons, Duncan's Irregular Horse, the 8th Light Cavalry and the Scinde Horse.

On the right of the front line under Gilbert, Harvey, and Penny extended the line with the 30th Native Infantry, eight heavy guns and then the 70th Native Infantry and 2nd Europeans. Fordyce's battery came next and then Harvey's 31st, 8th and 52nd Native Infantry, with the 10th Foot in the centre. Extending the line to the right through the village of Goriah was Mackenzie's battery and the mounted formations of Lockwood's and Harvey's brigades. Lockwood's Brigade was in the second line with the 45th, 51st and 72nd Native Light Infantry stiffened by the 32nd Foot around Killadar with Dawe's Battery. The 45th and 69th Native Infantry, 5th and 6th Light Cavalry and the Bombay Field Battery were held in the rear.

In line behind Mola lay the 14th Dragoons, 1st Light Cavalry, a squadron of the 11th Cavalry and a squadron of the 4th Cavalry. From the British line the Sikhs could be seen stirring, with movement on all the high ground and atop the houses of the small villages which barred the line of approach.

The Sikh artillery could not contain themselves at the sight of the British line being dressed and forming up. As soon as the British started off towards the city, some four miles distant across the level plain, they evoked a fierce if premature storm of fire. The British line advanced, orderly as a parade-ground drill back in Hyde Park, and reached a cluster of houses. The Sikh defenders melted away leaving their guns to do what execution they could. This was little, for the British line

was halted while details of the location and range of the Sikh guns were noted by the British artillerymen. Once they were fully satisfied the British guns were taken forward under cover of a thin line of skirmishes to engage the enemy on their own. By 9 am they were in position only some 800 yards from the Sikh line and Dawes's battery started the proceedings, the other batteries soon joining in.

Ludlow's and Robertson's 9pdrs were in front of Jumna and Loonpoor and pounded the Sikh guns at that crucial bend in the dry *nullah* to good effect. To their right across the gully Lane's horse artillery was even closer, while Huthwaite's heavy guns were before Kalra and pounded the enemy centre mercilessly. Fordyce, Anderson and McKenzie penetrated the closest to the Sikh defences on the extreme right while Warner's battery wheeled right to the edge of the wet *nullah* to keep the enemy pinned down around Malkwala and prevent any flanking by their horsemen. Lockwood and Hearsy's mounted men took station in his immediate rear to back this move. The same function was performed on the far left by the Scinde Horse, Duncan and Huishes' Horse while Blood's guns and the Light Field Batteries made good play before Narawala.

The fierce artillery duel which followed lasted for two and a half hours. There was no quarter on either side and the exposed British gunners suffered heavily but in return their more accurate and regular fire took a heavy toll of the Sikh defences although they were far from broken at this point. While this deadly duel was going on the long lines of British infantry were ordered to lie down while the shot and shell of the Sikh guns thundered in frustrated fury over their heads tearing up the ploughed fields and cornfields alike, and showering the redcoated figures with debris and earth from their detonations, but actually causing few casualties in their

The immaculate initial advance of the British foot regiments across the open plain.

ranks.

Such a pace could not be indefinitely maintained and eventually amid the roaring and crashing of the guns some slackening of fire could be detected. At 11:30 therefore the order was given for the line to again advance, the artillery accompanying the infantry. The men raised themselves stiffly and dressed their ranks once more. As they moved out again the Sikh infantry also came out and prepared to face them. Corporal Ryan relates events at this crucial period of the battle thus:

'The infantry was now ordered to advance; and as we went forward we could see the enemy forming their line to receive us. They commenced firing at a long range of musketry. We advanced and did not discharge a shot till within 150 yards or less, when we opened such a murderous and well-directed fire that they fell by hundreds. They, on their part, kept up a good fire but it was badly directed; as most of their balls went over our heads. With levelled bayonets we charged; but they could not stand the shock of cold steel.'

In some parts of the line so well had the British gunners done their job that little remained for the infantry to do but to occupy abandoned territory. This was particularly the case on the left and Campbell's men did not find it necessary to fire a shot. A threatening move by the Afghan cavalry was soon dispersed by a barrage by the Horse Artillery followed up with a fierce charge by the Scinde Horse with the 9th Lancers in close support. The native horsemen burst open the enemy squadrons and scattered them in complete disorder which soon turned to a rout. Thackwell was easily able to turn this flank and once more the British guns were deployed forward to enfilade that strong point on the bend, thus contributing to the fall of that position which had most stoutly contested the advance of the British centre.

On the far right too the conditions of the ground precluded any great sweeping movements by the Sikh cavalry although some thirty or so horsemen actually did make a considerable penetration and even momentarily seemed to threaten Gough and his staff in the rear. This no doubt brought a gleam to the old gentleman's eye (he was apparently no longer on the roof) but this alarm was short-lived for Lt Stannus led a troop of the 5th Light Cavalry out to meet this daring bunch of horsemen and cut them to bits.

It was at the fortified villages in the Sikh centre that the battle was most bitterly contested. Here, despite the hurricane of shot that had swept through them, the Sikh defenders made their firmest stand defending each house with some tenacity and skill. Some of the heaviest British casualties were suffered here when an advance unit was sent against the village of Burra Kalra thinking it abandoned. Such was not the case and the hidden defenders rose up and poured in a heavy fire on the surprised infantry. Heavy firing continued and was only finally broken by a full charge of the 2nd European Light Infantry led by Brigadier Penny and Major Steele that swept through the village in a determined rush.

A similar story of heroism on both sides took place

The British field artillery was brought forward into line and at point-blank range out-duelled the Sikh emplaced guns until the infantry could advance.

at the sister village of Chota Kalra against which another desperate attack had to be launched with fixed bayonets by Colonel Franks and the 10th Foot. A brilliant day for British gunners was maintained as whenever a rally was made by the Sikhs their massing infantry was immediately assailed at close range by the Horse Artillery and broken up before it could become dangerous.

It was hot work indeed for an hour but by 12:30 the Sikhs had had enough and soon a general movement to the rear was obvious. The British pushed forward through the shattered enemy defences toward the city itself. As Corporal Ryan relates, the carnage they found there revealed just how complete had been their victory:

'. . . the dead and dying lay strewed all over the ground in heaps. In some places might be seen men lying in whole ranks, as they fell; and in more than one place I saw artillerymen and horses one upon another, as they had been shot down by whole batteries at the time their guns were dismounted. The carriages lay broken and scattered in all directions. The enemy as they retreated made daring attempts to stand at the villages; but they were stormed, and very few escaped, for they were all either shot or bayoneted.'

The city was quickly occupied, and with it enormous booty in the form of guns, ammunition and the like was taken. The great tented area outside was similarly found to be abandoned with little regard to future needs. No doubt the hungry 32nd and others found suitable recompense among the loot contained therein. The few guns and armaments that were taken away in the hasty withdrawal subsequently had to be surrendered as the

pursuit by the British cavalry was hot and eager. For some twelve miles beyond the city the fleeing Sikh columns were harried and cut down by the score and never had a chance to rally. The chase continued until darkness brought a merciful end to the slaughter and never has so much sabring resulted from an enemy collapse! War with a vengeance had been promised to the Sikhs and that is precisely what Shere Singh's disintegrating army received.

The immediate advance of the main force was halted beyond Lalwali and Mahomedpoor at 16:00 and Lord Gough rode among the ranks of his victorious soldiers after ordering a dram of grog be served to each man. He was in cheerful mood, his original plan having been carried through with both precision and panache. A more total victory over a fierce foe could not be remembered. Nor was it accompanied on this occasion by any great loss of British life. The total rout that was Goojerat cost the Gough forces but five officers and 91 men killed and 24 officers and 646 men wounded. This casualty list was higher than he had anticipated, but it was no bloodbath, at least not on the British side. For the Sikhs it is estimated that they fielded some 21,000 troops of all arms and at least 3,100 of these lay dead on the field, with as many again severely wounded or cut down in flight.

To his weary men Gough declared that the enemy's teeth were finally drawn. And so it proved.

A Sikh painting showing a skirmish in the Sikh wars with the RHA in the foreground and the disciplined ranks of their own infantry in the background.

FINALE

Gough, his victory won, was determined to follow it up and bring the war to a quick conclusion. The enemy was to be given no chance to reform beyond the Jhelum. To this effect he despatched a flying column of 12,000 men under Gilbert to keep Shere Singh under continual pressure. At the same time George Lawrence, who had been used as an unofficial emissary by both sides while under parole (which did not prevent him telling Gough *before* the battle that the Sikhs feared the British artillery), sought out the Sirdar and informed him of Gough's terms for the laying down of the Sikhs' arms. These were brief enough, 'Unconditional Surrender'.

It says much for the enormity of their defeat that Singh was forced to accept this. On 12 March he, along with the other Sikh commanders, surrendered the remnants of their force to Gilbert and Campbell. Pershawar was surrendered a few days later, while the Sikhs' Afghan allies to whom it had been promised, vanished back over the border to bide their time for their own vengeance. Thus, a three month campaign by a tiny British force, utterly routed the most powerful nationalist force in India. Shere and Chutter Singh were later exiled for further subversive plotting but the Khasla itself was laid low for the next ninety years of British India.

It was Lord Gough's last battle and a fitting climax to his long career. On 31 March he addressed a long farewell to his much-loved troops in which he re-iterated that their persons and services were engraved in his heart and affections.

The feeling was reciprocated among all ranks. P. Keay of the Bengal Artillery wrote:

'There was no danger, no matter, how great, nor any undertaking, however desperate it might be, but they would have attempted it under him; indeed, when he was present, they looked upon success as being certain, and it was not as a commander alone that he was respected, but as a kind-feeling and good-hearted old man, who took a lively interest in the welfare of all those who were under him . . . .'

The much later verdict of history could find no better summary than that of Sir John Fortescue: 'As a tactician if he be judged by his last and most successful battle, he must certainly receive his meed of praise'. With that verdict we can surely agree. As for the Sikhs, once resigned to defeat and the annexation which inevitably followed they became among the most loyal of the subjected nations in India and stood by the British at the time of the Mutiny. Today, their aspirations of statehood and their own homeland are still denied them.

Chapter Two

THE ALMA

20 September 1854

THE BACKGROUND

General Gough was born at Limerick in 1779 and, lacking any formal education joined the City Militia at fourteen. Two years later he was serving with the 78th Highlanders at the capture of the Cape of Good Hope and later, with the 8th Regt, he also saw action in the West Indies before being promoted to Major in 1805. He fought in all major battles of the Peninsular War. Even here his actions were marked with heavy casualties and so if the butcher's bill he presented for his quick, but far from cheap, victories in India caused an outcry at home, the old General could be excused for thinking that there was more cant than cavill about them. This was especially so when, a scant five years later, public outcry was again raised and this time resulted in the far greater bloodletting of the Crimean War fought by men of Gough's vintage, who followed the same dictums and policies, but this time directed against a European opponent of equal strength and power.

Although some historians claim that Britain 'drifted' into the conflict with Russia there seems little doubt that behind the declaration of war, made on 28 March 1854, were the traditional British policies of maintaining maritime dominance and fear of Russian encroachment,

The highlight of the battle as The Guards regiments advance in stately splendour through the decimated ranks of their British comrades to finally carry the heights and send the Russians into retreat.

Almost as splendid a sight as the British Army, the assembled fleet of transports and warships is here seen embarking the troops at Varna.

either via the Dardanelles into the Mediterranean or by way of Afghanistan as a threat to India. Throughout the 19th century any hints of a move in either direction by the Czars were certain to evoke an immediate response in Whitehall. Thus it was that an obscure argument between Nicholas, Czar of All the Russias, and Emperor Louis Napoleon of France over who should exercise the right to uphold various Christian values in the Holy Land against the stricture of the Ponte and the Sultan's insensitive decrees, escalated, despite the assembly at Vienna, into all-out conflict. Britain, then fast approaching the pinnacle of her power, together with France, ranged herself on the side of Turkey. The latter had declared war on Russia, the feared 'Colossus of the North', when two Russian Army Corps crossed the River Pruth and occupied the Principalities of Moldavia and Wallachia. Britain immediately raised an army, appointed General Lord Raglan, aged 66 and a veteran of the Peninsula and Waterloo, as its C-in-C and despatched it to join with a French army, under Marshal A. J. Leroy de St Arnaud, camped out in the cholera-ridden swamps outside Varna to stem any Russian advance on the Bosphorus. However much Britain drifted into the war, however little enthusiasm might publicly have initially been espoused by the Queen or *The Times*, the magnificent army of 27,000 men had been despatched overseas amid scenes of near hysteria in the streets and in Parliament. The public, which had damned Gough for spilling so much British blood crushing the Sikhs, now bayed for more to be spilt in

order to teach the ferocious Bear a lesson not to bully lesser nations, or, as the Prince Consort expressed it, to 'Vindicate the Public Law of Europe'. Stubborn Turkish resistance at the siege of Silistria, inspired by some British officers, coupled with raging cholera, had forced the Russians to withdraw from the Principalities as early as 23 June but the great British public was not to be denied its victory.

The respective Allied Governments therefore directed their forces to the important Russian naval base of Sebastopol on the southern tip of the Crimean Peninsula across the Black Sea from Bulgaria in order to reduce that fortress. Therefore, borne by an imposing fleet of almost 400 merchant ships with naval escort, the two armies duly embarked and set off without even so much as a landing place agreed upon. The respective commanders had hardly conversed with each other, let alone made and joint plans. Their sole strategy was to land and march on the fortress while always keeping the sea on their flank. This was very much a British way of waging war, a re-run of the Peninsular Campaign. The dominance of the Royal Navy, would, as ever, ensure an unrestricted flow of men and supplies along the lines of communication which, although longer than Russian land lines, were much faster and more reliable. The defenders of Sebastopol would have to sortie out

and fight or endure a siege that they could not ultimately win. It was inevitable that the British would fight the war this way, with much the same weapons and with the same tactics, line against column, as were used in the Napoleonic wars forty years earlier. Britain had not conducted a major land campaign since.

The first battle, the crossing of the river Alma, brought victory and was won, more by the dogged courage of the British foot soldier than by any tactical originality or brilliance on the part of any of their leaders. Though fought with courage, tenacity and pluck any fruits of this battle were immediately squandered by the failure to follow up this initial success and the rest of the campaign bogged down in a dour struggle with the incomparable army decimated, not by the enemy but by disease and neglect. The earlier disbanding of the army's Land Transport Corps ensured that when the troops did eventually stumble ashore on Thursday the 14 September at the aptly named Kalamita Bay, it was two days before even the limited numbers of tents were put ashore to afford them rudimentary protection from the elements. By contrast both their French and Turkish allies went ashore with ample supplies of both.

Some 800 men had died of cholera before the short voyage from the Varna and, although fresh drafts had made up these numbers, it still raged among the British troops in their new environment. Lack of accommodation, coupled with a heavy downpour on their first night ashore, and a cold wind heralding the first hints of the onset of winter, ensured that sickness

The huge assembly of fighting units was put ashore on the Crimea on 14th September, with absolutely no attempt at interference by the over-confident Russian army.

compromised that splendid array of 27,000 men before the campaign had even started. It also brought home to the more optimistic that it was late in the year to begin such a campaign despite the invariable cries of 'twelve week operation and the boys, being home by Christmas' that always seem to accompany British troops at the commencement of long wars.

Thus, when the first British troops of the Light Division (either the 23rd Regt of Foot or the No1 Company of Royal Fusiliers, both claiming the honour) splashed ashore, or were carried piggy-back by sailors from the boats, at around 11am that day under the shadow of what became known as 'The Old Fort', all they had to oppose the enemy and sustain themselves were what they carried. This consisted of a rolled blanket with a few personal effects, three days' rations, 50 rounds of ammunition and a rifle. Thanks to the timely intervention of General Airey, the Quartermaster-General, a brief encounter with a party of watching Cossack horsemen resulted in the capture of a small convoy of fourteen carts, laden with brushwood and fruit, along with the bullocks. The traditional Russian burnt-earth policy was put into effect once the Allies were seen to land and farmhouses and crops were seen blazing in the distance. Despite this, foraging produced some 300 local waggons which became the only supply train the British possessed. They had subsistance for three days' marching and ammunition for one or two battles. Everything else was afloat.

More than supplies were lacking. Intelligence was almost totally non-existent. Sebastapol looked a logical enough target from London or Paris, but the bleak, black and inhospitable terrain of the Crimean Peninsula was not amicable to invaders. Living off the land was not likely to succeed but more pertinent was the fact that the general topography of the area was virtually a closed book to both Raglan and St Arnaud and neither took very energetic steps to remedy this failing. The Light Division was marched inland from the Old Fort for six miles to act as an outpost against any immediate Russian response to the landing but little other preliminary reconnaissance seems to have been carried out.

If the British went to war in their usual confused and amateur fashion then criticism should also be directed against the Russian commander, Prince Menschikov, for allowing such a shambles to go unpunished. Nothing was done over a period of four days to oppose the landing of an Allied force of 63,000 men and 128 guns. It is said that he intended to allow them to extend themselves first, by marching from their primitive base until they were exhausted. He would then fall on them at a point favourable to himself. Another allegation is that the Russians were taken by surprise by the Allied landing, but as the fleet had previously accepted the surrender of the port of Eupatoria further north and the sailing of so mighty a fleet from Bulgaria had been freely reported, this seems doubtful.

Whether surprised or not the Prince quickly recovered. His fortress command was one of the most powerful in the world and he had at his disposal a large garrison to man the great redoubts bristling with heavy guns. There was also the Russian Black Sea fleet under Admiral Vorniloff who was eager to put to sea and tackle the Allied convoy. Such a naval sortie might well have resulted in the loss of the Russian fleet, but it could have also resulted in some damage to the vital transports on which the whole Allied force was totally dependant. It would have been worth a gamble. Instead the Prince adopted the traditional Russian policy of the land animal. Rather than risk the ships in a sea battle he ordered them scuttled across the harbour entrance to block it. Their sailors joined the Russian soldiers ashore as infantrymen, a policy we have seen repeated often enough and adopted in both World Wars.

Menschikov, only recently appointed to the command, decided to pull back on his powerful forts. No plans had been made to defend Sebastapol from the

Prince Menschikov, C-in-C of the Russian army at Sebastapol. He marched north confident of holding the invaders on the heights above the river Alma.

northern side, nonetheless any army approaching from that direction by the coastal road must cross five natural barriers to do so. These barriers were the rivers Balganak, Alma, Katcha, Belbek and Tchernaya, all of which flowed down from the hills in the hinterland and ran parallel to each other directly to the sea at right angles to the coast. The Tchernaya was perhaps not a barrier as such forming as it did the natural roadstead north of the town. The only alternative approach was a diversion inland via Bakshisarai and the post road south to Balaclava where it met the Pronso Road from the sheltered harbour of Yalta, the most logical base for any invader. The Prince's Cossack patrols quickly established the fact that the Allies were on the move on the coastal road with the ships acting as seaborne cavalry on the right flank.

THE BATTLEFIELD

Menschikov was given four days to select the spot on which the Allied advance would be halted, their armies defeated and the threat to his fortress terminated before its walls were even sighted by the Allies. The spot he chose was the south bank of the Alma river and thither he despatched the cream of his army, 33,500 infantrymen, almost 5,000 cavalry and 96 guns. It was

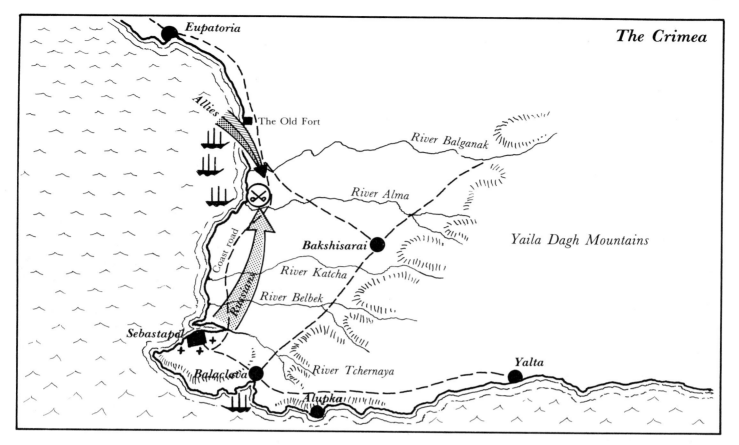

The Crimea

The Allies landed to the north of Sebastapol near the Old Fort, and moved south along the coast road until they reached the river Alma.

easy to see why. Where the stream flowed down from the hills it followed a broad path which marked its winter flood extent. But the Alma itself in September was merely a trickle with a few deep pools at intervals along its straggling length. Where it crossed the main post road, along which the Allies were advancing, it cut a swathe along the foot of a steep escarpment to the south continuing on to empty into the Black Sea. The northern slope which the invaders must descend was a gentle slope. Facing them across the bottom of the narrow but fertile vale and the trickle of water with its various fording places was a seemingly formidable barrier. It was here that the Russians chose to make their stand.

The Russian C-in-C had divided his force into three subordinate commands. The western group lay with its flank on the sea and was commanded by General Kiriakov. He had about 10,000 infantrymen and 32 guns in four field batteries. He was assumed to have the simplest job, holding the heights themselves. The central group was commanded by General Gorchakov with the same numbers of both infantry and guns as the western

group. Gorchakov's task was to block the most obvious approach, the main Eupatoria to Sebastopol coast road. Finally the eastern group, under the command of General Kvetzenski, held the right of the Russian line and was by far the strongest group as the natural defences were fewer here. Kvetzenski had at his disposal some 40 field guns and a heavy siege group with 14 heavier weapons which he made primitive efforts to emplace. The regular troops at his disposal comprised some 13,000 infantry and were supported by two battalions of sailors from the immobilised fleet. He also had the cavalry, some 3,400 horsemen in total.

Looking north from the heights of Alma, which rose breath-taking and almost sheer in places to 350 feet, the Russians had a clear view across the magnificent panorama of the cornfields and orchards through which were advancing the Allied armies. On the left the heights rose sharply from the river's mouth opposite which lay the village of Almatamack. The river could be crossed by fords and bridges on either side of the village. The river mouth itself was considered impassable. It was not. A sandbar lay athwart it which proved eminently suitable for the transport of men and horses. Behind the front ridges of the heights on the Russian bank lay the village of Ulokol Akles from which no direct view of the river

41

could be had. Here Menschikov placed one battalion from the Minsk Regt.

This unit could see neither the river nor the vine-clad shoulder leading to the abrupt face of the heights, which they regarded as unscalable. Nor could they observe the approaches to the numerous ravines and gulleys which cut into its face. These, in effect, provided to any determined opponent a steep but nontheless scalable approach by way of country tracks to the top of the cliffs. The battalion could have blocked these tracks quite simply but they did not. They seemed to have been stationed back in the village merely as a precaution against a possible attack whch their C-in-C had already dismissed in his mind as remote. The same disregard for even the most elementary defence was displayed by the Prince along the rest of the two-mile long heights facing the river. The clifftops were bare of Russian soldiers all along the crests in front of the village of Ulokol Touiets far to the rear. This showed complacency verging on arrogance. Such negligence deserved to be punished and it was.

To the right of the isolated battalion held back near the coast at Ulokol Akles, eight battalions were concentrated, in complete contrast, well forward on the slopes below a 400ft high prominance, known as Telegraph Hill (named for an incomplete semaphore station which was located on its peak). These units comprised four battalions from the Taroutine Regt and a reserve of four more battalions, placed at the foot of the hill in among the vineyards. After an inspection by General Kiriakov, these had begun to shuffle back up the hill to more suitable ground—an unofficial move. Supporting these foot soldiers were two batteries of guns (16 pieces) placed south of the river at about one mile from the bridge which was just about in range.

Next along the Russian line, and facing the ford and bridge on either side of the village of Bourliouk on the north bank, were four more battalions of the Borodino Regt. Another four battalions were placed immediately to the rear of Telegraph Hill as a reserve. These were from the Moscow Regt and they too could not see the river or the crossings. To their right ran the main road to Sebastopol and along this road Menschikov had placed a battery of 16 guns and also his strongest infantry concentration. Seven battalions, three from the Minsk Regt to the west and four from the Volhynia Regt to the east, were placed either side of the road ready to block any Allied march. To the right of the post road the ground again rose steeply to the 450ft Kourganie Hill and on the lower reaches on this prominence, and to its left and about 600 yds from the river itself, an outwork

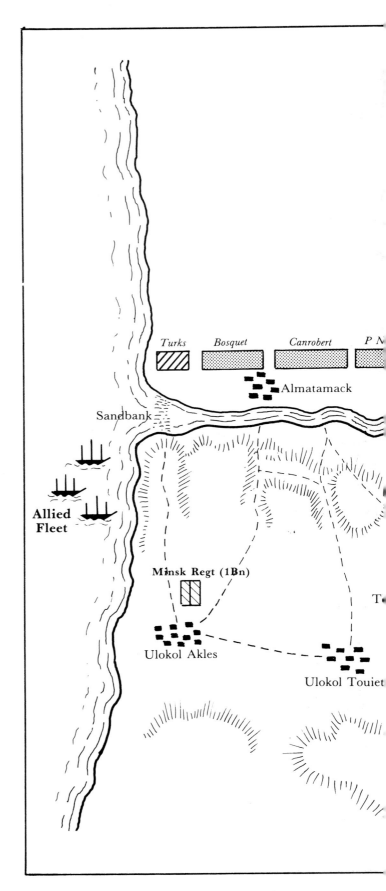

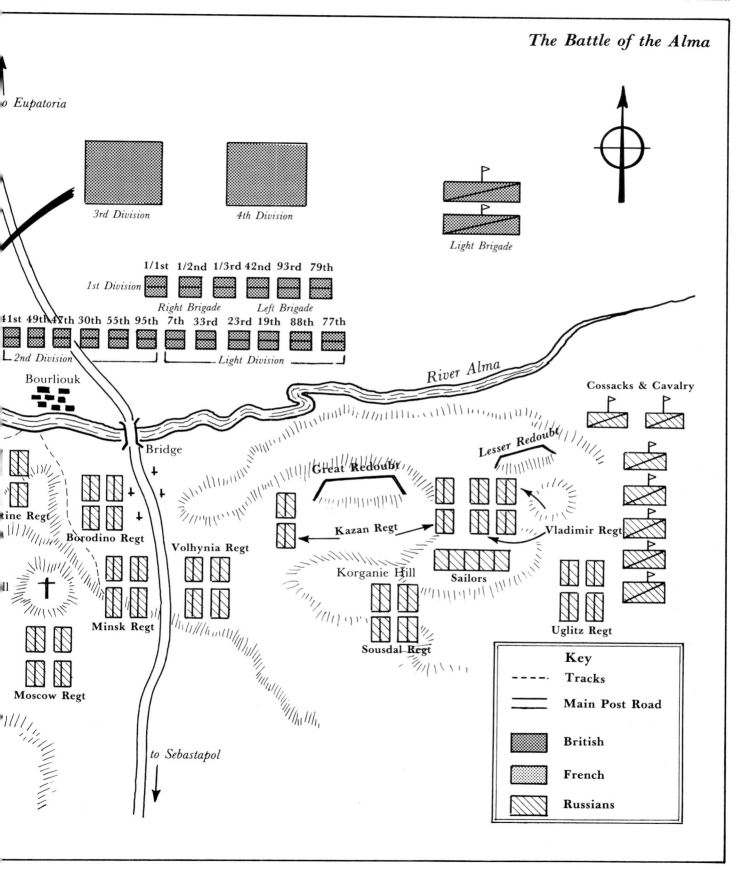

The Battle of the Alma

to Eupatoria

3rd Division

4th Division

Light Brigade

1/1st 1/2nd 1/3rd 42nd 93rd 79th

1st Division

Right Brigade   Left Brigade

41st 49th 47th 30th 55th 95th 7th 33rd 23rd 19th 88th 77th

2nd Division   Light Division

Bourliouk

River Alma

Cossacks & Cavalry

Bridge

Lesser Redoubt

Great Redoubt

tine Regt

Borodino Regt

Kazan Regt

Vladimir Regt

Volhynia Regt

Korganie Hill

Sailors

Minsk Regt

Uglitz Regt

Moscow Regt

Sousdal Regt

to Sebastapol

Key

- - - - Tracks

———— Main Post Road

British

French

Russians

43

had been hastily constructed. It was a broad, shallow entrenchment with a three foot high breastwork, one of few that the Russians had deigned to throw up, so confident were they in the natural defence of the area. This was graced by the extravagant title of 'The Great Redoubt'. Here two battalions of the Kazan Regt were placed on either side, and forward of the work, which contained no fewer than fourteen 32pdr guns and a few 24pdr howitzers. In reserve lay two further battalions of the Vladimir Regt and two batteries of 16 field guns.

Further right, and below Kourganie Hill, a small entrenchment, termed 'The Lesser Redoubt' had been constructed at an angle to prevent any flanking approach. It held a battery of eight 32pdr guns with two further battalions of the Vladimir Regt *en echelon* to its left. To the rear were two battalions of sailors from the fleet who had been organised into foot soldiers and behind them lay the four battalions of the Sousdal Regt with another group of four battalions from the Uglitz Regt completing the line to their right.

So confident were the Russians in the strength of their position that they even invited a party of civilians, including women, from Sebastopol to view the expected annihilation of the invaders from specially prepared stands atop Telegraph Hill! That such confidence was proved totally unfounded is history, but how daunting did the Russian positions appear from the Allied side of the Alma? One Peninsular veteran is said to have sworn that they were the most formidable he had encountered and that included Torres Vedras. However neither Lord Raglan nor St Arnaud was intimidated.

THE ALLIES

It is doubtful whether anything much would have intimidated the British C-in-C. Stout-hearted, kind and inoffensive he was, but the sound of gunfire re-awakened old memories. He had served in the Peninsular campaign and lost an arm at Waterloo. Forty years of being an armchair warrior had included a period as the Duke of Wellington's secretary so he should have been fully *au fait* with the task that faced him. He worried about his men and about upsetting his subordinates and he lacked a firm hand. He had never commanded troops in the field and this, coupled with his barely concealed detestation of his French allies, resulted in but the vaguest direction of the battle from the top.

The Allied armies had formed line of march on 19 September, with the French and the 8,000 strong Turkish contingent closest to the sea. Marshal St Arnaud, as senior ranking officer, claimed the honour

Lord Raglan. A kindly but vague soldier he had been too long behind a desk and was out of touch and sympathy with the men he led and loved.

of the right flank but lacked the cavalry to provide an effective flanking screen. He was thus forced to concede that place to Raglan. The French force, some 25,000 strong, therefore advanced somewhat ahead of the British with their flank to the sea, their 1st Division leading, followed by the 3rd Division, the baggage train, and the 4th Division bringing up the rear. Behind them were placed the Turks.

The British fronted their formation with the 1st and 2nd Battalions of the Rifle Brigade and this skirmishing line was followed by the British divisions in pairs, each marching in double companies from the centre, the Light, 1st and 4th Divisions to the right, the 2nd and 3rd Divisions to the left with the baggage train to their rear. On the right flank and to the rear of the whole force were deployed the cavalry. It was in this formation that the first trip wire, the river Balganak, was approached and crossed with nothing more severe than a slight cavalry skirmish between four squadrons of the 11th Hussars and 13th Light Dragoons on one side and some 2,000 Cossacks on the other.

This accomplished, the Allies made camp before approaching the next check, the Alma itself. Although in the main their scouting was desultory the Allies had briefly reconnoitred the next river crossing, after observers on the accompanying ships offshore had spotted the hasty Russian preparations on the heights. They had also spotted a path up the cliff and the sand bar across the river's mouth. Scouting parties from several British regiments had located the main concentrations of the Russian army on their centre and

The French C-in-C, Marshal de St Arnaud. He had an impossible job trying to co-ordinate tactics with Raglan. In the end he gave up trying!

right and nobody seemed to doubt that a major battle was inevitable the following day.

Not inappropriately at this late stage some sort of council of war was held that evening, but as Raglan made no movement from his own HQ, the French commander was forced to ride over with his Chief-of-Staff, Col Trochu, to seek enlightenment from his British counterpart as to what his plans were for the expected clash on the morrow. St Arnaud had already made his own plans, based on the crucial information relayed to him from a French man-'o-war off the river mouth. Briefly it involved an early morning assault by all three Allied armies. The French would create a diversion by attacking with their 2nd Division and the Turkish contingent at the point the Russians would least expect it, over the 'uncrossable' river mouth and up the

'unscalable' cliff face. While this was being accomplished, and Russian attention diverted, he suggested that Raglan would find it appropriate to cross the river on the enemy right and roll up his line from there with an enveloping movement. With both the enemy flanks turned the French would advance in the centre to complete the rout.

The snags to this audacious plan were probably very apparent to Raglan. It involved the deployment of all his five divisions in the pre-dawn darkness, with the probable confusion this would cause, and their advance against an enemy position only vaguely scouted but known to be of immense strength. If so it was not in the gentle Lord's nature to come out and say so directly. He might disparage the French but he had agreed to co-operate with them, even if that co-operation fell far short of subordinating the British army to direct French orders. Instead of commenting, favourably or unfavourably, he contented himself merely with a general assurance that the French could rely on the British Army's co-operation. St Arnaud, probably desperate to get any kind of commitment or decision from his aloof and taciturn fellow commander, took this as Raglan's agreement to his own idea and rode off to complete his preparations. Lord Raglan himself had no such commitments in his mind other than to attack only when and where he was ready. Nor did he deign to discuss even this notion with his own commanders, let alone his allies, and so he went to bed. Thus was the battle of Alma prepared!

Fortunately for the Allies the Russian C-in-C's own

On the extreme left of their line, the seemingly impregnable heights above the Alma in front of the village of Ulokol Akles led the Russians to neglect their own defences, with disastrous results.

misplaced confidence and lack of aggressive imagination precluded any pre-emptive attack by him, which might had it been made have caused some confusion in the Allied camp. It also gave Raglan ample daylight next day to make a much more concrete survey of his opponents' lines. In defence of his Lordship's and indeed perhaps the 'British' way of going about things, infuriating as it was for their allies, the second look revealed the heavy concentrations of Russian horsemen on the enemy right flank and thus ruled out any foolhardy rush by the British in that direction. It would surely have proved costly.

And so the British slept on while the French and Turkish armies were early astir and on the move. Not until midday did the British advance. St Arnaud rode over to the centre and again conferred with Raglan in another desperate attempt to glean, by hint or default, just why he had not moved his men as early as planned, and what exactly the British were going to do. Now he found out that the British C-in-C had his own ideas. Studying the masses of horsemen beyond the Kourganie, the numbers of which far exceeded his own cavalry, Raglan informed the French Marshal that he had no intention of attempting to turn the position.

Among historians there has been a fierce debate on the contribution of the French that day. We are here deliberately concerned only with the British Army, not because of contempt for the French contribution but because of the limited parameters of this study, but briefly, their work should be mentioned. Whereas Raglan considered that they did little but 'Toot, toot' on their trumpets, others contend that their advance, which proceeded as St Arnaud had outlined, although not as early or as firmly as he had indicated, did gain the unprotected Russian flank atop the heights with hardly any loss. It did draw off a small number of Russian troops, (eight battalions from the vicinity of the Kourganie), and once some very well-handled French artillery joined the infantry there, did inflict some loss on the Russian columns parading aimlessly about.

However there are those who go to the other extreme and say that this was not crucial to whole outcome of the battle but it was clearly a menacing posturing which did little else but act as a diversion which, after all, is all that was ever originally claimed for it by the French commander. Therefore it still remains the case, in this writer's opinion, that the Battle of the Alma was principally a British victory over the Russian Army rather than a predominantly Allied triumph. This argument no doubt will continue. Let us return to the British soldiers in the field.

BRITISH DISPOSITIONS

The glittering array of British Regiments that comprised the 'Army of the East', assembled on that lovely autumn day, was the pick of the Victorian Army. Rank upon rank they assembled as if on a parade ground under the eyes of the Queen herself. The weak sun glistened alike on the brilliant scarlet jackets and white cross belts of the infantry, the blue and gold of the hussars, lancers and light dragoons, the scarlet and brass of the heavy dragoons, the green files of the Riflemen, the rank upon rank of shako, bearskin and bayonet. The pride of the Empire lay awaiting the word to advance toward the little stream and assault the forbidding heights beyond it. The Queen herself wrote:

'I feel so *proud* of my dear noble Troops, who, they say, bear their privations, and sad disease which still haunts them, with such courage and good humour.' She could do little to help them evade the cold grasp of sickness and death but her pride in their achievements was later reflected by the institution of a new supreme award for individual bravery in the field, the Victoria Cross. The cross was (and still is) made from metal from captured Russian cannons and was approved by Her Majesty in January 1856. She originated the simple motto 'For Valour'. Valiant they proved themselves that day, though disgracefully accommodated and cared for, and indifferently led. Given little direction they proved themselves worthy of all the praise their Queen bestowed on them.

The initial advance was made in the Grand Divisions order of battle of the previous day but as the units moved forward they inclined slightly to thier right to close a gap which had opened between the British and French wings. This was achieved after about an hour and the whole force then moved down in parallel towards the river under a baking noon-day sun and in a hushed silence, until the last hillock was breasted and the Alma lay before them with the Russian heights' glowering above and beyond.

The French began to cross the Alma at 14:20 hours near the smallholding christened the 'White Farmhouse' but they might have been on another planet as far as the bulk of the British army, officers or men, were concerned. Ordered to load ball cartridge the columns then stood patiently in the heat surveying the ground before them. From their positions the land sloped gently down through vineyards separated here and there with stone walls and bisected on the British right by the post road. Slightly to the right of this lay the village of Bourliouk. Massed troops could be seen manouvering

Photography was in its infancy during the Crimean War but many splendid plates are available. Here is a battery of British horse-drawn artillery.

on the heights like grey caterpillers as the Russian battalions were marched and counter-marched to their positions.

During a brief British advance, the first Russian round shot began to swish through the air to arrive with a suddenness that at first alarmed and then amused the troops as the cannon balls bounced towards them. The soldiers had time to see them coming as one Norfolk private was later to recall:

'As soon as the enemy's round shot came hopping along we simply did the polite thing—opened out and allowed them to pass on—there is nothing lost by politeness, even on a battlefield. As we kept advancing, we had to move our pins to get out of their way; and presently they began to pitch their shot and shell right amongst us, and our men began to fall.'

The advance was halted while the armies deployed into line from the right. Much practiced precision drill enabled each divisional column to extend into line from its centre and to form two continuous lines, each 2,500 men strong, along a mile-long frontage. The two leading divisions, the 2nd and the Light were thus dressed correctly and without hurry while the shot fell yet more thickly among them. The rear divisions were still out of range of the enemy guns and were stood at ease awaiting their turn. Impressive as this manouevre was under fire, the earlier inclination to the right to close with their French allies had been over-done and the

British 2nd Division found itself cramped on its right by the division under Prince Napoleon holding the French left. The 2nd Division, pushing to its left to compensate, in turn crowded into its neighbour, the Light Division, so that the 95th Regt of the former, overlapped the extreme right formation of the latter, the 7th Fusiliers. Lt-Gen Sir George Brown commanding the Light Division eventually ordered his men here to take ground to the left in fours to compensate but this bunching was never to be satisfactorily overcome in the conditions then prevailing.

While all this orderly shuffling was taking place the placid ranks gradually began to thin as the enemy artillery fire increased and as the range was found became more effective. Sgt Gowing of the Royal Fusiliers related:

'I know that I felt horribly sick—a cold shivering running through my veins—and I must acknowledge that I felt very uncomfortable; but I am happy to say that feeling passed off as soon as I began to get warm to it. It was very exciting work, and the sights were sickening; I hope I shall never witness such another scene. We were now fairly under the enemy's fire— our poor fellows began to fall fast all around me. We had deployed into line, and lay down, in order to avoid the hurricane of shot and shell that was being poured into us.'

Capt Hugh Hibbert of the same regiment recorded in similar fashion that, 'the worst part of the whole affair was the lying down in lines before we received the order to advance' He painted a graphic picture of how Russian shells bursting overhead were, 'blowing men to pieces, arms, legs, and brains in all directions'.

It was worse for many of the officers, for, in true tradition of their kind at the time, they scorned taking cover with their men but remained seated or standing out in front.

Attempts by some batteries of 9pdrs, which were spurred forward to engage the enemy guns, failed due to their lack of elevation and work by a rocket battery proved just as ineffective. Not for the first time the British 'Tommies' had to lie and take it for an hour and a half while awaiting their commander's pleasure. He, in turn, was awaiting the results of the French advance. These were a long time coming and the sight of his brave men being blown asunder as they lay hugging the ground in their long ranks caused much pain to the kindly C-in-C. Like Gough he deliberately exposed himself (and his staff officers) by riding about, conspicuous in his cocked hat and blue frocked coat in order to draw some of that dreadful cannonade to himself.

Finally word reached him that the French were pinned down on the heights, taking casualties and were in danger of being thrown back in disorder. Their losses later proved much exaggerated and their position far more tenable than stated, but the reports had the desired effect on the British commander who now elected to join his Allies in the fight. He took up station to the right of the post road in the rear of the 2nd Division and, at 14:45, delivered his last order of the whole battle to General Airey:

'The infantry will advance.'

The exact composition of the British force at this stage was as follows:

In addition to the skirmishing line of the 1st and 2nd Battalions of the Rifle Brigade led on horseback by Colonel A. J. Lawrence and Major W. S. Norcott on the right of the front line, abuting onto the French left, was the 2nd Division, which was under the command of Lt-Gen Sir George De Lacey Evans. The Right Brigade, (Brig-Gen H. W. Adams), consisted of (from right to left) the 41st (Welsh Regt), the 49th (Royal Berkshires), and the 47th (Loyal North Lancs) Regts of Foot. The Left Brigade (Brig-Gen J. L. Pennefather) was made up of the 30th (East Lancs), 55th (Border Regt) and 95th (Sherwood Foresters) Regts of Foot.

Next in line, slightly behind the alignment of the 2nd, lay the Light Division, with the Right Brigade (Brig-Gen W. J. Codrington) consisting of the 7th (Royal Fusiliers) 33rd (Duke of Wellington's) and 23rd (Royal Welsh Fusiliers) Regts of Foot, while the Left Brigade (Brig-Gen George Buller) comprised the 19th (Green Howards), 88th (Connaught Rangers) and 77th

Hot-blooded and impetuous, Sir Colin Campbell led the Highland Brigade with typical dash and fire.

(Middlesex) Regts of Foot. A pair of field guns were placed on the flank of each division. The two thin, scarlet lines stretched out across the valley floor for two miles.

Meanwhile the three divisions comprising the rear formations had been ordered by Raglan to take position. The 3rd was to fall back in alignment with the 4th and together constitute a large reserve. The 1st Division was to extend into line as the second line of the attack. This order was supplemented by a later instruction to support the Light Division and thus the 1st Division, with two guns again on either flank, formed a shortened second line but with the emphasis more to the left-hand side.

As deployed the 1st Division, commanded by General

Lieutenant-General Sir Richard England commanded the 3rd Division which initially waited in reserve.

Lieutenant-General De Lacey Evans, whose 2nd Division was on the British right of Allied centre.

HRH Duke of Cambridge, had the Right Brigade (Brig-Gen H. J. Bentinck) with the 1/1 (Grenadier), 1/2 (Scots Fusilier) and the 1/3 (Coldstream) Foot Guards and the Left Brigade (General Sir Colin Campbell, whom we have met before) with the 42nd (Black Watch), 93rd (Argyll and Sutherland Highlanders) and 79th (Cameron Highlanders) Regts of Foot.

The British Cavalry, (Maj-Gen Lord Lucan) was present with the 4th Hussars, 8th Hussars, 11th Hussars and 17th Lancers. At the Alma they were represented in the form of General Earl Cardigan's Light Brigade. Bristling with suppressed indignation at being totally ignored throughout the whole proceedings, he had

General Sir George Brown leads from horseback as the regiments struggled up towards the Russian guns.

deployed his command to screen the British left and was in position there but somewhat back from the front British line, ready for action. He could see the hordes of Russian cavalry but, being given no orders prior to the battle and receiving no orders until it was almost over, and then those being to withdraw, his magnificent command was to play no part at all. All this was also of course to Lucan's fury, and the cruel *sobriquet* of 'Lord Look-On' began to circulate. Lord Raglan had decided to keep his cavalry 'in a bandbox', not to hazard them and this decision (as usual uncommunicated to his subordinates) he resolutely stuck to, leaving the 'Cherry Pickers' and the rest to remain nothing but ornate and frustrated observers throughout. They were to have their day later in the campaign.

In reserve waited the 3rd (Maj-Gen Sir Richard England) and 4th (Maj-Gen Sir George Cathcart) Grand Divisions. England had the 1st (Royal Scots), 28th (Gloucesters), 38th (South Staffs), 44th (Essex Regt), 50th (West Kents) and 68th (Durham Light Infantry) Regts of Foot, while Cathcart had an incomplete formation consisting of only the 4th (King's Own), 20th (Lancashire Fusiliers), 21st (Royal Scots Fusiliers), 63rd (Manchester) Regt and parts of the 46th (Duke of Cornwall's Light Infantry) Regts of Foot, with attached guns. The Royal Artillery had in total two batteries of horse and eight batteries of field artillery.

On receiving Raglan's order to advance, and with a few more enlightening words from General Airey, Capt L. E. Nolan spurred his horse towards the respective commanders of the forward divisions. They in turn instructed their brigadiers to move their men forward across the river by the most direct route. Beyond that, nothing!

The two ranks were thereupon ordered to rise and once more the line was rigorously dressed amidst shot and shell, the bugle calls sounded and, in immaculate step twenty thousand pairs of feet moved forward towards the enemy. The long line was rent by Russian fire again and again, grape and shot taking a dozen men at a time. but each great gap torn in their impeccable ranks was deliberately closed and the lines continued to move forward in stately and awesome discipline.

Only where the two divisions still slightly overlapped was there a different impression and here the bunching of regiments gave even choicer targets to the Russian gunners. Another inconvenience was the setting fire to the village of Bourliouk immediately in the face of the advancing companies of Riflemen, with the 49th Foot hard at their heels. The houses burst into flame and smoke and a fusilade of musketry blossomed out from hidden defenders. Colonel Lawrence had his men fix bayonets and the burning hamlet was cleared in a rush and found empty the enemy having fired one more hasty volley and then fled. The battle had commenced in earnest.

THE RUSSIAN FOE

Much of the subsequent battle was fought at very close quarters between groups of infantrymen blazing away into each others ranks, not from the protection of the trenches or embrasures, or even walls and trees, but in the open and in their pre-determined formations. These formations were of course mainly line for the British redcoats and close-packed columns for the grey-clad Russian soldiers.

The natural characteristics of the nations coloured the men's actions. The British soldier was often the sweepings of the streets but once in the Army a certain pride in his regiment became commonplace. He might lack much, but he was fed, clothed and, in the main, cared for by his officers, albeit often in a condescending way. But it is important to remember events in the context of the times and, the average Tommy Atkins was a resigned but loyal and proud soldier. His officers might be incompetent and unapproachable, or they might be highly professional but answerable to superiors who did not have a clue. But by and large those officers would lead by example, exposing themselves to the same danges as their men, and those men, although almost robot-like in their obedience, would give their lives for their country, their officers, their comrades and, above all else, their regimental colour.

Organisd more by battalion than by regiment there was no such rallying point for the Russian soldier. There were no such feelings of *camaraderie* between the average Russian infantryman and his officers. The gulf was almost unbridgeable and for the most part the peasant from the Steppes turned soldier was treated disgracefully. Open contempt was expressed by officers for their men. No records exist to record feelings but overall the dull mass of the peasant stock was by no means as knowlegeable or as 'sharp' as the soldiers of the British Empire. Cockney cocksureness and wit, Highland pride and aggressiveness, and Welsh comradeship and sentimentality all formed bonds which only reinforced regimental pride and the feeling of 'family'. Russian opposite numbers were bullied and maltreated and sent to battle regardless of loss or consequence.

There was no lack of bravery in the Russian ranks. Dour and unimaginative they might be but when ordered they advanced in clumsy and close-packed columns into certain death initially without wavering. The limitless resource of their population in itself however tended to belittle individualism and, the leadership had gone, either through death or cowardice, then the Russian soldier lacked the resource to take any initiative of his own. It was then that he cracked and, when no obvious alternative presented itself, retreated.

The British line enabled the maximum fire power to be brought to bear whereas the Russian formations, though often many times the number of the British, could reply effectively with only their outermost ranks. Thus 1,000 Russians in column might oppose fewer than 500 British soldiers in line. But every British rifle could be brought to bear whereas the Russians could respond with but a tenth of that number, the bulk of the men within the column being masked by their comrades. It was not only this method of fighting that handicapped the Russians in this, and subsequent battles. Most British regiments had the newly acquired Minie rifles, with a far greater range and carrying power than the ancient 1832 smooth-bore muskets of their opponent. These had just been converted from flintlock to percussion. It was a weapon that did little damage at more than 100 yards.

The mass recruitment that had taken place in response to the Allied declaration of war also meant that a high percentage of Russian battalions were composed of fresh, raw recruits straight from the farms. They could barely drill and had little or no shooting practice. They tended to be marshalled into the inner ranks of the columns with the veterans forming the outer ranks. This resulted in their being easily led from point to point, but, seeing little and able to do even less, when the outer ranks fell, as they inevitably did, the columns were reduced to aimless masses of men who either melted away or died *en masse*.

Their officers had learnt even fewer tactics than the British. Used to moving their men about in dense columns they could not understand that the two lines of men dressed in red, advancing in silence and order through the most severe fire, were all that there was. Many were convinced that they were but the first two lines of a vast array of columns like their own. Thus impossible odds were faced down by the British, not solely through pluck and dogged tenacity, but also because of the ignorance of their opponents.

The Russian artillery was better handled and, had it received more support when required, might have proven as decisive as had been expected. It caused almost all the British losses but once it had been overrun or forced to retire the Russian Army had nothing up its sleeve to take its place. The great mass of Russian cavalry, so daunting to Raglan, ought to have played a great part but, like the British horsemen, the Cossacks and the Hussars were kept on a very short leash and contributed little or nothing to the day's events other than further inhibiting Raglan when the decisive moment of breakthrough came. Subsequent battles and encounters however revealed them to have the same lack of aggression and initiative as their infantry counterparts.

THE FIRST ASSAULT

The 2nd Division on the British right found the blazing houses and the heavy smoke pall a hazard to their immaculate advance. Each of the three regiments of the right-hand brigade adopted its own solution to this problem. Most of the 41st and some of the 49th proceeded straight ahead and pressed on through the vineyards towards the river without having to break ranks other that a slight veering to the right by the latter regiment. To their left however elements of the 49th, along with the 47th had to make a more violent detour and pushed in towards the 30th and 55th Regts of the left-hand brigade. In order to squeeze through the narrow gap between the village and the road they were forced to reform in fours. In this compact formation they proved an easy target for the eighteen guns of the Russian battery deployed beyond the bridge. They were also visible to the batteries deployed on the Kourganie and about Telegraph Hill. A valiant effort at counter-battery fire worked by the field artillery came to naught. Thus the advance of the 2nd Division was delayed and was not aided by the fact that the river curved outward toward the enemy hills at this point. The British ranks were steadily reduced by continuous rounds of grape and canister until they had crossed this lethal bottleneck and plunged, determined and angry, into the water.

The leftward movement around the village caused bunching in Pennefather's Brigade, as the 30th and 55th encroached upon their left-hand neighbours and the Royal Fusiliers, on the right of the Light Division and already masked by the 95th, found their forward progress still further hampered. This was too much for their commanding officer, Colonel Lacey Yea, who at once ordered his men forward through the ranks of the 95th.

The left-handed section of the 95th, whose ranks had been buffeted from both sides and upon whom a virtual rain of shell was falling cutting down men by the score along with many of the officers, had baulked from crossing by the road bridge because of fears that the enemy had mined it. After some hesitation they were rallied by Capt Champion who called out 'Come on 95th, show them the way', and they pressed across the river. In so doing they veered over behind the advancing ranks of the 7th and came up with the men of the 33rd Regt who were now across and facing the lower slopes of that formidable strongpoint, the Great Redoubt. Thus the 7th and portions of the 95th changed places, the former coming up between the left- and right-hand portions of the 95th.

In the lee of the foothills the soaking-wet soldiers at last found some protection from the hail of shell. They took shelter here to gain breath, having crossed the river largely intact thus fulfilling the order given them. They were some 600 yards from the Russian 18 gun battery and they began firing to pick off the gunners. In this they were reinforced by Capt H. A. Turner's two 9pdr guns which anticipating Raglan's order quickly positioned themselves to enfilade the Russian battery. They opened fire at long range and with the third shot detonated an ammunition wagon with a spectacular explosion. The Russian gunners whipped up their horses and retired in some disorder, their departure greatly hastened by the further advance of General Evans's brigades. The infantry were now ordered forward up the bank, the officers there laying out markers again with meticulous care and ordering and dressing the line before leading their men forward up the hill and along the roadway. This time there was no pause, no faltering and no stopping the thin red line.

Meantme left of this peerless deployment some harder fighting had been going on. The Royal Fusiliers found themselves separated from their colleagues of the Light Division and fought their own desperate and private war at the left-hand extremity of the 2nd Division. Having crossed the river ahead of the 95th they found themselves assailed by a line of Russian sharpshooters from the crest of a steep bank. Men fell thick and fast until the colour was firmly planted atop the bank and the men swarmed up and over, exterminating their tormentors.

However their troubles were far from over. Directly ahead of them now they could make out more than double their number of Russian troops marching steadily down the slope towards them. This densely-packed mass consisted of battalions of the Kazan Regt. This column of élite Russian troops, 'The Grand Duke Michael's Regt', had been moved down the slope as part of a flanking movement by which the enemy hoped to enfilade the British regiments of the left-hand attack which were storming the Great Redoubt. The Kazan Regt was formed in two columns of two battalions apiece and descended on both sides of this British salient.

The Alma

However, the left-hand Russian column suddenly found itself flanked in turn by the sudden appearance of the Fusiliers.

Undaunted by the odds against them the 7th were wheeled by Colonel Lacy Yea to face this mass and, at a range of only a few yards, they were immediately formed into the standard two ranks. Puzzled, the head of the Russian column halted and then, face to face across the broken ground of the lower slope, red line and grey line exchanged volley upon volley, Minie against musket, at point-blank range with a grim and dogged determination. So close were the two combattants that from time to time frustration got the better of men. Those so affected would then dash over from their own battalion to engage in hand-to-hand combat with their opposite numbers. For example, Capt The Hon William Monck 'sprang forward from his place on the left and rushed up to the enemy's massed battalion, ran his sword through a man in the front rank and struck another with his fist. He was then shot dead by a musket fired from the second rank of the column'. If this sounds vainglorious and a useless waste then the reader must try to place himself both in the context of the time and of the battle. Full of elation, with the enemy clearly before him and frustrated at the slowness of the steady fire in collapsing their ranks, the hot blood of the young officer proved too much for his self-restraint and he paid the price accordingly. Even at such close quarters pistol shots were missing their targets and while the British Minie might penetrate the thick coats of the Russian soldiers it would only take out one man at a time. In return the smaller volume of fire that the restricted Russian front ranks could deliver lacked much penetration power, even at that range, and the long thin line gave them a less concentrated target.

They battled on. Other Royal Fusiliers had become detached in the general mêlée of crossing the river and became involved in the taking of the redoubt itself as did Sgt Gowring. He gives a graphic account of the fighting at this stage as they struggled out of the river and up the hill.

'How I got out I cannot say, as the banks were very steep and slippery. We were now enveloped in smoke, and could not see much. Up the hill we went, step by step, but with fearful carnage. The fighting now became very exciting, our artillery playing over our heads, and we firing and advancing all the time. The smoke was now so great that we could hardly see what we were doing, and our poor fellows were falling all around. It was a dirty, rugged hill. We got mixed up with the 95th. Some one called out, 'Come on young

95th, the old 7th are in front.' The fighting was now desperate. General Sir George Brown, Brigadier Codrington, our noble Colonel Yea and, in fact, all our mounted officers, were encouraging us to move on; and, at last, with a ringing cheer we topped the heights, and into the enemy's battery we jumped.'

Indeed the main assault on the Great Redoubt was, as he states, a very scrambled affair with elements of the 95th and 7th Regiments on the British right of this attack combining with a direct frontal rush by the 23rd and 33rd from the rest of the Light Division's right-hand brigade and with good work on the left by the extreme right-hand regiment of General Codrington's left-hand brigade, the gallant 19th. Here the battle was at its bloodiest.

Mounted on his white horse Codrington sought General Brown but failed to find him in the confusion. Ignoring the hail of fire that swept down from the heights on himself and his regiments floundering out of the water and stumbling over the rock and debris littering the far bank, Codrington rallied the British infantry by example and ordered the brigade to fix bayonets and advance forthwith. In fact Brown was of the same mind, surviving a fall when his horse went down and being helped back into the saddle by a rifleman. How such officers lived

Line versus column. The classic disposition of the British redcoats against the great masses of the Russians as the 23rd Foot advance up the hill.

through these mad moments is a miracle, but they did and, cheered by their men, led the foot troops in a wild madcap dash up the slope into the very muzzles of the Russian cannon belching smoke and flame from the earthworks.

Up they went in a far from orderly scramble, but up they went. From the British reserve divisions Sir Colin Campbell was as aghast as his Russian opponents at the manner of the attack, 'Those regiments are not moving like British soldiers!', he was heard to exclaim, but both sides could at least admit to the efficiency of the results of the advance, no matter how disorderly. At first the Russian defenders could hardly believe their eyes at such tactics, which appeared suicidal, and indeed if their own dense columns had attempted such a manoeuvre it would have resulted in blood-letting on a huge scale. Even the thin lines of the scarlet and white suffered ghastly losses in this incredibly brave dash but steadily the shot-swept, open ground, some 500 yards of bare slope,was covered. Panic began to set in at the twelve guns. Officers screamed at the gunners to lower their sights and sweep

away the audacious lines with grape but, as the barrels came down, so the British infantrymen redoubled their efforts and, although salvoes tore gaping gaps in their bunched ranks, they kept coming. To the Russians such tactics could not be understood or countered by orthodox means and soon cavalry horses were desperately pressed into service to pull the apparently doomed guns to safety.

In order to retrieve the situation the Russian commanders ordered down the four batallions of the Kazan Regt, deployed on either flank of the Great Redoubt. We have seen how the left-hand column were brought up sharp by the 7th. On the Russian right a similar role was played by the 19th Regt which poured volley after volley into the advancing mass in exactly the same manner as the 7th were doing but with even more effect. One Russian officer, Capt Hodasevich, lamented, 'We did not think it possible for men to be found with such firmness of morale to be able to attack in this apparently weak formation our massive columns'. But it soon became apparent to him, and others on the Russian side, including the incredulous civilians atop Telegraph Hill itself, that it was the massive grey columns who could not stand the pace and not the slender scarlet lines.

Capt R Gipps wrote:

'The 19th were shooting with keen deliberation almost as if it was a sport, and men from the other battalions came over to the left to join in. Before long, Russians in the outside ranks began to fall and the column moved ponderously away round the east side of Kourgani Hill, leaving a score of inert figures sprawled on the ground'.

In the centre the final rush now carried the redoubt with Lt Henry Anstruther falling as he crossed the parapet with the uncased colours of the 23rd Regt. Despite having one arm shot away in the final dash Capt A. T. Heyland of the 95th was able to complete the attack and laid claim to one of two Russian guns that were too slow limbering up, the other being taken by Capt E. W. Bell of the 23rd. Into the redoubt poured the 2,000 men of the 23rd, 33rd and 95th with stragglers from other regiments. It was a moment of triumph!

On the extreme left of the British advance two other regiments played a decisive part in this achievement, albeit in a less spectacular manner. The 77th and 88th went up the slope to the left of the Great Redoubt without the protection of the steep bank at the river's edge (to give them a breathing and rallying space) as existed downstream. Thus their ranks were sorely thinned as they went forward, but their advance was a more orderly and measured one for all that. 'Gentleman George'

Buller was very conscious of his crucial responsibility of preventing the British advance from being taken in the flank and accordingly, as soon as his regiments were clear of the water, he allowed this obligation to inhibit him a great deal more than was subsequently proved necessary. True his orders were merely to cross the river but, like his companion generals to his right, it should have been obvious to him that once this was achieved he should press home the attack. His brigade had far fewer natural obstacles to surmount in order to achieve this, although due to the bend of the Alma at this point, some men had to cross the meanderings twice. Once over and in good order, the lack of cover between the river and the track below the slope called for very rapid movement.

This Buller apparently failed to comprehend. In his uncertainty he even had to ask his ADC, Lt Henry Clifford, what he should do next! While he was mulling over Clifford's advice, which was of course to match Codrington's advance, his brigadiers took matters into their own hands. Colonel T. G. Egerton wheeled the 77th round to the left on spotting an advancing Russian column and thus effectively sealed the British left. When Buller finally decided to order the advance, Egerton remained where he was, indeed he ordered his men to lie down to avoid the artillery fire from above, such disobedience being fully justified within a short while by the sighting of what was taken to be elements of the massive Russian cavalry presence forming up further up the hill to charge.

To meet this Buller ordered the 88th Regt to form square and as Buller was within their ranks, this they reluctantly did. Forming square to repel cavalry was sensible enough, but no horsemen materialised and the 88th was, in this formation, extremely vulnerable to the guns of the Lesser Redoubt above them. The 19th were also ordered to form a square for the same purpose but their commanding officer, Major W. S. Norcott, saw that this would put them in a suicidal position under the guns of both Russian redoubts. He turned a blind eye to this instruction in the same manner as had Egerton. Norcott's own solution was to get his men up the hill and clear the guns as fast as he could. Thus the 19th joined the right-hand brigade of the Light Division in that gallant final charge and cleared the ground to the left of the Great Redoubt and, as we have seen, were thus instrumental in parrying the actual Russian riposte, the two battalions of the Kazan Regt.

Thus stood the British line at the end of the first phase of the fighting. By courage, pluck and dogged determination, in spite of some generals but inspired by others, the British infantry had crossed the river, overcome both natural obstacles and the fiercest opposition of both Russian artillery and infantry, had forced the retreat of two enemy formations and halted a third. It was a magnificent achievement. Now consolidation was required and firm, swift support before the Russians regained their composure.

Already there were signs that they had recovered from their initial shock. They still held the higher ground, still had most of their guns intact, had huge masses of foot soldiers yet to be committed, and, despite the despatch of one column on a wild-goose chase across to the French front, had ample reserves to throw back the slender row of British troops clinging precariously to their hard-won positions. Nor, despite both Raglan's and Buller's forebodings, had they yet committed their superior force of cavalry. At this point the battle of the Alma surely hung in the balance. Which side would move first to swing the balance one way or the other?

THE RUSSIAN COUNTER-ATTACK

The British losses, both dead and wounded, had been enormous. The men endured the greatest distress before they allowed themselves to withdraw from the attack. Cowardice was levelled by some officers in the minutes that followed, confusion is blamed by most historians while another view is that the events which followed were triggered off by either a traitorous or panic-stricken officer. We shall never be certain. But we can be sure of events recorded at the time, or shortly afterwards, and one such incident typifies the courage of the British soldier.

On the British right the 2nd Division's casualties had included the Assistant Quarter-Master-General, Colonel Percy Herbert. On his deathbed many years later he related what took place between himself and two soldiers of the 47th Foot.

He said that while he was lying wounded on the ground, utterly unable to move hand or foot, he saw a number of soldiers passing him going to the rear; and from the numbers thought that they must be turning tail. He called to them to stop; when two men who had passed him, turned and in spite of there being a heavy fire of bullets passing over the ground between them and the spot where he was lying, came back to show that they were not running away, but going to the rear owing to being severely wounded, one being shot in the jaw, the other severely wounded in the breast by part of a shell. Both these men belonged to the 47th Regt. He said that these poor wounded men coming back through that storm of bullets, merely because they were called by an officer, who was lying on the ground, himself wounded and unable to move, was a fact so honourable to the British Army, and to the regiment to which these men belonged, that he considered that it ought to be known.

And so it should be.

The two British Divisions had commenced their gallant crossing of the river at 15:00 or thereabouts, the Great Redoubt falling a quarter of an hour later and all the leading British line being over the Alma by 15:30. It was not until then that the incredulous Russian generals regained their composure sufficiently to order a counter-attack against the hard-won toeholds. As we have seen this initially consisted of the two wings of the Kazan Regt plodding down the slopes on either side of the redoubt and being held on one side and driven back on the other.

The Russian artillery pieces were now emplaced in new defensive places further up the slopes. They were unlimbered and soon re-commenced firing, directing much of their shot and shell against their former positions, which were covered with massed redcoats, and they began to exact a heavy toll. Some of the British infantry, already mixed up in the final scamper into the redoubt, began seeking a more sheltered place to continue the fight, now clearly defensive, until such time as the support should come up to take over the ground that had been won at such severe cost. Alas, the reserve divisions were late in being ordered forward, which proved almost fatal to the whole outcome of the battle.

Courage and euphoria had carried the leading waves forward to achieve the impossible. They had already endured one prolonged bout of shelling without the chance to respond. After their advance it was too much to expect that they should now be left to endure a second on their own. While General Codrington shared the expectation of quick support, and was equally let-down when it failed to appear, he continued to rally his men to hold their ground despite the bombardment.

The shelling was reinforced at this point of the battle by the commitment of fresh Russian forces to counter-attack. These were the 3,000 or so infantrymen of two regiments of Vladimir Regt, who were seen approaching in column, eight abreast, from around the edge of Kourganie Hill and heading straight for the left-hand side of the redoubt, bayonets fixed. In their midst they bore the Ikon of St Sergius. As they came ponderously on they were met with but a scattered fusillade from the British line, for initially they were, somewhat remarkably, mistaken for a French column. It must be

Russian regiments took their holy ikons into battle and prayed to their saints as they marched.

emphasised that, even from the extreme British right, and even on Lord Raglan's exposed hilltop in advance of the British 2nd Division, no sign could be had of the French troops so they could be anywhere as far as the average 'Tommy' was concerned.

It is less explicable that the Russian grey mass could be mistaken for the French blue columns, other than in the confusion of the bombardment and drifting smoke and the general confusion of battle. The Russian column did not fire but advanced slowly with bayonets fixed which may have helped cause doubt in one horseborne officer's mind. Nonetheless this initial mistake let the Vladimir Regt off lightly as they tramped steadily down the slope, for, instead of suffering the massed fire of the Minies that was punishing the flanking columns of the Kazan Regt so much, they advanced practically unopposed.

Not all the confusion was on the British side at this point however. Witness the strange story of how two Russian generals, Gorchakov and Kvetzenski, both claimed to have led this column's attack. It would seem that, completely oblivious to one another on either side of the dense mass, both men urged the column forward, each on his own initiative. The Russian trooper stoically obeyed the General closest to him which was fine while both were giving basically the same instructions; 'March forward!'. Later it was, not surprisingly, to lead to considerable confusion!

The original British error of mistaking the Russian mass for French troops was reinforced by the bugle call 'Cease Fire'. The Russians seemed as amazed at the lack of response by the British as they had been at their initial assault and, seemingly suspecting a ploy, perhaps to outflank them, came to a halt. This standoff lasted

General Gortschakov, one of the two generals who independently led the Kazan Regiment counter-attack which briefly re-took the 'Great Redoubt'.

only a short time and them the mysterious British bugler sounded 'Retreat'! Despite desperate efforts by some officers of the 23rd to hold the men and continue the defence of the redoubt's parapet, most men did as they had been trained day and night to do, they obeyed their bugle calls. But they did not panic, did not rush to the rear as has been alleged elsewhere. For the most part it was a steady and orderly retreat down the slope, but it was still a withdrawal *en masse* and the great press of men doggedly retiring swept with them men like those of the Rifle Brigade who wished to stand and fight. This withdrawal continued despite all efforts by some of the surviving officers of various regiments, to stem the tide. Men such as Col H. G. Chester of the 23rd Foot for example, were perfectly able to see that the approaching mass was the enemy and not their French Allies and urged his men to re-commence firing. But he, and other officers like him, who bravely showed themselves in the open waving the swords in an effort to turn the tide of men streaming to the rear, were shot dead where they stood. The red wave continued to ebb down the hill, here and there little knots turning to fire back before retreating further.

Triumphantly the Russians re-entered the redoubt, some even breaking ranks to chase after the British whom they thought had been broken and were withdrawing in disorder. These Russians were in for a shock, a much-delayed shock, but nonetheless a profound and decisive one. Finally, having overcome their suspicions of British motives, the long grey-coated columns of the Vladimir

Regt inched their way forward again over the redoubt to stolidly press home their new advantage. Sgt Gowing recalled:

'We were mobbed out of the battery, and a part of the way down the hill again; and then we had some desperate fighting. We lay down and blazed into their huge columns as hard as we could load and fire...'

On the left flank of the redoubt the 77th and 88th remained stoically in their defensive positions despite the eagerness of the troops to be let off the leash. On the right, Yea's gallant men were still eyeball to eyeball with their opponents and exchanging shot for shot with telling effect. Further to the right the 2nd Division was now finally established on the far bank of the river and Lord Raglan was on his hummock far in advance of any of his men with a lofty disdain for his own safety. But where was the 1st Division?

THE ADVANCE OF THE 1ST DIVISION

Loyal to the only order issued to him by his Commanding Officer, to 'support the front line', the Duke of Cambridge was rather lethargic in carrying out this crucial function. Because of this the 1st Division arrived in line at the crucial juncture, the British withdrawal, instead of earlier when they might have prevented its taking place at all. However they arrived in the nick of time and their intervention, although tardy, was magnificent.

The Division had, in response to Raglan's perfunctory command, been formed into two ranks. As befitted the proud regiments which comprised this elite force, this was done with panache and precision, both the Foot Guards and the Highlanders being neatly dressed into impeccable order before proceeding forward across the little gardens and through the vineyards over the bodies of their predecessors, and in fact had caught up with the leading division on the far bank. In order to prevent an intolerable mix-up the Duke ordered the Division to halt its stately progress and to lie down to await events. The Duke wished to see how the leading attack developed before further committing his force but the opinion was expressed (by General Airey to the Commander of the Guards Brigade, General H. J. Bentinck), that too great a gap ought not to develop although, like everything else in Raglan's scheme of vagueness, no set gap had been laid down.

Nonetheless this conversation prompted the Duke to resume the advance of the 1st Division, but the damage had already been done. On their deployment the Highland Regts formed the far left with the Guards in

The Duke of Cambridge cheers on the Guards as they advance in steady order towards the battle-line. The failure of the 1st Division to move rapidly in support of the initial assault was particularly costly.

Below: The advance of the 42nd Royal Highland Regiment of Foot at bayonet point. At the Alma the Black Watch added yet another honour to their unrivalled history.

their usual position on the right of the line. Reading from left to right as the Division advanced, the British second line comprised the 79th (Cameron Highlanders), 93rd (Argyll and Sutherland Highlanders) and the 42nd (The Black Watch). Then came the Coldstream Guards, Scots Fusilier Guards and the Grenadier Guards. The two lines they formed extended from the rear of the 77th of the Light Division across to the rear of the 7th and the 95th of the 2nd Division. It was a considerable overlap and complicated the deployment of the 3rd Division in the rear of the 2nd Division, thus severely limiting the part they played. The 3rd Division deployed into line in the order, left to right, 4th, 44th, 28th, 38th, 50th and 1st Regts of Foot, and their right was so far over that it was in effect supporting Prince Napoleon's regiments about White Farm as much as the 2nd Division.

The walls and gardens, and the opportunity presented by the road bridge, all encroached upon the original immaculate line and the 1st Division crossed the river in as many different ways as there were regiments. The 2nd and 3rd Grenadiers for example went over by the bridge in fours while their comrades waded over in line, as did the Scots Fusilier Guards, who claimed the honour of being the first of the Division to reach the far bank.

The advance of the Highland Brigade on the Allied left flank, with steady-aimed fire being directed into the Russian ranks at close quarters.

The Scots Guards, according to their own historian, were instructed to get over the river, 'in any way they could do so and reform on the far side', and this they did. The Coldstreams went across the river in columns of platoons and reformed on the far bank.

The Highland Brigade's three regiments crossed in echelon, with the Black Watch on the right slightly in advance of the Argyll and Sutherland Highlanders to their left and the Camerons in turn slightly behind and to the left of them. Thus they passed behind the 77th and 88th in their static line and square respectively, acting as flank guards against the still-expected intervention by the Russian horsemen. Soon the Highland Brigades were storming up the steep crest and driving back the Russians foot by foot, waved on by Campbell in his tartan breeks and brandishing his sword, shouting to his men, 'We'll hae nane but Hieland bonnets here!'.

The Scots Fusilier Guards were still in the process of re-dressing their lines below the redoubt when the crisis broke about them and they were hastily urged forward before their new dressing had been completed. General Bentinck initiated the movement of the Scots Fusiliers following an urgent plea from General Codrington as

his regiments began pulling back. Bentinck, on horseback, was soon gesticulating and shouting to his men, 'Forward, Fusiliers, what are you waiting for?' Nothing daunted by such a slur, in a mass rather than a line, with the colours and No4 Company in the lead and the others strung out behind them in a semi-circle, the men struggled to fix bayonets as they clambered the steep slopes toward the enemy redoubt, being hindered by the mass of British troops withdrawing as well as Russian fire.

As they swept through the retreating British ranks they came into bayonet contact with the more rash of the Russian advance troops and split them readily and liberally as the Russians blundered into them. However their impetus, crucial as it was in stemming the rot, left them dangerously exposed with their flanks unsupported and faced by the great mass of the Vladimir Regt, itself still largely intact. Before the Grenadiers could come up in support again a mistake was made by an officer (again undetected) who ordered the Fusiliers to fall back. Some obeyed, others disregarded this order and stood their ground steadily. This little group stood like a small red

Colours flying, drums beating and officers well up, the Guards advance in a steady and unstoppable line.

Capt Lindsay, who won the Victoria Cross, is here depicted urging his men onward at the Alma.

island as the grey hordes of the Vladimir surged and broke all around them threatening to engulf them totally.

The soldiers surrounding the colours wheeled into line and stood their ground as excited Russians jumped out of the redoubt determined to take the standard. Two battalions of the Kazan Regt which had earlier been forced to retire made a belated reappearance in a vain attempt to regain their honour and they joined in the attack on the Fusilier vanguard. The fighting here for the next few minutes was intense, in some cases hand-to-hand. Twenty-four bullet holes were found in the colour after the battle, but this also indicated the high shooting of the enemy musketry and accounted for the survival of this gallant little band in the face of overwhelming numbers. Even so it is on record that every NCO save one sergeant was hit in this brief crisis. But just when it seemed they must be trampled under, relief again arrived in the nick of time.

The Coldstream and Grenadiers had not been so rushed and had formed their lines more deliberately on their markers in the shelter of the dead ground. They

were able to advance in comparative order, followed by the re-formed lines of the Rifle Brigade and the Light Divisions, and thus relieved this little crisis, passing the Fusiliers as they began re-forming in turn. The Guards' history comments on Codrington's men:

'though forced to retire behind the advancing line of the Guards many took the earliest opportunity of again facing the enemy and as gap after gap was made in the ranks there were many eager volunteers from Codrington's and Pennefather's Brigades ready to fill the vacant places.'

It is as well this was so because the Russians were not finished. Under the direct leadership of General Gorchakov the Vladimir Regt ponderously marched their way into a gap which had opened between the bunched-up Fusiliers and the other relieving Guards formations. The threat was enormous but at least it had the effect of stopping the Russian artillery fire for fear of hitting their own men which afforded the British some relief. Nonetheless this was another very dangerous moment but the 1st Division rose to it superbly. The Grenadiers, under Colonel The Hon F. Hood, stopped and brought its left flank round into line down one side of the solid Russian mass.

One account of this triumphant movement gives a graphic description of the close-range fighting of those days:

'Our gallant Regiment stood in line as if in Hyde Park, the enemy coming down with 80 or 100 yards and firing from behind the hill as well. We delivered our fire and they dropped by dozens, another and another volley and the cool determined stand we made in that awful bottom cut them down in crowds, as they came on.'

The Coldstreams reacted in a similar way, halting in line and facing across the head of the Russian column at an angle. Thus the Russians were assailed once more by lines of red-clad musket men pouring a steady series of controlled volleys into their ranks. The thickset bodies with their ankle-length greatcoats began to pile up in heaps and the column shuddered to a complete halt in the face of such withering fire.

As the Kazan column veered away so Hood could wheel more of his line and concentrate yet more Minies on the Vladimir Regt. For a few minutes the Russians stood solidly and died, then the rear ranks began to give way and soon the column was in dispirited retirement. Although the fighting was less bloody the Highland Brigades on the left were also steadily advancing, still in echelon and they forced the Russians to abandon in turn the Lesser Redoubt. Almost at the same time the

Guards advanced, firing as they went, sixteen aimed volleys from each man as they strode up the hill, a solid line of tall, scarlet figures topped by the great bearskins, an unforgettable and unstoppable wave. In next to no time the Grenadiers had re-entered the Great Redoubt, capturing the solitary gun they found there. Once more this strongpoint was in British hands and, this time, permanently so.

The inertia that had kept the British cavalry almost static throughout the battle, was matched, but with far less reason or justification, by that of General Menshkov and the great hordes of riders who waited poised beyond the British left flank. Throughout, they remained unused, and failed to fall on the advancing Highlanders' flanks. Thus Campbell was able to lead his men on to the higher ground, the Black Watch pausing only to re-dress into line before once more flanking a Russian column, two battalions of the Kazan Regt again, and enfilading it with that steady and deadly fire until it broke. In the same manner the other two Highland Regts came upon, and administered another thrashing to, a reserve Russian column, this time the fresh Sousdal Regt.

The advance of this enemy column at first threatened to take the leading 42nd in their flanks but the situation was saved by the 93rd coming up in echelon which poured, 'a murderous fire' into the Russian masses who had no answer to the line's fire and they fled before the kilted warriors could come to close quarters and use the bayonet.

One Russian regiment remained unbroken, the four battalions of the Uglitz Regt which had been in the shelter of the Kourganie. Their commander scorned his own withdrawal and began to form his men into another huge column to bar further advance. Whether the Uglitz would have fared any better than the others in such a situation will never be known for at this moment, an opportune deployment of artillery came about which placed the matter beyond dispute.

VICTORY—AND FAILURE

It was the guns of two batteries of the Royal Horse Artillery that delivered the *coup de grâce* on the British left. Like many British units this day it had received absolutely no instructions from its Commander-in-Chief and so, on the pure initiative of its commander alone, a battery crossed the river and selected the massing Russian horde as a perfect target. Soon rounds of grape and shot were cutting great swathes through the ranks of the Uglitz until they in turn broke and streamed back down the hills, following the astounded Russian civilians and dismayed Russian generals back to Sebastopol, numbed by their unexpected and overwhelming defeat.

Arthur Tremayne was to write that he 'never saw a more ghastly sight than rows of Russians with their skulls blown off.'

Only General Kiriakov remained calm and organised a rearguard with eight battalions and thirty guns on the

The advance of the Guards. Delayed by the need to dress their ranks, they arrived on the scene just at the right moment to swing the course of the battle finally and decisively to the Allies.

ridge overlooking the post road. Here it could not influence events at the actual battlefront but it would have provided a formidable breakwater to bar any Allied follow-up. They need not have bothered. No order was given to press home the British victory. The surviving Russians were allowed to return to Sebastopol, dispirited, but largely intact.

The fleeting moment passed, never to return. As Mrs Armytage said:

'Spectators from the town had come out to witness the anticipated certain victory over the bold invaders, instead of which the day ended in a general retreat of the Russians, and saw the Allies resting on the battlefield where they had earned the first laurels of the campaign, and had defeated the Russians between the hours of twelve and four, inflicting a moral defeat far greater even than the actual victory of the day; for the Russians had felt quite confident that the position was so strong that its capture was impossible, and the inhabitants of the Crimea expected to see the Allies driven back into the sea instead of their own army being routed in less than four hours.'

Many claim that the whole campaign could have been concluded with a vigorous follow-up by the Allies, but is this so? The French had had enough, despite suffering few casualties, far fewer than 600 killed and wounded they claimed for themselves. Indeed they were barely engaged in earnest. Nonetheless their troops sat down on the heights and took off their packs. Clearly if there was to be a pursuit it would have to be a solely British affair.

Although British losses had been severe, the Light Division recording 878, 2nd Division 495 and the 1st Division 439 officers, the men the 3rd Division, although deployed had not taken part in the fight, the 4th Division was fully intact and the cavalry, to their lasting fury, had to content themselves with cantering in the wake of the infantry and being curtly ordered to refrain from any pursuit of the fleeing Russians.

But if the British had taken losses then the Russian had suffered a ghastly carnage, some 5,700 being the final casualty figures given for them, including over a thousand left wounded who later died. There was little sympathy for them as Gowring recalled at the time.

'The wounded Russian behaved worse than the brute beasts of the field; they shot some of our officers and men just after they had done all they could for them, but they did not live long to talk of what they had done, for they were at once shot or bayoneted.'

It would seem that Raglan missed a good opportunity to crown his long career with a decisive victory. His men had won a victory for him, many say in spite of him, but he lacked the 'killer touch' and the ruthlessness of his mentor, the Iron Duke. His kindly nature perhaps forbade him asking yet more from his soldiers who had given and achieved so much. Yet perhaps it would have been wiser to be cruel rather than kind and finished it there and then. Restraint, whether for this reason, or for the much-quoted version that he failed to send British troops forward, 'for the sake of accord between the Allies' resulted in a long winter siege campaign and the slaughter, through disease and illness along with hopelessly rash assaults on the fortresses, which ultimately decimated the ranks of the proud army he was trying to protect far more than any clinching battle on the 20 September would have done.

Raglan paid the ultimate price, shared by so many of his men. After the ignominy of the failure to take the Redan the following summer, he caught cholera and died ten days later, on 28 June. But if he cared for his men, it was not the obvious caring and sharing that men like Campbell and old Gough conveyed to the troops and Raglan was not much mourned by the men he led, or failed to lead, at the victory of the Alma.

VICTORY OF THE ALMA.

Chapter Three

TAKU FORTS

21 August 1860

ONCE BITTEN

The small wars that took place in China have been much debated and censured of late with modern critics concentrating on the Opium trade factor, at the expense of any other, as the main reason for their taking place. A more objective study would seem to place the continuance of dealing in this 'pernicious article', as it was termed, as incidental to the wars rather than as the main British *raison d'être* for military action. As in so many cases in the 18th and 19th centuries, trade followed the flag, but, should that trade be thwarted in any way, particularly when coupled with a challenge to Britain's military might, war was likely to follow.

Expeditions to 'Far Cathay' had been undertaken from the time of Marco Polo and if by the mid 1800s the majority of that trade was British, this merely reflected her position in the world at the time. This picture was a happy one of unprecedented boom and expansion. This wealth and true enterprise was backed by the largest navy the world had ever seen which gave her undisputed command of the world's trade routes. The port of London was therefore packed with ships from all the remote corners of the globe and included vessels from the upper reaches of the Pei-Ho river in China

The exterior of the Taku Forts, showing its ditches and protective wooden-spiked palisades. Primitive in construction they proved formidable to the troops wading through the mud and dykes of the flat estuary.

which could be navigated almost as far as the Anting Gate in Peking itself.

The common acceptance of the time was that wherever there was enough water for a ship to float, the Red or White Ensign would be present and predominant. Any craft flying these flags or owned by British interests was guaranteed the right of protection much as a Roman citizen enjoyed immunity in the heyday of that empire. Much sensitivity was displayed by Her Majesty's Government, and indeed by the Queen herself, in respect of any violation of this established fact. *Pax Britannica* existed, not only in theory, but in fact and if that meant overall peaceful and benevolent overseeing of the world's sea routes, then occasionally that same dominance required a small and sharp flexing of the muscles to prove that it was founded on strength, and not rhetoric. One such show of strength took place in China in 1856 and from that stemmed the subsequent heroic failures and dour victories in that country, that characterise so much of English military history.

Chinese and British attitudes in the preceding years found little common ground. China considered itself as the centre of the civilised world and saw all foreigners, including the British as mere barbarians. Britain, busy creating an empire which would rule two-thirds of the known world beyond China, felt that whatever the Chinese view, the practicalities of the situation showed their roles in reverse light. Still these differences did not matter as long as unhindered trade was permitted. Much to Britain's anger, the Chinese imposed increasingly stiff regulations against all foreign trading incursions and this eventually led to the war of 1842.

In this campaign superior British arms had quickly crushed the numerically stronger Chinese forces, resulting in the capture of Canton and the ceding of Hong Kong. In the next phase later that same year General Sir Hugh Gough commanded from India a miniscule British force which quickly took in succession the cities of Amoy, Tinghae and Chinghae, culminating in an assault on Ningpo which Sir Hugh took with a force of only 800 men, who attacked under a burning sun that itself caused twenty deaths from sunstroke in a single day. On 9 August of that year Nanking was brought under siege. The city was surrounded by a twelve mile wall and defended by 12,000 Imperial troops and yet old Sir Hugh's resolute little army had so cowed the wily Mandarins that rather than put their defences to the test they immediately sued for peace. Sir Hugh sailed back to India to resume his campaigning but the peace that followed was certainly fragile in view of the continued tension and misunderstandings between the two powers.

Commissioner Yea. He showed all the usual Chinese guile and wiliness in dragging out protracted negotiations to keep the 'Barbarians' from marching on Peking.

In 1856 the *lorcha* (or schooner) *Arrow* was boarded by Chinese authorities on the spurious grounds that among her Chinese crew were a number of pirates. Twelve of them were forcibly taken from the vessel by Commissioner Yea's troops and put on trial. They were subsequently found to be innocent and were released but by then the damage had been done. The *Arrow* claimed to be a British registered vessel, operating out of Hong Kong and this meant that the British flag had, in theory, been violated as no consultation had been made prior to her seizure. Too late, it was found that her registration had lapsed and so technically the British were as much in error as the Chinese.

Sir John Bowring, commanding the Far East station, had no hesitation in demanding the repatriation of the *Arrow*'s crew and failing this, threatened hostilities. The contemptuous reply from Imperial Commissioner Yea ended any hopes that the incident could be diplomatically ignored and events rapidly moved from negotiation to confrontation. Once again the initial fighting took place around Canton commencing with the Royal Navy's Commander-in-Chief, Sir Michael Seymour, bringing his ships into action and, on 23 October, conducting a

Sir John Bowring who later became the Governor of Hong Kong, which the British gained through the peace treaties with the manchu.

bombardment of the Barrier forts. These were constructed to protect the mouth of all the major Chinese rivers, being their main arteries of trade and commerce. On this occasion the British warships quickly prevailed and moved on up-river towards the city itself.

On 29 October an assault was made by a Naval landing party of 200 Royal Marines led by Capt Penrose, Royal Marine Light Infantry, and a number of seamen.

They managed to penetrate the walls before being forced back by superior numbers. But further attacks continued and one by one the city's defences succumbed to fire from the warships and frequent skirmishes by landing parties. A fleet of war junks lying under the protection of the forts was also attacked by British boats and wiped out and the Bogue forts, which contained some 200 guns, were also taken, again with minimal loss.

Unable to defeat the British directly the intractable Yea ordered that, in revenge, British factories within the city be put to the torch. In retaliation the British themselves fired areas of the city. Skirmishing continued for some considerable time, a typical example of which took place on 14 December and which gives some idea of the type of fighting which took place in Canton at this time. One survivor described the scene thus:

'The Chinese, who were maddened by the loss of property and life, manned the house tops to hurl bricks and stones down on our heads, and the Chinese soldiers who were very thick, tried hard to cut us off; but as they had only spears we knocked them down like ninepins. Our party lost two men killed and one mortally wounded. The Chinese got the bodies, and cut off their heads for the reward. We were obliged to make such a sharp retreat that we could not recover their bodies although the Marines offered to go and try.'

Such fighting could never result in the occupation of the whole city by such a small force and it was clear that only that would force a change of attitude by the Chinese authorities. While the fighting dragged on, trade itself, the continuance of which was the mainstay of British policy, was directly affected and it thus behove Sir Michael, if he could, to make a quick end to the affair. He therefore appealed to the Governor-General of India for 5,000 soldiers and for the Admiralty to send out a fleet of gunboats to enable him to make a final assault.

The naval forces assembled by May 1857, and Commodore Elliot attacked a fleet of war junks in Escape Creek, all of which were destroyed. The outbreak of the Mutiny in India caused delay to further operations as Lord Elgin, who was on his way to China as Special Plenipotentiary, was diverted to India along with many of the troops. Once this 'incident' had been resolved Lord Elgin and fresh troops arrived in China at the end of September and the negotiations re-commenced.

Commissioner Yea's response to British overtures was

The Royal Navy brings modern ordnance to bear all along China's coast and up her major rivers.

again so disdainful that the British opened a heavy fire on the city's river walls and outer forts on 25 December. A large Chinese fleet existed at the nearby city of Fatsan, where some eighty large war junks lay manned by 6,000 seamen and soldiers ready to fight. The British attacked these vessels towards the end of the year. Seymour's fleet moved up the Canton river and the gunboats under the newly arrived Commodore Henry Keppel, inflicted a severe defeat on the enemy, sinking and burning all but three of the Chinese vessels. Subsequent operations in January 1858 resulted in the fall of the city and the capture of Yea himself. He was sent to Calcutta in chains, already having been thrown out of office by his Emperor and denounced for '. . . dallying with the barbarians'.

Having antagonised the British, the Chinese compounded their error by murdering a French missionary and so, as in the Crimea, once more the two 'natural enemies' found themselves allied against an eastern power. Lord Elgin and the French official, Baron Gros, then sent their conditions of peace to the Imperial Palace at Peking in the north but the Emperor did not deign to acknowledge their receipt nor reply and so operations shifted to the north and the combined Allied fleets anchored off the Pei-Ho river forts in April, 1858. Sir Michael Seymour demanded the surrender of the Taku Forts and, receiving no reply, made plans for their seizure.

The forts themselves were in a commanding position and were powerfully built, comprising a mile-long complex of earthworks and batteries, but when the attack was made on 20 May, the 32pdr guns, backed up by mortars and rockets, quickly silenced the enemy artillery, with less than an hour's steady firing sufficing to achieve this. The landing parties were sent in, again Royal Marines and sailors from the fleets, and for the loss of only twenty-one British and sixty-seven French (fifty of which were killed by an explosion in a magazine while they were occupying a fort) the Taku Forts fell into the Allies' hands easily.

This proved effective and the Emperor permitted an unratified peace treaty to be signed some forty miles up the river towards his capital, at Tientsin. The campaign successfully concluded, Sir Michael went home and was succeeded by Admiral Sir James Hope. The latter had greatly distinguished himself in operations against the Buenos Aires dictator, Rosas, on the Parana River in 1845, where the battle of Obligado involved the forcing of river defences in much the same manner as on the Pei-Ho, but Hope found his new job much more difficult to accomplish than Seymour had. The Chinese were not to be caught out twice!

THE BRITISH REPULSED

Admiral Hope arrived on station on 18 June and at once made a detailed reconnaissance of the river and the Chinese defences. He was greatly disturbed to find that, under cover of the continuing peace negotiations, the Chinese had been busily reinforcing the forts' already formidable defences. The forts situated on the north bank of the river had extra guns mounted to menace with enfilading fire any ships attempting to reduce the forts lower down on the south bank. Furthermore, to thwart attempts by attackers to land by boat on the stinking mudflats to the rear of these forts, two deep ditches had been dug completely encompassing the rear, or land side, of the forts. The innermost ditch was reinforced with large, pointed, wooden stakes and both trenches became water-filled due to the low-lying nature of the land. A further broad ring of spiked bamboo obstructions filled the space between the crenellated walls and the innermost ditch. In addition, to restrict maritime operations by the Allied fleets, a heavy chain boom was thrown across the mouth of the river between the two banks connecting the forts. Inside the walls a central artillery platform, a *cavalier,* existed with ramps leading up to it so that the guns could be manhandled up to fire in any direction. There were thought to be fifty-eight guns of varying calibres mounted there.

No concealment was possible for any force approaching these strongpoints. The landscape was a dreary spread of muddy flats much of which was inundated at high tide. It was criss-crossed with drainage ditches. This left great areas mere swampland and impassable. There were salt workings to the north stretching almost to the raised causeway that carried the track between Sin-Ho and Peh-Tang further up the coast. A coastal approach was out of the question. Beyond this causeway was a wide plain deteriorating into further swamps, crossed from east to west by a passable cart track. Along the north bank of the Pei-Ho another raised causeway followed the course of the river until it reached Teng-Ku. From there a track ran due south to a bridge of boats which linked the north bank to Tung-Ku and the Great South Fort.

Surveying this bleak expanse of almost liquid plain it is not really surprising that Admiral Hope decided that a waterborne assault under cover of the gunboats and across the shortest space of land available in the manner of the previous attack, was the method most likely to succeed with the limited forces at his disposal. He laid his plans accordingly. The boom was to be blown under cover of darkness, the walls breached by a fierce cannonade and some 700 Royal Marines were to be landed by small boats as close to the walls as possible and thence to storm the breaches. In the light of the

Chinese lack of stomach to stand and fight shown in the earlier capture this was thought to be quite feasible by the senior naval officers, despite the new defence works and obstructions.

Not all the attacking force were of Admiral Hope's mind however. Colonel Lemon of the 1st Battalion Royal Marine Light Infantry, just out from India, whose men were to bear the brunt of the assault, protested vehemently against this plan which seemed to him practically suicidal. The landing of his 400 men, plus a reinforced battalion of a further 300 Royal Marines from the ships of the fleet, against a forewarned enemy under heavy fire, across a muddy waste through which just to advance involved great effort, does indeed appear, in retrospect, more than rash. It conjures up in the mind a miniature Passchendaele, and so it was to prove. All really rested on whether the Chinese defenders would run or resist. In the event they chose to stand and fight!

The Admiral continued to demand the removal of the boom and the safe passage of his fleet in order to transport the British Envoy, Mr Bruce, to Tientsin so that the recently signed peace treaty could be ratified at Peking as previously agreed. The Chinese stalled, continually strengthened their defences, hoping thus to postpone for ever the finalisation of the treaty and its conditions. Clearly force was the only thing that the Mandarins understood and Admiral Hope therefore determined that the attack must take place after all.

So it was that on 24 June, the British Fleet led by the gunboats closed on the boom and prepared for action. That night Capt Wilkes blew open the boom and examined an inner raft. He was fired on and had to withdraw but the way was open for the bombarding fleet. Accordingly, at first light, the warships *Cormorant* and *Nimrod,* with nine gunboats, took up their stations. They were divided into a right- and left-hand attack, with Admiral Hope embarked aboard the *Plover* so he could direct operations from close inshore. The right attack was led by Capt Shadwell aboard the *Banterer* while the left was under the command of Capt Vansittart aboard the *Forester.* Accompanying them was the French gunboat *Duchayla* commanded by Capt Tricault, which took part in the assault, and, as a neutral observer, the United States' gunboat *Toeywan* commanded by Flag Officer Tatnall. Although the combined fire-power of the warships was formidable the tide had not been included

Early landing craft. British troops disembark from a Royal Navy gunboat in preparation for a landing, this time at Canton. Against the Taku Forts however such methods led to disaster.

in the calculations and as the attack was made at the slack, the bombarding ships were at a far lower level than the defending Chinese guns which made their counter-battery work less effective than it should have been.

This second major miscalculation by the Admiral prolonged the bombardment time needed and exposed the ships to a longer period of intense fire from all the Chinese forts. Nor did the state of the tide assist in navigation and even the shallow-draft gunboats soon began to come to grief on the sandbars and flats that lay athwart their approaches. Both the *Banterer* and the *Starling* were quickly aground and unable to take part in the bombardment.

At 14:00 the gunboat *Opossum* was ordered to advance and pull up the stakes in front of the boom, which, it had been found, the Chinese had repaired during the early hours. As she did so, all the guns in both Chinese batteries opened a heavy fire on the leading ships. The intense cross-fire soon caused casualties. The flagship, *HMS Plover* was hard hit, her Commanding Officer, Lt Rasen, killed and only nine of her forty-man crew remained uninjured. The wounded included Admiral Hope himself who was hit in the thigh. The American

To prepare for the capture of the Taku Forts, at the mouth of the Pei-Ho river, a fierce bombardment was made by the Allied fleet.

Captain embarked in a boat from his own ship in the thick of the fight and visited Hope aboard his stricken ship, the American coxswain being killed by Chinese fire while alongside. He also took off some of the British wounded, justifying his actions later by the now famous statement that 'Blood is thicker than water'. The injured British admiral then sent his damaged vessel downstream to fetch reinforcements while he transferred his flag to the *Opossum* which was ordered to get closer in to the forts. She too came under heavy fire and the gallant old Admiral was hit a second time. The *Opossum* fouled her screw and started drifting out of the battle zone down-river. Nonetheless Hope continued in command until loss of blood forced him to relinquish his command to Capt Shadwell and he was taken aboard the *Cormorant*.

Return Chinese fire cost the British several of their gunboats. Here the Nimrod *together with the French* Avalanche *engage the forts.*

The Chinese gunnery was extremely effective. The *Kestrel* was pounded and left sinking, the *Lee* was hard hit and had to be run aground and the *Haughty* was also badly damaged and forced out of line. Things were going badly awry for the British force. The *Opossum* and *Plover* meanwhile resumed their places and the bombardment continued apace until the enemy guns finally fell silent. Believing them to be largely disabled, the two senior captains on the spot decided that the boats should be launched to deliver the *coup de grâce*. Hope gave his sanction over Lemon's more soldierly advice and accordingly the ships' bluejackets began to pull away on their oars, as each boat crammed to the gunnels with Royal Marines, made its way towards those distant walls, lined with Chinese marksmen. However, many Chinese guns, far from being disabled, had merely ceased firing to await better targets, which were now generously provided.

Soon after 19:00 that evening the long lines of boats approached the mud flats on the north bank of the Pei-Ho River and landed the troops who advanced in a series of files towards the forts. In the twilight all surviving guns opened fire on the columns of white shakoed and neckclothed Marines as they slithered and slid their way across the morass accompanied by parties of men carrying primitive scaling ladders. Musket and shot cut swathes through the ranks struggling in the soft cloying mud up to their ankles and often their knees. Every one of the three senior officers was shot down, Capt Vansittart losing a leg and four lieutenants killed outright. The command thus devolved upon Commander Commerell who determined to persevere. He led the first division on and the survivors, only 150 strong, managed to scramble across the first ditch, which was dry.

They scrambled out in the face of more intense fire and less than a third of the little force made it to the next obstruction, the second ditch, filled to the brim with water. They were stuck, the fire poured down, the mocking bamboo stakes stood on the other side in case any should manage to flounder across. The majority had not managed to keep their cartridges dry and their rifles were useless. Moreover most of the ladder parties had been killed or wounded in any event.

Only a single scaling ladder reached the walls and it was immediately thrown up, some ten Marines gallantly attempting the forlorn hope of climbing it. Eight fell dead and the ladder was thrown down. It was a massacre. The reserve division under Capt Wilkes fared little better and soon it was obvious that the attack had been a fiasco. By now night had fallen which helped shield some of the wounded crawling back through the mire to the relative safety of the boats but Chinese blue lights were much in evidence from the forts revealing the struggling groups of survivors in their pitiless glare and many men were hit a second time as they tried to gain sanctuary while many of the boats themselves were holed and disabled. Lt H. L. Evans, RMLI, returned three times into that hellish scene to bring out wounded men. Because this was a defeat he was not awarded the Victoria Cross for his gallantry, although it was commonly said thereafter that many men had been awarded it for less.

Eighty men had been killed and 350 wounded, three gunboats, *Cormorant*, *Lee* and *Plover*, had been lost and another 100 men wounded in the ships before the fleet withdrew. Three more damaged vessels, *Haughty*, *Kestrel* and *Starling* were pulled off with the help of a high tide next day and salvaged. It had been a humiliating disaster. As they withdrew they left behind them in the night those squat walls, menacing, fearsome, and now, a symbol of Chinese tenacity and victory.

The flat landing boats full of RMLI are towed up-river under a covering bombardment prior to the landing itself on the stinking mudflats, before the unsuccessful assault on the forts.

A NEW HOPE

There was little the discomforted British force could do but retire, mainly to Hong Kong, to lick its wounds. In Parliament the defeat aroused the passions of the pacifists and little Englanders and Mr Bright stood up to denounce both the Plenipotentiaries and the naval officers alike for gross incompetence and warned the British Government not to make partnership with another power, presumably France. But it was again too late for such sentiments to carry any great sway and vengeance for cruel deceit was more the feeling in the nation. It seemed obvious that with a water-borne landing discredited the job must be carried out by the Army with the Navy supplying the supporting role, much as in the Crimea. It was equally obvious, after the evils of the Crimea and its criminal mismanagement of supply and shelter, that a competent officer must be given command of the operation and a competent general must take command in the field.

Fortunately for Victorian pride the right men were found to fill both positions, and, moreover, their subordinates included many of the ablest and brightest of the new generation of Army leaders destined for great things in the second half of the 19th century. Earl Elgin and Baron Gros continued their diplomatic roles but the British land forces were placed under command of Sir John Michel and Sir Robert Napier, while Admiral Hope, having recovered, survived the defeat with his reputation almost intact, to continue as naval C-in-C. The French forces were smaller than the British and again caused irritation, doing little of the fighting but claiming maximum glory. They were commanded by General de Montauban.

A large fleet was assembled, which included units of the Indian Navy and troops were called in from distant stations, chiefly India but also the Cape and England, while most of the allied troops came directly from France itself. All were concentrated in China by March, 1860. Preparations then continued and detailed plans were made up until June, when the war was resumed. The British deployed some 13,000 European and Sepoy troops, excluding a garrison of 5,000 left at Hong Kong, while the French deployed some 6,700 soldiers, many of them colonial. The British forces in the field were placed under the very able command of General Sir Hope Grant and included the King's Dragoon Guards, and two Sikh Cavalry Regiments under the command of two Mutiny heroes, Fane and Probyn. There were six battalions of infantry and field and siege batteries of the Royal Artillery who were destined to play a

Sir Robert Cornelis Napier, who had served at the battle of Goojerat and was later to become 1st Baron of Magdala but here seen at the time of his triumph at the Taku Forts in China.

particularly valuable role.

On 28 July, 1860, the assembled force arrived back off the Pei-Ho River and anchored within twenty miles of the Taku Forts. They were unmolested when they began landing at Peh-Tang, in the Gulf of Pechili on the 31st of that month.

General Sir Robert Napier had been born in Ceylon (Sri Lanka) in 1810, the son of an artillery major, and at the age of eighteen the young sapper officer had sailed to India to join the Bengal Engineers. He was clever and methodical, with an artistic flair, both painting and poetry featuring in his spare time hobbies. He was a widower with six children. He had served and fought hard, having his horse shot from under him before being wounded in the infantry charge at Ferozeshah. He was present at Googerat also in the second war and was rewarded by promotion to Brigade Major. There followed several frontier expeditions against rebellious tribes. As a Colonel he had served as military secretary to Maj-Gen Outram during the Mutiny and was at the siege of Lucknow where his conduct and skill had earned him the rank of Brigadier-General and a KCB from the Queen. He had followed this up with more Indian campaigns and was rewarded with command of the 2nd Division in China in 1860.

Other young bloods on Grant's team included Garnet Wolseley, eagerly seeking fresh glories after campaigning in Burma, the Crimea and the Mutiny and a future field marshal and C-in-C of the British Army; Major Probyn whom we have already noted was most highly thought

The Army Commander-in-Chief was Sir Hope Grant. His task was not made easier by the fact that his French opposite number disagreed with every plan he made. In the end the French fell into line.

of as a cavalry leader, commanding one of the two irregular cavalry regiments, and destined to win the Victoria Cross; and Colonel Stephenson, of the Scots Fusilier Guards, acting as Grant's senior staff officer. There was also Lt-Col Gerald Graham, another VC holder was later to become a lieutenant-general and, later in the campaign, Charles 'Chinese' Gordon, then a young engineer officer, was to join. So Grant had strong, intelligent backing to enable him to carry out his task.

An exceptionally able man, he was to experience no great difficulties in planning his operations, caring for his men, preparing his advances or winning his battles.

Like most preceding and succeeding British generals with a French army for comrades-in-arms however, he was to experience his greatest problems trying to win the war his way against the advice and desires of his ally! Like Lord Raglan before him he had to cope not just with their 'toot-tooting' on their bugles, but their outward obsession with glory in all its forms. At all the major encounters they made certain that they had a small force present who contributed little.

Sir Hope Grant was born in Scotland in 1808 and, after attending school in Switzerland with no great success, had joined the 9th Lancers as an eighteen-year-old cornet, where he remained for thirty-two years attaining the rank of Major-General. He became an expert cavalry officer, very tall, lean and straight, but he was a soldier's soldier rather than a dandy and knew his trade backwards. He had fought in China before earning a CB and the two Sikh wars saw his name featured in most of the bloody encounters. During the Mutiny he shone as leader of the Movable Column and was also at the relief of Lucknow. However, his muddled way of giving orders and the fact that he was not conversant with map reading did not make his arguments with de Montauban on the correct battle plan any easier to follow. Luckily his sub-ordinates fully made up for his lack in these matters.

Sir Hope Grant with his staff at the time of the march on Peking. Attempts to negotiate with the Chinese officials led to repeated acts of treachery. The city was finally occupied and the firing of the Summer Palace was fully justified, but totally misunderstood at home, both at the time and ever since.

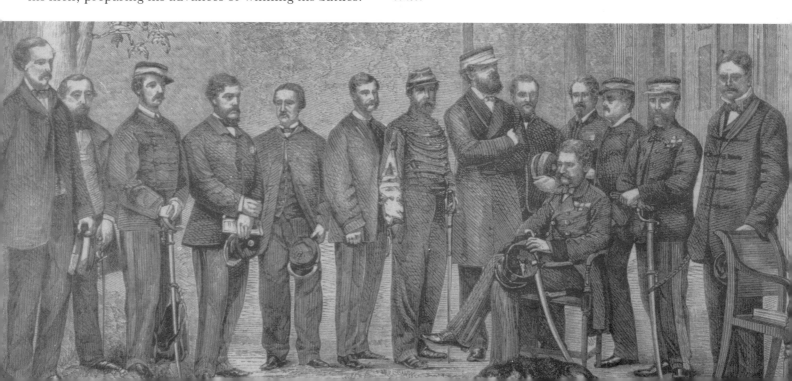

The full strength of the British and Empire forces was established by July, 1860. Because the land over which they were fighting was fertile further inland, the Allies did not encounter the same problems of foraging as usual, nor were the distances from base to front line such that enormous transport problems overwhelmed them, as we shall see was experienced in campaigns such as the Zululand expedition. But to keep the troops supplied a Canton Coolie Corps was set up and run most effectively for the duration. Thus, by July the British were, in most respects, fully prepared to take the field and avenge the shame of the preceeding year.

SCHEMES, STRATEGEMS AND FIRST STRIKE

It was largely at the instigation of Napier that Sir Hope Grant laid his plans based on a land attack against the north bank fort, '...and not on the south bank, as his colleague, General Montauban, desired', for Napier, '...an experienced and skilful officer...', had foreseen that victory would follow. Overall direction of the campaign was left to Grant and neither the War Office nor Whitehall interfered. The Prime Minister, Palmerston, shared the viewpoint of the Secretary of State for War, Sidney Herbert, who had advised Grant that: 'All I can undertake is that you shall be honestly and heartily supported at home'. In the Cabinet, Lord John Russell completed this refreshing trinity with a similar *carte blanche* extended to Lord Elgin. Grant and Elgin also seemed to have been on cordial terms with mutual understanding prevailing throughout.

It was as well that Grant was given such a respite (one can imagine how a Churchill figure in the Government of the time would have dabbled and coerced!) for harmony from London was more than compensated for by disharmony with his French colleague. Nor did his immunity from outside influence extend to Horse Guards

---

British Forces deployed against the Taku Forts

INFANTRY
1st (Royal Scots) Regiment of Foot
2nd (Queen's Royal) Regiment of Foot
3rd (East Kent-The Buffs) Regiment of Foot
44th Regiment of Foot (the Essex Regiment)
60th (King's Royal Rifle Corps)
67th Regiment of Foot (the Royal Hampshire Regiment)
70th (Surrey) Regiment of Foot
99th Regiment of Foot
1st Battalion Royal Marine Light Infantry
Six Punjab regiments including the 8th Punjab Infantry

CAVALRY
King's Dragoon Guards (two squadrons)
Fane's Horse (Sikhs, Parthans and Punjabi Mussulmen, later the 19th Bengal Cavalry)
Probyn's Horse (Sikhs, nicknamed by the Chinese the 'Black Princes')

ARTILLERY
Two batteries of the new Armstrong rifled breech-loading 12pdrs, under Capt Barry and Capt I. Milward, supplemented by the normal smooth-bore 9pdrs under Capt Stirling in the field artillery and a Rocket Battery. Siege train under Major Guy Rotten, with two batteries of 24pdr howitzers commanded by Capt C. Govan and Capt J. Desbrough respectively
Madras Mountain Train battery under Capt H. Hicks

ENGINEERS
23rd Company Royal Engineers and the Madras Sappers and Miners under Capt Shaw Stewart (responsible for setting up of the base and camp and in constructing suitable causeway roads on which to move the British and Allied armies around the quagmire surrounding the fortifications themselves).

and the Duke of Cambridge, a notorious meddler and behind the scenes string-puller throughout his long tenure of office of the Commander-in-Chief. He played a large part in the placing of officers, as did Lord Clyde (formerly Sir Colin Campbell) now C-in-C India, under the Viceroy, from whose resources much of Grant's strength was drawn. Lord Clyde also took the opportunity to advance the careers of some of his favourites, much to Wolseley's disgust. He described such appointments as being made by '...a bigotted Scotchman with a host of greedy friends...'.

The traditional friction between the British and the French was apparent, even before the campaign started, due mainly to the leisurely way the smaller French contingent made its way to the war zone. Grant's exasperation was very apparent when he wrote petulantly to Herbert that, '...(between ourselves)...', it was a '...great bore being tied down by the French...', in that way. Their force was, '...so small...', (the French had tried to get the British to cut the size of their contingent to better match the French but this request was ignored), and by the time it eventually reached China, '...in all probability a five months' voyage...', it would be of little value to him. He was asked to be

The Allied armies came principally from India where the Mutiny had just been effectively put down. The cavalry horses did not take well to the long sea voyage.

patient and to co-operate to the fullest with his opposite number, even to the extent of commanding on alternate days, but this condition was quietly dropped later in the campaign as being both impractical and counter-productive.

In practice de Montauban and Hope Grant did largely hit it off, but the continual dilatory performance of the French, even after they had reached the Far East, stretched the latter's goodwill to the limits. No such hesitancy attended their later involvement in the actual battles however for they strove to be first in the field of glory, if not in the field of fire! The original British plan was to land their forces north of the Pei-Ho River at the town of Talien-Whan but the French commander decreed his force would go ashore south of the forts, at the port of Chefoo. Both were on the Gulf of Pechili but the landing sites reflected the initial disagreements of the Allies as to the best course the land campaign should follow.

In the light of the continued Chinese intransigence only an armed march on Peking and the Imperial Palace itself would seem to suffice to bring the Celestial Emperor to his pig-headed senses and plans were made for a step-by-step advance up the Pei-Ho. The biggest obstacles were the Taku Forts and these, to the British, were also the greatest prizes to avenge their earlier humiliation. The French had not been so affected of course and they sought the line of least resistance and most acclamation.

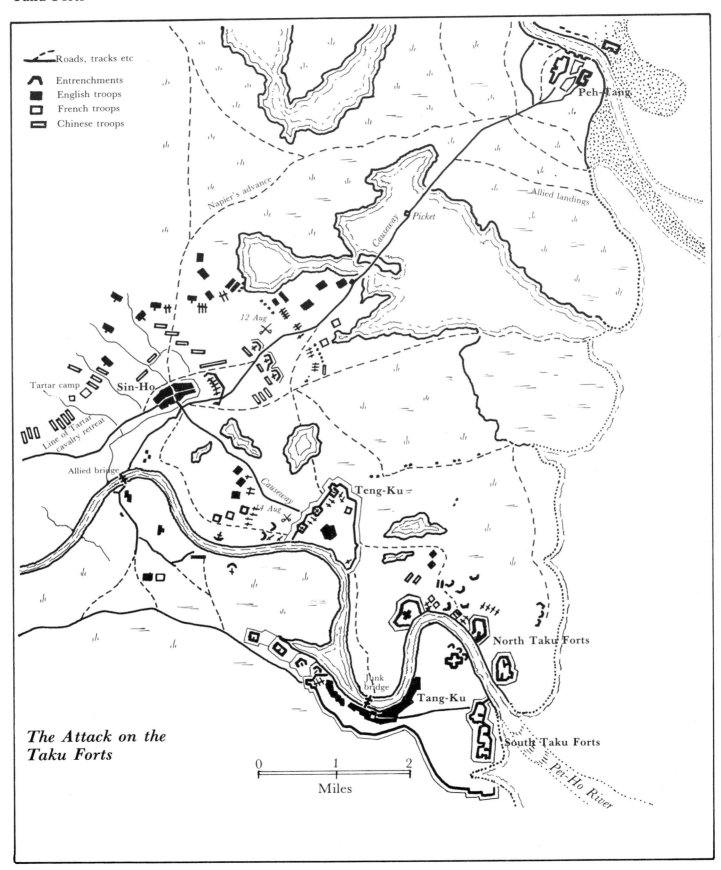

Roads, tracks etc
Entrenchments
English troops
French troops
Chinese troops

Napier's advance

Causeway *Picket*

Allied landings

Peh-Tang

12 Aug

Tartar camp

Sin-Ho

*Line of Tartar
cavalry retreat*

Allied bridge

Causeway

14 Aug

Teng-Ku

North Taku Forts

*Junk
bridge*

Tang-Ku

South Taku Forts

Pei-Ho River

*The Attack on the
Taku Forts*

0   1   2

Miles

If Peking could have been taken by avoiding the Taku Forts they would have done it, but it was not possible. However both French and British were in complete agreement that the forts must somehow this time be taken from the rear.

Despite his protestations and arguments for the southern approach, in the end de Montauban landed to the north disembarking at Peh-Tang where the Allies set up a great encampment. In the subsequent detailed planning for the assault on the forts themselves the Frenchman again expressed vehement opposition, but Grant was not disuaded and merely explained in detail what *his* army planned to do and left it to the volatile Gaul to decide whether to co-operate or not. In the event, despite much gesturing, the French again complied and so it continued almost to the end. The British just got on with the job.

None of the blight of disease decimated the army's ranks in China as it had done in the Crimea, although dysentery and malaria were much feared and had raged through unfortunate regiments based further south in earlier years. Every opportunity was made to prepare the men for dangers. Lessons had been absorbed from the 1842 campaign and, with several hospital ships on station offshore to which the wounded and sick were hastily evacuated, the health of the army held up in a remarkable manner.

From Peh-Tang to Taku stretched eight dreary miles of salt and black silt. D. F. Rennie recalled four years later his first distant glimpse of those glowering and eerie fortifications. '...Looking out for land I saw in the distant haze three dark masses, apparently equidistant from each other and of symmetrical shape, looming obscurely above the horizon. I looked at them through my glass and concluded they were the Taku forts'.

General Sutton's brigade, the first troops ashore, soon sampled the stinking knee-deep mud and spent a night trying to sleep in the open on a dank, damp causeway. The town of Peh-Tang itself was soon occupied and divided equally between the two armies. The Chinese made no attempt to dispute the town but the causeway towards Sin-Ho was breached for a considerable way along its length and defensive positions thrown up to either side. The defenders were counting on the Allies' being forced to make a direct assault along the causeway, and in such circumstances were confident of holding them without fear of being outflanked.

But outflanked they were! About half a mile down the causeway, Wolseley and a cavalry squadron came upon a rough cart track that branched off from the straight causeway itself and snaked west through the swamps and lagoons, past some joss poles and ancient tombs. It skirted the southern bank of a wide creek to the north and dropped back down behind Sin-Ho from the north across an open plain which proved quite suitable for the deployment of horses. A Tartar camp with an estimated 20,000 enemy cavalry stood to the west of Sin-Ho. Such a large force posed a powerful threat. Between this camp and the loop of the Pei-Ho River was an area criss-crossed with canals and water gardens in advance of the hard ground south of the town, adjacent to the southbound causeway leading to Teng-Ku. The British engineers worked hard for two days strengthening the track and making it suitable for the passage of a large force of troops. The work was carried out under a protecting screen to prevent the Chinese getting wind of what was afoot.

Under the 'Buggins' Turn' agreement reached by the respective commanders in the field, it was agreed the British should lead off the attack and so, on 12 August, when all was ready, the initial skirmishing began.

Sir John Michel took the 1st Division down the causeway in a head-on attack on the defence works there while Napier took his division round by the cart track and came in from the rear. All this was well done and quickly accomplished with the minimum of both fighting and losses. The Chinese defence works once assaulted proved to be far less formidable than feared, being not much more than entrenched outposts. The defenders indeed offered little resistance. When Napier's force marched in from the north only a small part of the expected huge mass of Tartar horsemen put in an appearance.

Napier's Second Division had left their billets at 04:00 that morning. A skirmishing party of 200 men of the 3rd Buffs, commanded by Lt-Col Sargent, with two of the new Armstrong 12pdr guns of Capt Milward's battery preceded the main body. The main force followed the brigades, being advanced in line of continuous columns, and consisting of four more Armstrong's, the 23rd Company, Royal Engineers; the bulk of the 3rd Buffs, the 8th Punjab Infantry, the 44th Regiment of Foot; Rotten's Rocket Battery; the Royal Marine contingent and the Madras Sappers and Miners. Protecting the flanks of the extended column was the 67th Regiment of Foot, and bringing up the rear, reserve ammunition parties, hospital stretchers and the rear guard. Out on the plain to the right jingled the resplendent horsemen of the King's Dragoon Guards, Probyn's Horse; and three 9pdr field guns of Capt Stirling's battery with Fane's Horse as flankers.

The causeway proved daunting, the '...deep

tenacious mud . . .', making movement so difficult that it took three-and-a-half hours before the rear of the column cleared the Peh-Tang gate. Off the causeway things got worse. Napier recorded that:

> 'The Commander-in-Chief was himself a witness of the extreme difficulties which had to be overcome in extricating the troops from the inundated town and advancing thence through the deep mud, in which gun wheels frequently were embedded axle deep. It cost two hours' hard labour to the troops to traverse the first two miles.'

Napier was aware of the Tartar horde to his front, so a halt was made to enable the rear to struggle through the heavy ground to close up. By first light his whole division had re-assembled and rested, so he rode forward to scan the flat landscape to the south. The 1st Division was advancing along the causeway to his left and he saw masses of Chinese troops in the trenches there and also deployed in front of Sin-Ho itself. He himself was undetected, and the enemy had been neatly out-manouevered by the simple expedient of marching troops where they thought troops could not march. Like the Russians on the Alma they were too confident in the natural terrain to take even the most elementary precautions.

The First Division now moved due south both to take Chinese forces in the flank and to cut off their line of retreat. At 1,500 yards range, Milward's Armstrongs commenced firing, the first time these guns had been fired in anger. Napier recorded that, ' . . . the range and accuracy of its fire excited the admiration of the force'. Grant expressed similar views in a later assessment to the Duke of Cambridge, ' . . . Their precision is most excellent and their range very great. When the percussion shell explodes nothing can be more effective . . .'.

But these guns had problems. The dampness of the battlefield affected the charges, causing several premature breech explosions and fatalities among their gunners. The explosions threw up huge columns of mud and earth and looked awe-inspiring but the nature of the ground muffled the blast effects of the heavy shells and casualties among the Chinese were far fewer than expected. Although great work was done by these weapons in this campaign, they were not adopted by the Army, which reverted again to muzzle loaders, which were reliable, proven and above all, easy to manufacture. British pluck and know-how would somehow compensate for the rest!

The early shells detonated among the Tartar cavalry caused some initial shock but these stoic Asiatics soon regained their composure and rallied. They soon streamed by a hidden track across the marsh and quickly

The Chinese had numerous cavalry, mainly Tartar horsemen. Although heavily outnumbered, the King's Dragoon Guards soon put them to flight.

formed into a regular line thereby encircling the British northern force, completing the ring with further horsemen who ' . . . hitherto had kept out of sight . . .', and who, ' . . . seemed to rise in position from the plain'.

Brigadier Pattle, commanding the British cavalry, at once led out his smaller force to meet this mounted mass, detaching a part to protect the British right rear. Napier told him to take any opportunity offered to charge and

Test firing a Whitworth 3-pdr gun. The British artillery was most effective during the war in China.

with dead and dying men and ponies.

These attacks seen off in no uncertain manner, Napier resumed his advance to the western end of Sin-Ho itself, joining forces with the 1st Division which had broken through on the causeway. No Chinese or Mongolian infantry were encountered at close quarters, having apparently cut and run once their cavalry had been beaten off.

Sin-Ho was thus entered by the Allied armies in a single day. In the grounds were discovered the hastily abandoned trappings of the Chinese Commander-in-Chief, General San-ko-lin-sin but that was all. It had all been very easy and marred only by more grumbling by the French about the state of the ground they were to advance over and their holding back all bar a token force of 1,000 men. They were not needed.

THE SOLDIERS OF THE EMPEROR

The Celestial Empire, although Manchu, relied a great deal on Tartar and Mongol forces both for its mass of cavalry and for its infantry. In the main, both arms were very primitively equipped, matchlocks being the principal firearm used. Although some were quite dexterous in its use it was hardly an adequate weapon to pit against the British Minie. The majority of the Emperor's infantry however had to make do with medieval weapons, the short Tartar bow, able to be used from the saddle and a few self-loading crossbows but in the main swords, spears and pikes. Large round shields were carried, often intricately decorated with dragon motifs and the like. These were sometimes made of brass

Typical Chinese cavalry and foot soldiers. Horsemen relied on the traditional bow and swords while a few of the infantry had primitive muskets.

disperse the enemy horsemen if he could and this very soon, he did. The Armstrongs continued to assail them and when the King's Dragoon Guards put spurs to mounts and charged full tilt at them they scattered and dispersed very fast, using the old trick of turning in their saddles to fire their muskets and bows at the pursuing British cavalry. Their short, sturdy, little pony mounts were able to outdistance the Dragoons' fine horses, not yet fit from the long sea voyage, but the threat was dispersed. While this stirring work was in progress another body of enemy horsemen had come round to attack the isolated detachment of Capt Stirling's half-battery of 9pdrs which, being out of range, had not played a part in the battle. Their only escort was some thirty mounted Sikhs of Fane's Horse under the command of Lt MacGregor but they were very boldly and ably handled, charging the vastly superior force of Tartars with resolution, routing them and inflicting heavy losses, thus saving the gunners. MacGregor and many of his men were injured in this fierce little battle, but none was killed.

Another group of determined Tartars advanced upon the Buffs holding the left front position, despite the attentions of two Armstrongs under Lt Harvey and showers of rockets from the battery of Capt Rotten. These horsemen pressed to within 450 yards of the British line taking severe casualties from the musketry of the Buffs and won the sincere admiration of the British soldiers for their courage. A similar brave assault was made against Brigadier Reeves's 4th Brigade but the steady, disciplined fire of the British infantry exacted a heavy toll from the horsemen who eventually veered away and took to their heels leaving the ground littered and very heavy. It is little wonder then that only when closely pressed in the open without the means of withdrawal could the enemy infantry be persuaded to stand and fight. Their only chance was at close-quarters and on the rare occasions when hand-to-hand work was called for they proved as brave a foe as any.

Their great preponderance of horseman was always a threat, but after their severe handling by Napier on the first day of the battle they were wary and elusive, preferring to concentrate in small, isolated detachments rather than again make suicidal charges against massed Minie fire, and who can blame them? They could certainly never be ignored but the King's Dragoon Guards, although but a fraction of their number, never lost the initiative and soon earned a great reputation for 'Tartar-sticking'.

The true strength of the Chinese defences lay in the forts themselves, and in the artillery emplaced therein. This was almost exclusively Chinese manned and the bloody repulse of the British naval squadron and the Royal Marines the year before had testified to their efficiency. Nobody treated them lightly a second time. Of course nothing they possessed could match the 12pdrs for range and power but nonetheless the forts between them mounted a formidable array of weapons, smooth-bore 32pdrs, ancient mortars and the Chinese *Gingall*.

The last was a versatile piece used both in the field and from behind fortifications. It had a long barrel which fired a 1lb solid shot, and gun and mounting could be quickly taken apart and carried into battle on two ponies, making it very versatile. Its range, however, was poor. The 'stink pots', fire grenades with long chains which were whirled around the heads of the carriers and then released, were also mainly close-range weapons.

Their dress was traditional, the Tartar cavalry being described as wearing long under garments of dark material with a lighter, padded jacket over the top, blue trousers and black Tartar boots. They wore black silk Chinese hats with the brims turned up all round and two squirrels' tails projecting from the rear. Their spears were decorated with red horse-hair affixed to the shafts.

The gunners wore simple smocks with crossbelts and round pouches. Pigtails of course were then common among all Chinese. Reports that the gunners were tied to their guns to prevent them running away have always been made about our enemies and the Chinese War was no exception. These reports were completely false, the port-fires for the cannon being lengths of ropeyarn fastened to the gunners' wrists. Their poor performance in the open when faced by a strong European force should not detract from the overall skill and bravery of

A typical Mandarin at the time of the 1860 war in China, distant, aloof and above all, evasive. The Governor-General of Kwang-Tung and Kwang-i, Lea-On.

the Chinese armies about Taku. Earlier they had, under the same General San-ko-lin-sin (which Thomas Atkins immediately turned into 'Sam Collinson'), inflicted a defeat on a rebellious army at Taiping. San-ko-lin-sin was a typical Tartar mandarin, outwardly contemptuous of his foe, proud and autocratic, but secretly fearing he had more than met his match in the Allied forces. Chinese justice was rough justice. A pair of soldiers from the Buffs was captured by a cavalry patrol the day after the battle and they were taken before him. One of them, Pte John Moyse, who refused to perform the obsequious *kow-tow* was summarily beheaded.

With such men representing the Manchu dynasty it was clear that nothing but total defeat would bring about a peace. For their part the Chinese, Mongols and Tartars had no doubts about the justice of their cause. They were fighting to defend their Emperor and their land, not just against an invading army, but an army of 'Barbarians'. It is hard even now to understand the contempt and horror with which the average Chinese viewed the European soldiers. Many civilians committed suicide rather than face subjugation by such 'monsters', and the

Despite the fact they were at war, the Chinese never missed an opportunity to trade. Here opportunists ply their wares to Allied troops in camp.

looting and general behaviour of the French soldiers, unfettered by their officers, did much to reinforce the Chinese viewpoint. Fortunately the British soldiers behaved much better and were disciplined and correct in the main, but all the 'foreign devils' were tarred with the same brush.

Immediately after Sin-Ho had been occupied the French, now that it was their turn, rushed off down the road toward the next fortified town, Teng-Ku, in the hope of carrying it cheaply by surprise attack. Teng-Ku could only be reached via the raised causeway which ran parallel to the river at this point, although there was firm ground between the two. Alas for *élan,* the Chinese were well-prepared with 45 guns mounted behind the three-mile crenellated wall fortifications, reinforced by a long, deep trench running up from the river and curving round to the swampy ground to the north.

The French stopped – it was again the British turn – and they moved forward in concert with the British 1st Division, the British covering the hard ground to the right and the French again on the causeway itself. The engineers particularly distinguished themselves in

this campaign and again it was their bridging work across the various small dykes that helped facilitate the advance up to the walls of Tang-Ku. Flanking fire from a Chinese battery and a pair of beached war junks on the other side of the river was quickly silenced by a storming party. Sapping was conducted under the cover of darkness to bring the Allied trenches right under the Chinese defences, while the ditch was rendered ineffective by damming it at the river entrance.

The Allies attacked next day, under covering fire from 36 guns. The walls were soon breached in numerous places and the Chinese guns dismounted or silenced as the Royal Artillery moved forward steadily by alternate battery positions to point-blank range. Both the French and British infantry succeeded in gaining access to the fort by daring use of scaling ladders. The remaining defenders then forsook the walls abandoning their cannon, and made off down the causeway, crossing the Pei-Ho by a bridge of boats and taking refuge in the South Fort. This neat little action was achieved without any Allied losses whatsoever but some fifty or so Chinese lay dead in the fortifications.

It was time for the final blow.

THE FINAL PREPARATIONS

Careful preparation by the sappers was once again the key to the final stage and the culmination of the Allied effort. For four days after the occupation of Sin-Ho on 14 August, much dedicated work was done by the Royal Engineers under Graham, who was himself wounded in the process. Pontoon bridges were erected over the many canals and ditches interlacing the low-lying hinterland. Whole new embanked roads were built for the passage of artillery, one running west from Teng-Ku into the dismal salt marsh north of the North Taku forts, which the tide inundated daily. This causeway was extended through the wet-lands until the firmer ground at the rear of the forts was reached, all work being subjected to the enemy's fire. In the bend of the Pei-Ho river the three northern forts were ranged *en echelon* to give mutual covering fire, and Hope saw clearly that to capture the central northern fort would give him an advantageous site from which to concentrate further efforts on the two strongholds on either side of the estuary closest to the sea, while isolating the most upstream position.

Napier marched his division comprising Milward's battery, the Madras Mountain Train, 23rd Company Royal Engineers, a company of Madras Sappers, and the 67th Regt out of Teng-Ku on 19 August until they reached the series of canals which beset the enemy position. Here the engineers again got to work, under the direction of Lt-Col Mann, and made a series of passages across these obstructions. During the night the whole force advanced to within 800 yards of the fort. Attempts to work round through the salt workings, canals and reservoirs on the Chinese right proved impossible and the enemy's left flank was protected by a small Tartar cantonment, itself under protection of the guns on the right bank.

Final preparations were made next day while a peaceful surrender of the forts was sought by Grant. Mr Parkes, the official interpreter and Capt Graham were sent forward under a flag of truce but the Chinese General was as scornful as ever and they returned empty-handed. At 11:00 the guns in the forts opened a heavy fire on the front-line positions as a further response, both north and south forts taking part in a prolonged carronade. Nothing could be done but to carry the Taku forts by fire and storm!

The British replied with a few rounds at 2,000 yards from Milward's battery. The Chinese fire made little impact and caused not a single British casualty but it did reveal their exact strength and disposition to the watching British commanders who adjusted their plans accordingly. This helped considerably in the subsequent placings of their own heavy weapons for the battle on the morrow. The final bridges were thrown across the canal at the same time. The 2nd Division was reinforced on the 20th by Govan's battery, Pennycuick's battery, Bedingfield's battery, Rotten's Rocket battery, a company of Madras Sappers, the 44th Regt and the Royal Marine Light Infantry, the batteries being passed to the front and emplaced, save for a single 8in gun which became so bogged down that it was incapable of being extracted until the following day.

The French had again disagreed with Grant's plans and suggested the alternative strategy of attacking the entrenchments around Tung-Ku town on the south bank of the river, then moving to take the Southern Forts. A bridge of boats was built higher up the river, below Sin-Ho, to facilitate the passage of the bulk of the Allied armies to this side of the Pei-Ho river for such an eventuality. Thus, argued de Montauban, the Chinese would be hemmed in and unable to escape in any direction. Grant was in no doubt that such a policy would be both costly in Allied lives and risky. With the northern attack the river protected their right flank. He would not be party to another 'mad dash' by the French. De Montauban went through the usual antics, but finally gave way, covering his back by writing to his Government of his own plan in case Grant's assault

A cartoon or sketch of General Sir Hope Grant mounted on a Chinese steed at the time of the battle for Sin-Ho and the assault on the Taku Forts.

failed.

Eventually, the main attack was undertaken by 2,500 British troops and 1,000 French with artillery support from all the main field and siege guns, six batteries in all, and by gunboats and rocket-equipped boats of the Royal Navy on the river. The Chinese would thus be prevented from moving all their guns to the landward side of the forts.

The French commander, General Collineau, visited Napier at dusk on the 20th and both generals toured the front to become fully acquainted with the terrain and the plans. Major Greathead, the *aide-de-camp* was detached to conduct the French contingent into position accordingly. Grant visited the 2nd Division's forward positions early on the 20th and the final deployment of the artillery was decided.

THE FORTS FALL

On the 21st August 1860 the attack commenced. The first British infantry filed out of their positions at 04:00, the right wing of the 67th and 44th Regts moved under cover of the canals near the mortar battery, and the left wing of the 44th, 67th and one-half of the RMLI forming their support was placed under cover of the canals close to Milward's guns. The Royal Engineers, Sappers and the rest of the Royal Marines, the former with materials, the latter with pontoons, were readied behind them, to move forward with the assault waves and speed their passage. Almost immediately these British movements were spotted by the alert garrison and the Chinese guns commenced a heavy fire. Milward's battery responded. The late arrival of the French again delayed the British attack.

By 06:00 all the British guns were heavily engaged, and General Collineau's force was now in place on the right with the French guns firing. Despite the great length of wall at the forts not all the enemy guns were occupied and a few free cannon began troubling the French right with well-directed shots. These cannons were quickly taken under fire by Capt Barry's guns from the town before they could do much harm.

From the muzzles of all the Allied guns; 8in mortars, 32, 24, 12 and 9pdrs, roared a heavy bombardment of shot and shell which smashed down on the Chinese gunners, while the guns of the warships added their quota. One spectacular direct hit by an 8in shell on the fort's arsenal caused an enormous explosion which wreathed the fort in smoke. This caused a temporary lull in the return fire from the Chinese guns, but they resolutely came back again after a short interval, although firing was much reduced. A similar result was obtained by the gunboats on the more distant fort.

With Chinese fire perceptibly slackening Napier moved his field guns forward to within 450 yards of the fort and, as the assault further developed, more British guns were moved forward until all were ultimately ranged in a row facing the northern walls of the fort at close quarters. From north to south were ranged the following batteries: Govan's, Barry's, Rotten's and Hicks's Madras artillery. They had orders to concentrate on the left of the gateway to effect a breach. Sir John Campbell's howitzers were sent to support the French storming column to the right and were much praised by the French commander for their good work here.

In the interim the British skirmishing line advanced to within 300 yards of the Chinese works, with the French similarly making progress supported by two of Capt Desborough's guns. But the Taku Forts were tough nuts to crack. The light artillery pieces were having little effect on the walls so Napier brought forward an 8in howitzer while the 9pdrs followed the skirmish lines even closer until they were at the edge of the outer, water-filled ditch.

Even with such formidable covering fire these deep

Deployment of Artillery against the Taku Forts

Number 1 Battery:
Six French 24pdr guns closest to the river bend, sheltered by the Tartar village and supported by Major Guy Rotten's Rocket battery. These to fire in direct support of the French infantry which was to advance down the north bank of the river to the right of the track. In addition, two of Barry's guns and two of Govan's 9pdrs placed at the south-east angle of Tang-Ku walls to cover the right of the French advance.

Number 2 Battery:
Major C. Pennycuick's guns, to provide direct support to the British 2nd Division marching in alignment with the French but left of the track.
Capt J. Desborough's battery with three 8in mortars. In advance of these and close to the river and the forts' northern flank to be sited to batter the Chinese defences from 500 yards range.

Number 3 Battery:
Two 32pdrs and two 8in howitzers under Capt J. Bedingfield located north of the track, to play on the north fort and effect a breach for the assault parties.

Number 4 Battery:
Two 24pdrs from Capt Govan's battery and two from Capt Desborough's positioned due north of the fort assaulted to provide covering fire.

Number 5 Battery:
Capt I. Milward's four Armstrong guns sited well back but with the range to reach the forts with ease, and to direct counter-battery fire to silence the enemy guns of the most northern fort.

Number 6 Battery:
One 8in gun, two of Capt Barry's Armstrongs and two French 24pdr guns placed to cover the British right and to attack the southern forts and the guns on the south bank of the river.

The low-lying but formidable Taku Forts after the main attack. The wilderness of mud and water shows the difficulties the Allies had in approaching them.

dykes were hazardous. The Royal Marine party, under the command of Lt-Col Gascoigne, RM, bravely came forward down the line of the causeway carrying the pontoon bridge, but the Chinese soldiers manning the walls opened such a severe fire upon them that half were killed and wounded in an instant and they were forced to retire. Among the casualties in this little foray were Lt-Col Travers, RMLI and again Major Graham, RE. Royal Marine Sergeant Henry Trent was wounded at this time, but still made persistent efforts to get the pontoon forward until hit a second time and forced to desist.

The assault goes in. While parties seek ways to gain the tops of the walls the artillery produces a satisfactory explosion inside one fort. Meanwhile further reinforcements make their way along the causeways through the mire.

The only hope lay in the ladder parties under Lt Pritchard, RE, and these were at once brought forward. They passed their ladders across the ditches to the right of the British line. The 44th, led by Lt-Col McMahon, and 67th, under Lt-Col Knox, then pressed forward across this rickety ramp. Others, like Knox himself, chose to swim across to advance on the main gate itself. Brigadier Reeves, well up in front with his men, fell wounded at the edge of the ditch at this period, as did Capt Brooke, Napier's ADC.

The French also used ladder-bridges to cross. Both armies therefore effected a lodgment under the Chinese ramparts, but how to proceed further was a new problem. The walls were not yet fully breached, the gates were built up internally and could not be stormed and a heavy fire continued to be directed down on the crouching infantry by the unabashed defenders. Napier described the Chinese soldiers' resistance at this point as, '...noble, and vigorous...'. The French attempted to escalade the angle of the fort but were repulsed. Desperate measures were called for and once again the Royal Artillery responded with a will.

Two howitzers were brought as far forward as possible despite the fire from the walls, and were reinforced by two of Govan's 9pdrs, together with a small rocket battery under Lt G. G. Hannen, all being manhandled to within 80 yards of the enemy rampart. Here the gunners cooly opened fire directly over the heads of their own infantry, smashing the parapet where the enemy defenders clustered most thickly and knocking chunks off the walls.

This was all hot work and splendidly done. Gunners William Lawlers, McNally and John Walsh were all hit but continued to serve their guns. Totally accurate enemy fire at such range would have killed all gunners outright. This brave action from the British artillerymen certainly tipped the scales and resolved a potentially nasty situation. With fire from matchlock and bow thus

Chinese gunners, who fought bravely and diligently, lie dead around their guns, cut down as the infantry scaled the walls. Note the abandoned crossbow and shield.

Another view of the interior of the North Taku Fort after its fall to British storming parties with the bodies of its defenders still strewn about.

minimised, the renewed escalade by the French and the British, now through a partial breach near the gate, became practicable. Lt N. Burslem of the 67th was the first Englishman to enter the fort, but was severely wounded and forced back. Lt Rogers of the 44th was the first to fully establish himself inside the fort and was closely followed by Pte J. McDougall of the 44th and Lt E. H. Lenon of the 67th. The few remaining Chinese guns on the *cavalier* had now fallen silent, repeatedly hit by British shells. The British infantry were able to storm it, Lt Chaplin planting there the colour of the 67th Regt.

The surviving garrison, desperate because there was no other means of escape for them other than by dropping over their own walls on the river side or crossing their own defence ditches, stakes and abattis, while under severe fire from the Allied infantry and artillery, fiercely contested every step forward. Not surprisingly the defenders suffered heavy loss of life in making their exit, and the manner and place of their slaughter was particularly satisfying to those Royal Marines who had survived the previous year's assault.

By 08:30 this fort had fallen and, as General Hope Grant had predicted, its occupation proved the key to the remaining Chinese works. The captured Chinese guns were now turned upon their companions in the southern fort while the heavy guns of the British batteries shifted to continue their good work against the same target. To consolidate his position Napier now moved forward fresh regiments, the Buffs and the 8th Punjab

Infantry, under Brigadier Jephson. But before a further assault could be undertaken on either of the forts on their flanks a host of white flags suddenly appeared above their walls and enemy guns ceased firing.

MOPPING UP

At first, with the appearance of the white flags, it seemed that the battle was over, but account was not taken of traditional Chinese duplicity and when the willing interpreter, Mr Parkes, went to the gate of the northern-most fort to deliver the surrender ultimatum he was sent away with a flea in his ear. Preparations were then put in hand for a direct, methodical assault on the larger fort. However, while the British were moving their guns and infantry into the assault positions, the French went off half-cock again on their own, and this time their headlong dash without regard to plan or orders paid a handsome dividend. They managed to effect an immediate entrance to the fort through an embrasure before the surprised defenders under the impression there was a truce, could rally and thus by 10:30 a second fort had fallen without a fight or a shot fired in anger.

Nothing daunted by his former rebuff, Grant sent peace envoys, including Lord Elgin's private secretary, H. B. Loch, across the river to the town on the south bank to treat with the Chinese Governor-General of Chihli Province, Hang-Fu. The wily Governor knew his forces had been massively defeated and was well aware

Negotiations! Every foot of the journey from the mouth of the Pei-Ho to the walls of Peking itself was a constant clash with the Chinese. While the Emperor skulked in the background his envoys procrastinated and laid ambushes and treacherous tricks. All to no avail.

that with the northern forts in Allied hands his southern defence works could not long hold out on their own. Nonetheless, mindful of the fate of mandarins who dealt with the barbarians, he initially refused to take responsibility for the surrender. He claimed that this could only be undertaken by the C-in-C of his army, but that worthy had long since beat a hasty retreat up the Pei-Ho river, taking the bulk of the remaining Tartar horsemen with him.

However, Grant was by now well familiar with the tactics of Chinese diplomacy and, under threat of renewed assault on the 22nd, and with much patient work by Parkes in the background, Hang-Fu caved in and the Allied troops were able quickly to occupy the remaining forts without incident. They dismantled the Chinese heavy guns quickly, and removed the chains and barriers across the river mouth, allowing the Allied

fleet to enter the Pei-Ho peacefully, as they had wished to do eighteen months and many Chinese lives earlier. Continuing delaying tactics by Hang-Fu and by the Emperor himself, were ignored by Lord Elgin and eventually a meeting of the two envoys with representatives of the Manchus was again arranged at Tientsin. Further delaying tactics occurred, this time by three more Chinese envoys, who negotiated a treaty and then revealed they had no powers to sign it. Clearly they were playing for time, waiting for the onset of winter to stop the advance on the Chinese capital. Lord Elgin, Baron Gros and the Allied representatives would have no more of this farce and, led by the ships of Admiral Hope's river squadron, the Allied armies continued their advance north.

Still the Chinese continued to play the same game, resolutely urging the Allies to halt their forces and talk but Lord Elgin replied that he would not stop until he reached Ting-Chow, some ten miles below Peking itself. They were met by Prince Tsai who at first seemed to treat sincerely. However when under a flag of truce the Allied negotiators, Parkes, De Normann, Loch, *Times* correspondent Bowlby, three officers and a troop of cavalry, they were greeted not with politeness but the old evasiveness. They were also concerned to note that the Chinese, under the orders of General San-ko-lin-sin once more, were preparing a trap for the advance party of the Allies cutting down trees and assembling troops and cavalry in large numbers. While pretending not to realise what was happening some of the party managed to get away and warn Grant. The others were summarily attacked by their hosts who ignored the flag of truce and executed or imprisoned the Allied party. Hostilities were resumed.

The Chinese had seventy guns and the usual mass of horsemen and the little Allied force, the French on the right and the British on the left, was soon in danger of being overwhelmed. However, once more, the British irregular cavalry in their penny packet numbers, charged the enemy time and time again and broke them. The King's Dragoon Guards were brought up together with the Armstrong guns and the 99th Regt, and the battle of Chan-chia-wan was turned into another Chinese rout. Another fierce battle was fought on 21 September at the Pal-le-chiao bridge, when the pick of the Chinese Imperial Guard were thrown into the fight and duly sent packing by the French, again after the British artillery and cavalry had broken the main Tartar force.

The Emperor himself now fled his capital to Jehol in the north, but left his envoys, Prince Kung and Hang-ki, to negotiate. The British siege train was eventually brought up to deal with the huge, forbidding, forty-feet-high and sixty-feet-wide walls of the city. They were emplaced in front of the Anting Gate and, under the direct threat to demolish it and sack the city, the Chinese finally, but still reluctantly, agreed the Allied terms. Meanwhile the French had run wild again, looting the enormous complex of the Summer Palace, much to Grant's stern disapproval. The Emperor was enraged and ordered the execution of Parkes and Loch, but fortunately they had already been released. Napier marched in with 400 men and took possession of the Chinese capital.

The treaty was signed in the Hall of Ceremonies on 24 October 1860 by Prince Kung, the Emperor himself remaining sulking at Jehol. It included the ceding of Kowloon Territory to Britain and Tientsin was made an open port in addition to the original treaty terms. To

The final battle was for the Pa-Li-Chian bridge just eight miles from Peking itself. Here the French are seen storming the bridge and crossing the last natural barrier before the city. The Summer Palace complex was extensively looted.

punish the Emperor personally for the treacherous murder of the peace envoys and the war itself, Grant had the Yuen-ming-yuen Palace burnt to the ground. The world reacted in horror to this apparent vandalism and it is for this that the Third China War is chiefly remembered by modern historians.

With regard to the actual fighting, time and again a handful of British troops routed huge numbers of the Empire's best troops. They did not lack courage but they lacked good leadership. This was proven by Gordon in the years that followed. He took some 3,000 Chinese troops, put them in the hands of his own officers, dismissing most of the riff-raff white officers they had and in a short while built this force into the 'Ever-Victorious Army' that finally crushed the Taiping Rebellion and brought a lasting peace to that troubled land.

Grant received a GCB for his work. Napier, whose talent for good sound organisation on which sure and steady victories were built we shall meet again in the next chapter. The glowering Taku forts featured again in British operations in China during the Boxer Rebellion.

Chapter Four

MAGDALA

13 April 1868

HOSTAGE TAKING

During the period of Idi Amin's obscene dictatorship over the unfortunate people of the central African state of Uganda the Israeli Government took the daring decision to send in a rescue party by air to Entebbe airport and release the hostages being held there. Almost one hundred years prior to the Israeli operation another mentally-unstable dictator ruling an African nation had acted in much the same manner and, after a prolonged and lengthy period of patient negotiation, Great Britain had been forced to adopt the same measures as Israel to retrieve the situation. The time-scale of the operation was entirely different; it was a campaign of months not hours and, the country itself, Abyssinia, indeed the whole of the 'Dark Continent' was little known. Nonetheless in the context of the period, General Napier's campaign of 1868 was as brilliantly planned and executed as the Entebbe mission.

The dictator Theodore III was born Liz Kasa, the mentally disturbed son of a Kourarian official who became a cleric but who subsequently turned to theft and extortion. By murder and intrigue he elevated himself through the tangled web of Abyssinian politics until, at the age of thirty-eight, he felt secure enough

Panoramic view of the final storming of Magdala on Easter Monday, 13 April 1868. Despite the awesome natural barriers and Abyssinian defence, resistance was soon broken by Napier's British and Indian force.

to have himself proclaimed absolute ruler. He had his title expanded to King Theodore III, King of Ethiopia, King of Kings, Emperor and the Chosen of God. He embraced the Christian religion as a means to various ends including the conquest and subjugation of the surrounding Moslem tribes and states, including the Gallas. One of Theodore's other, unachieved, objectives was to lead an army to liberate Jerusalem from Turkish rule in the manner of the Crusaders of the Middle Ages. His main base was atop the remote and awesome mountain of Magdala which lies in northern Abyssinia between the Blue Nile in the west and the southern mouth of the Red Sea.

He quickly developed some military skill and became adept at putting his opponents to the sword and their settlements to the torch. Night attacks became his speciality and his cunning was matched only by his persecution mania. His cruelty and rapacity were fuelled by a growing insanity. It is likely that Theodore, if left alone, would have continued the way of most such African rulers until overthrown or slaughtered in turn by opponents or equally ambitious subordinates. Unfortunately Lord Palmerston's Government decided that a British envoy was necessary to represent the Union Flag in even this remote part of the globe and this gentleman, Walter Plowden, became not only British envoy, but allowed himself to be used by the King for his own ends. For a while all went well, the Queen herself sent the King gifts including a pair of pistols suitably engraved, but Theodore, blinded by his own visions, read more into these diplomatic gestures than was intended. Meanwhile Plowden had met his death while on an unauthorised mission for the King. Still no great harm had been done, but his successor, Capt Charles Cameron, proved himself less receptive to the King's wishes and he was therefore incarcerated and subjected to great torture.

This was compounded by further insults and disgraceful behaviour. A letter written in 1863, formally proposing an alliance between Theodore and the British Empire to begin the conquest of all the Moslem world, went astray in London and was not delivered until many months after its despatch. The Emperor convinced himself that this was a deliberate slight and the acknowledgement, via a Turkish intermediary Hormuzd Rassam, asking for the release of Cameron, was ignored. The floggings continued. Further prisoners were taken and kept in chains in huts at Magdala. There were German missionaries, various British officials on Cameron's staff, their wives, some lay preachers, quite a *pot-pourri* of individuals of different nationalities—but

many were British. Another letter from the King requested more specialists be sent to help him expand his growing army. Cannon and muskets were purchased from Europe, and artisans imported to forge more of the same and teach the warriors how to use them in combat.

At first Her Britannic Majesty's Government negotiated patiently but each approach only seemed to enrage the King to further insult. With the imprisoning of the envoy Rassam and his escort, young Lt Prideaux who had been sent to negotiate, patience snapped. On 13 August 1867, four years after the first unfortunate had been incarcerated, the Government decided to despatch an expeditionary force to rescue all the hostages. The proximity of Bombay to the seat of the trouble made it inevitable that the bulk of the troops would come from that theatre, and to command them they chose the local C-in-C, an officer of already high repute, Sir Robert Napier the conqueror of Peking, now

The mad King Theodore III eventually assembled a whole range of European hostages whom he kept under constant threat of death. He variously chained them, tortured them and marched them many hundreds of miles throughout southern Abyssinia before he decided to make his final stand on the mountain top at Magdala.

fifty-six and held in very high esteem. He was asked to prepare a report on how such an expedition could be mounted, and, in September, an official ultimatum was delivered to Theodore.

Theodore was scornful of the wrath his belligerent attitude had at last stirred up. He seemed not to realise just what he was taking on, or else his mental state overrode rationality. To avoid an outbreak of cholera he shifted his base north to Deba Tabor, south-east of Gondor, putting its Christian churches to the torch and instantly exterminating anyone his diseased mind felt had wronged him. This gradually included the bulk of

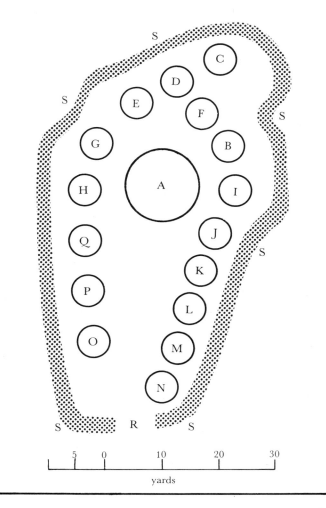

Ground plan of the Huts and enclosure which formed the prison of the British Mission in Magdala 1867.

A Kitchen, common to all.
B The Rev Rosenthal's Hut.
C Mr Rassam's Hut.
D & G. Itto Samuel's Huts.
E Dr Blanc and Lieut Prideaux's Huts.
F Office.
H Reception Room.
I Mr Stern's Hut.
J Capt. Cameron's Hut.
K Mr Keran's Hut.
L Pietro's Hut. In this hut the dead King was laid
M.N.O.P. Servant's Huts.
Q Guard Room.
R Gateway.
S. Enclosing Stockade.

Magdala

the civilian population as his army's need for food rapidly exceeded the available supply. While this genocide was taking place in one of the few remaining areas of Abyssinia the 'King of Kings' still controlled, across the Indian Ocean General Napier was busy assembling a small, but exceedingly workmanlike army to carry out his task and to bring about retribution.

In all, there were some 4,000 European troops with 9,000 Native troops, the latter mainly from Bombay, with a further 7,000 camp followers.

Weapons used by the British force contrasted sharply in type and range. The Native Infantry from India were, for the most part, still equipped exclusively with the old

Field-Marshal Lord Napier of Magdala, GCB, GCSI, towards the end of his long and most distinguished career. He was a careful, if somewhat over-prudent planner who left little to chance.

Seen below with his staff attending diligently to his instructions, Napier brought off a remarkable coup in marching an army through unknown terrain, storming an impregnable fortress and rescuing every hostage alive. All in a day's work for a Victorian general!

90

COMPOSITION AND DISPOSITION OF THE BRITISH ARMY AGAINST MAGDALA

Sir Robert Napier's Staff:
Colonel the Honorable F. A. Thesiger (later to become Lord Chelmsford) Deputy Adjutant-General.
Capt T. J. Holland, Assistant Quarter-Master-General
Lt Colonel M. A. Dillen, Military Secretary
Lt H. M. Hozier, Assistant Military Secretary
Brig-Gen W. L. Merewether, CB Political Officer
Major Grant, CB Intelligence Department
Capt Speedy, Amharic Interpreter
Lt R. Napier, (Aide de camp)
Lt W. Scott, (Aide de camp)
Lord C. Hamilton, (Aide de camp)
H. Q. Escort:
10th Company, Royal Engineers 3rd Bombay Light Cavalry—25 troopers

1st Division (Maj-Gen Sir Charles Staveley, KCB)
Lt-Col H. H. A. Wood, Assistant Adjutant-General,
Major R. Baigrie, Assistant Quarter-Master-General,
Pioneer Force, Colonel Field, 10th Native Infantry
Capt Macgregor, Deputy Assistant Quarter-Master-General
Lt Shewell, Commissary
Capt Goodfellow, Field Surgeon
Lt Jopp, Assistant Field Surgeon
Colonel R. Phayre, Deputy Quarter-Master-General
(to survey the road and country in its vicinity)

This force, to march two days in advance of the 1st Brigade, 1st Division
Troops:
3rd Light Cavalry—40 troopers
3rd Scinde Horse—40 troopers
3rd and 4th Companies Bombay Sappers and Miners
33rd Regt (2 Companies)
10th Native Infantry (HQ Wing)—200 men
23rd Punjabi Pioneers 1 Company

1st Brigade, 1st Division (Brig-Gen Schneider)
Capt Beville, Brevet Major
Capt Hogg, Deputy Assistant Quarter-Master-General
Major Mignou, Commissary

Troops:
3rd Dragoon Guards (HQ Wing)
3rd Light Cavalry
3rd Scind Horse
G/14 Battery Royal Artillery (four 12pdr, steel, breech-loading Armstrong mountain guns)
H/21 Battery Royal Artillery (six 7pdr guns)
4th (King's Own Royal) Regiment of Foot
33rd (Duke of Wellington's Regiment of Foot HQ and eight companies)
10th Company Royal Engineers
27th (Beloochies) Regt Native Light Infantry (HQ Wing)

2nd Brigade, (2nd Division Brig-Gen Wilby)
Capt William Hicks, Brevet Major (later the ill-famed Hicks Pasha slaughtered in the Sudan)
Capt Fawcett, Deputy Assistant Quarter-Master-General
Major Burdin, Commissary

Troops:
12th Bengal Cavalry (HQ Wing)
B/21 Battery, Royal Artillery (six 7pdr guns)
5/25 Battery, detached, with two 8in mortars
Rocket Battery Naval Brigade, (four rocket-tubes)
K Company Madras Sappers and Miners
23rd Regt (Punjab Pioneers) Native Light Infantry (HQ and seven companies)
27th Regt (Beloochies) Native Light Infantry (Wing)

2nd Division (Maj-Gen G. Malcolm, CB)
Major G. Brady, Assistant Adjutant-General
Major Tweed, Commissary
All troops at and between Senafe and Antoto.

Antalo Garrison (Brig-Gen Collings)
Major Quies, Brevet Major
Capt James, Deputy Assistant
               Quarter-Master-General
Lt. Hose, Commissary

Troops:
12th Bengal Cavalry (Wing)
5/25 Battery Royal Artillery
H Company Madras Sappers and Miners
45th (Sherwood Foresters) Regiment of Foot
(later joined 1st Division)
3rd Regt Native Infantry
10th Regt Native Infantry (Detachment)

Adigrat Garrison (Major Fairbrother)

Troops:
10th Bengal Cavalry, 1 squadron
G/14 Battery Royal Artillery, (2 guns)
2nd Company Bombay Sappers and Miners
25th Regt Native Infantry (Wing)

Senafe Garrison (Lt-Col Little,
         25th Native Light Infantry)
Lt Becke, Staff Officer
Capt Edwardes, Deputy Assistant
               Quarter-Master-General
Major Thacker, Commissary

Troops:
26th (Cameronian) Regiment of Foot
10th Bengal Cavalry, 1 squadron
1 Company Native Artillery
21st Punjab Native Infantry (3 companies)
10th Regt Native Infantry (Wing)
Royal Marine Battery (1 Company)
25th Native Light Infantry (HQ Wing)
Depots of all Regiments in Front

Zoola Command (Brig-Gen H. Stewart)
Capt Fellowes, Brevet Major
Major Roberts, Assistant Quarter-Master-General
Major Gammell, Deputy Assistant
               Quarter-Master-General
Capt Hawkes, Commissary
All troops at Zoola and in the passes.

Troops:
10th Bengal Cavalry (1 Squadron)
G Company Madras Sappers and Miners
1 Company Bombay Sappers and Miners
2nd Regt Native Infantry (Grenadiers)
18th Regt Native Infantry
21st Punjabi Pioneers (HQ and five companies)
5th Bombay Native Infantry
8th Bombay Native Infantry

smooth-bore, muzzle-loading muskets. They therefore adopted the old tactics of firing, charging with powder from one end of the mouth-torn paper cartridge, containing powder and ball, inserting the bullet and ramming down. A separate percussion cap then had to be inserted on the nipple, the hammer drawn back to full cock, the musket aimed and fired, again with deliberate volleys. Two rounds a minute for well-trained troops was the norm for such a complex procedure. Against fanatical opponents not too many volleys could be discharged before the enemy would be upon them. Soldiers therefore were taught to rely on the traditional British infantry weapon, the bayonet, to bring matters to a conclusion at close quarters. In the steady hands of the Punjabis the bayonet proved to be as good a friend to the Queen's Indian soldiers as to her white regiments.

By contrast British regiments of foot were being re-equipped with the new breech-loading rifle, the Snider-Enfield. This was a composite weapon, the old muzzle-loading Enfield being subject to a conversion. This was done because custom-built breechloaders were still undergoing trials in the British army, despite Continental conversion to the type following the outstanding Prussian victories over the Austrians in the recent war. The breech was cut away for a 2.5-inch length and into the trough a right-handed steel block was inserted. This had a striker which was operated by the original hammer and it fired a brass cartridge with its own percussion cap, also extracting the spent cartridge from the breech whereupon it was ejected by a swift arm movement. This increased the rate of fire dramatically to about eight or nine rounds per minute, quite outstanding for the period. It had an effective range of about eight to nine hundred yards but was usually fired from five to increase the killing effect. The new brass cartridges were packed in 70lb boxes for mule haulage and some two million rounds were sent out to India to equip the force. There was, however, considerable reluctance to equip Indian units, infantry or cavalry, with such a weapon. The Indian Mutiny was only two decades away and memories were long!

The decision to re-equip from muzzle-loaders to breech-loaders in the infantry was not copied in the artillery, which, despite the reverse trends abroad, had re-adopted muzzle-loaders. Thus it was this type of weapon which constituted the newest of the British guns in the force, which were 7pdr steel mountain guns, each with a thousand rounds of various types of shell, and again mule transported. However breech-loaders had proved themselves invaluable in the field, even if scorned at Horse Guards, and Napier saw to it that his force was equipped with some of these long-range weapons, 9pdr rifled Armstrongs, originally to have been drawn by horse. For the expected siege of the Abyssinian stronghold, two large 8in mortars were included in the force, and to transport these and also the 9 pdrs, some 44 trained elephants were included on the strength.

The Naval Brigade took into action more than three hundred Hale's war rockets. These were 6pdrs fired from 'rocket machines', or launchers. They were not noted for their accuracy but were spectacular in effect and, on the rare occasion they arrived on the target, could be highly effective, especially against massed infantry. Britain had been using such rocket batteries on and off for many years (notably in the American war of 1812) after being introduced to them at the wrong end by Tipu Sahib at Seringapatam in 1792. Opinion however was divided on their usefulness. In practice it did not seem to have daunted the Abyssinians much in the heat of battle, but it had a profound effect on the Emperor when one roared over his head and killed a horse close behind him.

For the main the British troops were still uniformed in the traditional and stirring scarlet with white facings but, as a hint of things to come, some regiments now wore the experimental warm-weather adaptation of drab khaki. This was a practice frowned upon by many senior officers, but which was under increasing consideration by the more 'progressively minded' officers. This was due, it should be said, more to the beneficial effects of reflecting the heat in the hot climate rather than for any camouflage requirements. The British 'Tommy' was still expected to stand straight and tall and face his opponent in line. Not for another twenty years was the experience at the hands of Boer marksmen to send the British soldier scrambling in the dirt to avoid unseen riflemen, and not until that traumatic event did the blending into the background reinforce the purely welfare benefits of replacing red with earth-coloured uniforms. The Native troops likewise followed their European cousins in the matter of dress, many of the Indian regiments exceeding in both boldness and visual display even the traditional red and blue of the British line regiments.

INTO THE DARKNESS

Apart from British envoys, and the various hostages' contacts, very few white men had ventured into the dark continent at this stage of the 19th century, in particular from the east. Much was therefore guesswork and much more completely unknown to Napier and his staff as they diligently planned their advance. So much could go wrong, for many the precedent of the Crimea boded evil and even if the little force could somehow penetrate the interior it was the Abyssinians who would choose the terrain that suited them best. They could stage ambushes, harry and wear down the British column long before Magdala itself was reached. At home the politicians, having agonised for many months on whether or not to do anything at all, now wanted everything done at a rush and above all else, cheaply. They voted two million pounds to do the job which was actually to cost eight-and-a-half million!

The establishment desired that: 'a flying column or a succession of flying columns should be pushed forward and operate to the front, so as to make a dash if possible and finish the business before the rains set in'.

Napier however, had no intention of sacrificing his career or the lives of his men to pander to the whims of old men in Whitehall who knew even less than he of the rugged terrain. He determined on a methodical and well-planned advance, with the well-being of his army, their supply, care and medical protection being, if anything, over-emphasised. If they were to face an unknown enemy in an unknown land then they would face them as a properly-supplied and equipped force in good health. The outcome would then be decided by superior generalship, not pure chance.

In a precise and detailed memorandum written on 6 September 1867, after due consideration of the task facing him, Napier spelt this out so there would be no doubt in London.

'The expedition will consist of a force that may be stated in round numbers: 4,000 British, 8,000 native troops; with at least an equal number of camp followers, and 25,000 head of cattle of various kinds. All of these cannot arrive at once, but it will be well to assume that one-fourth of the number may arrive together or within very short intervals. It is probable that as many as 150 transports may be assembled at one time.'

He then went on to enumerate exactly what points required attention, for the landing and setting up his base on the Red Sea coast, making it clear that he would expect all requirements to be fulfilled to his own satisfaction before he made his foray after the hostages. These were:

1: A good harbour or roadstead.
2: A good shore for landing.
3: A plentiful supply of good water as near the beach as possible and a report, as far as ascertainable, of its quality at all seasons.
4: A convenient, healthy locality for the depot of stores

on first landing, to be called Post No 1, with room for the sheds, encampment of troops, picketing of horses and other animals, immediately after their being landed, and pending their removal to a greater distance.

5: A suitable situation for the camp of the troops to protect the depot on shore.

6: A position, which will not interfere with the encampment of the troops, for the encampment of the native followers who will probably collect and remain during the expedition, as well as those who may merely halt on their way with the force.

7: A position for collecting and organising the land transport for the force as it is gradually landed, where large numbers of cattle can be picketed, fed, and watered; also herded for pasture in the day.

This gave London a good idea of how Napier was going about his business. There would obviously be no

The use of elephants brought from India to carry the heavy guns was another startling innovation and one that paid dividends on the long and difficult march into the interior of Abyssinia.

'flying columns' making 'dashes' of four hundred miles into the interior while Napier was in command! Back home Prime Minister Disraeli accepted this was the case, and, to give him his due, the Commander-in-Chief also gave his man in the field his full backing. Thus unencumbered with political impedimenta Napier could concentrate his masterly organising talents on his miltary baggage, which, as would be expected from the above, was considerable! Other hangers-on proved less easy to be rid of and eventually a considerable corps of the 'Gentlemen of the Press' attached themselves to the reluctant soldiers, among them Dr Austin representing *The Times,* the dry and formal Mr Whiteside of *The Morning Post,* G. A. Henty of *The Standard,* later to be well-known for his stirring tales of Empire written for youngsters, and Lt Shepherd of *The Times of India.* There was also an American reporter for the *New York Times,* H. M. Stanley, to earn lasting fame on the same continent with his search for the explorer Livingstone.

The landing place finally chosen was Zoola on the eastern side of Annesley Bay, a very large indentation on the coast twenty miles below Massawa on the Red Sea, (an advance survey party finding the latter port to be unsuitable), and special permission had to be obtained from the Egyptian Government for the British to utilise this anchorage. In all, more than two hundred sailing ships and seventy-five steamships were eventually required at a cost of almost half-a-million pounds per month, and, from 21 October until the end of the campaign, these vessels transported and landed some 62,220 men and 36,094 animals of various types to this isolated area of the African coast.

Among this *ménage* of four-footed supporters there were no fewer than 960 bullocks, 1,800 camels, almost 5,000 ponies and mules and the 44 elephants. The latter were brought in once first reports of the hinterland were studied. It was clear that mules and bullocks would be unable to haul heavy weapons over such terrain as the column was due to face. As the bulk of the embarkations were taking place at Bombay nothing could be simpler than to add these gentle giants to the roster of Napier's strength. Ninety German soldiers attached to the 33rd Regt of Foot, the dozen or so observers from six European nations, the despised but tolerated journalists, the Coolie Corps of labourers and the elephants lent the whole expedition an exotic air.

Elaborate measures were taken to transport and care for the elephants. Two sailing ships were specially converted at Bombay to carry them and special slings had to be made to hoist them aboard and into the ships' holds where they were carefully stabled back-to-back for

Various Abyssinian princes had armies of their own which could have threatened Napier's lines of communication. He pre-empted this by meeting with them and making them allies, like the Ras of Tigre seen here.

the voyage. Aboard ship each elephant was allocated its own *mahout* and coolie to care for it and beds of shingle were laid out. An allowance of 175lb hay, 20lb rice, 4lb gram, 2½ oz salt and forty gallons of water, was made for each beast. The first elephants, including *Roostum Khan* and *Shah Bux* arrived at Zoola aboard the transport *Goomtee* on 6 January, four days after HMS *Octavia* had disembarked Napier.

After being lowered from the ship into a barge and then towed to the pierhead by steam launch they had to be coaxed onto the structure of the 900yd long pier itself. After much trumpeting and uproar they were finally disembarked. Like the rest of the facilities, (an artificial island and a tramway etc) the pier was built especially for the job. Likewise the construction of a 5½ft gauge railway was undertaken by the sappers (with considerable help from the elephants and coolies) and steadily pushed inland to the forward base which was established at Senafe, 8,000ft up, and forty miles inland from the coast. This settlement stood at the head of the Koomayli Pass through the Abyssinian mountain range. Like all the bases established it was to be garrisoned and to act as a link in moving forward the column into the forbidding interior of the country. It was also far

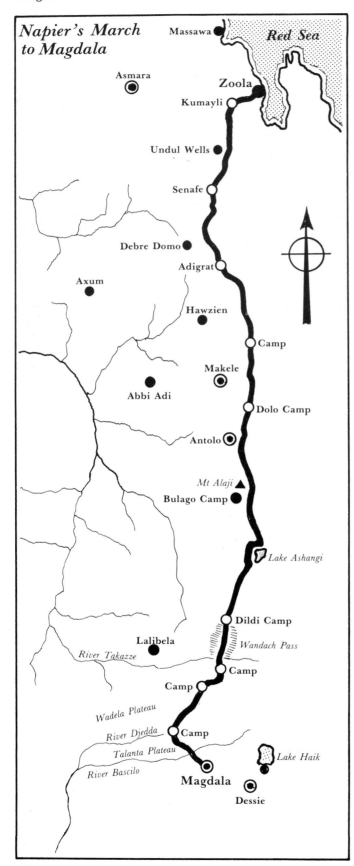

Napier's March to Magdala

Massawa
Red Sea
Asmara
Zoola
Kumayli
Undul Wells
Senafe
Debre Domo
Adigrat
Axum
Hawzien
Camp
Makele
Abbi Adi
Dolo Camp
Antolo
Mt Alaji
Bulago Camp
Lake Ashangi
Dildi Camp
Lalibela
Wandach Pass
River Takazze
Camp
Camp
Wadela Plateau
River Djedda
Camp
Talanta Plateau
Lake Haik
River Bascilo
Magdala
Dessie

Prince Kassai shows the noble profile of the Abyssinian royal house. He was won over by Napier's astute diplomacy.

healthier than Zoola, where a combination of indifference and non-cooperation by the Egyptian Governor and lethargy and disorganisation by the British Commissary was only finally overcome by the energetic urgings and proddings of General Sir Charles Stavesey, who arrived on 6 December, and by the arrival of Napier a month later.

One contemporary historian wrote:

'It is said that the gallant general astonished the home authorities by the requirements he sent for to ensure the comfort and health of his men; but the result proved the wisdom of his conduct.'

Diplomacy was needed to secure the passage of Napier's army from coast to target. The various provinces through which the little column had to pass were themselves hazardous enough, unopposed. Fighting a way through would have been impossible. The bulk of the force's food and water had to be carried the whole way. Luckily for the British, Theodore's autocratic and eccentric behaviour had not endeared him to his princes, most of whom detested him and so, far from proving a series of screens through which the invading army must fight, each prince was wooed by Napier, or impressed

Above: The Battle of Goojerat. In the distance the snow-capped mountains. In the left background the city itself and on the left the fortified villages. The flat and open plain devoid of cover can be clearly seen, a daunting prospect for troops to cross before they could get to grips with the enemy. The British infantry are drawn up in their patient lines while the horse artillery drive forward to duel with the hidden Sikh batteries. In the foreground a small bunch of mounted men audaciously try to work their way round to the British rear.

Right: Goojerat. The charge of the 3rd (King's Own) Light Dragoons which completed the rout of the Sikh Army after the artillery duel and the infantry advance had broken their prepared lines. The follow-up inflicted great loss on the demoralised Sikhs but isolated groups or individuals would always be found willing to sell their lives dearly.

Left: *The Alma. Illustrating representatives of the 38th (1st Staffordshire) Regiment of Foot in camp before the battle. Here they are shown with their yellow facings to the scarlet tunics. Whether they had such immaculate tenting at the time is doubtful.*

Below: *The Alma. Forward up the hill goes the thin red line, despite natural hazard of river, difficult terrain, fortifications and overwhelming odds. The massed grey ranks of the Russian defenders were at first surprised, then incredulous and finally amazed at such steady advance towards a seemingly impregnable position.*

Right: *The Alma. An inspection is carried out of the 1st Bn. 'The Devil's Own', the 88th (Connaught Rangers) Regiment before the battle.*

Bottom right: *The Alma. 'Forward 42nd.' The 1st Bn. of the 42nd, Royal Highland (The Black Watch) Regiment of Foot already had the most illustrious honours in the British Army prior to this battle. At the Alma they enhanced their already outstanding reputation. Here, urged on by their officers fully exposed on horseback, they storm up toward the Russian heights in an unstoppable kilted wave.*

Private – 23rd
(Royal Welch Fusiliers) Regt
The Alma – 1854

Private – 4th
(King's Own) Regt
Magdala – 1868

Private
Highland Light Infantry
Tel-el-Kebir – 1882

Private – 29th
(Worcestershire) Regt
Goojerat – 1849

Private – 44th
(East Essex) Regt
Taku Forts – 1860

Private – 94th
(Connaught Rangers) Regt
Ulundi – 1879

Private
York & Lancaster Regt
Tamaii – 1884

Sikh
Infantryman

Russian Infantryman
Grenadier Regt

Chinese
Infantryman

Abyssinian
Warrior

Zulu Warrior
in Gobamakhosi Regt

Egyptian
Infantryman

Beja
Tribesman

Right: The final advance on Theodore's mountain fastness. The redoubt atop its peak had to be approached by way of the narrow track dignified by the title 'The King's Road', and a series of steadily increasing slopes had to be taken cautiously before the final great slab with its defences could be stormed.

Below: The March to Magdala. The long column wends its way through a defile in straggling line of march. Note the mixture of uniforms and the elephants interspersed through the column. The exposed nature of such a march is obvious and its vulnerability to hostile ambush only too apparent. Fortunately the local chiefs were persuaded to refrain from intervening on behalf of the mad Emperor or the campaign might have been another Afghanistan.

Bottom right: The storming of the heights of Magdala. The seemingly impossible assault of the lofty fortress' walled defences proved far more simple than any of the British had dared to hope thanks to audacious work by the infantrymen on the spot. Nonetheless it was a daunting prospect at first.

Below: Ulundi. Lord Chelmsford was convinced that steady rifle fire delivered with precision by the British infantryman standing up to his foe in the 'Grand Old Style', would be more than a match for any native army, even one as formidable as the Zulu nation had shown itself to be. Earlier disasters tended to cloud the fact that when properly organised the Impi charge merely dashed itself to a bloody standstill in the face of disciplined volleys. Ulundi finally proved that courage, pluck and fanaticism was no match for the steady, aimed volley of the British redcoat.

Right: A panoramic view of Tel-el-Kebir as depicted in the artist's imagination. The Sweetwater Canal can be clearly seen to the right of the field of battle, and the great earthworks of Arabi's encampment stretching north from its banks. The advance redoubt close to the canal should have triggered advance warning but by good fortune it was by-passed in the darkness and the bold move of the night march paid off handsomely.

Far right, top: If Goojerat was won by the gunners then Tel-el-Kebir was won by the infantryman's friends, 'Butt 'n' Bayonet' but the dash and professionalism of the horse batteries was evident in the follow up and eagerness to get into the fight.

Far right, centre: The Black Watch at Tel-el-Kebir. The night march covered, the great open desert dawn's first light found the Highlanders in the ditches under the shadow of the earthworks. Here they took severe casualties before the final rush carried them into the Egyptian lines.

Right: 'All Sir Garnet'. General Wolseley, Britain's 'Only General' probably reached the height of his career with the victory over the Egyptians at Tel-el-Kebir. Certainly his careful planning, bold use of tactics and the overwhelming completeness of his victory presented the perfect example of how small colonial wars should be fought. He was never again to have such a total vindication of his methods and teaching.

Below: Tamaii. The crisis of the battle. The leading British square, split asunder not so much by the weight and suddenness of the Dervish attack from out of the gully, (in the foreground) but by the confused order to advance which only reached half of the companies, has been penetrated and thrown back. The Naval Brigade's machine guns have been captured and the Dervishes have been trying to work them, without success. The second British square has come up in support and broken the enemy attack with steady, aimed volleys while the first square re-forms.

Number Three Battery, 21st Brigade, Royal Artillery, under Capt L W Penn in camp during the long march from the Red Sea coast to Magdala.

by a show of strength, and won over. Thus the princes actually assisted the column with food and forage and became in effect allies of the British in deed if not name. Two such worthies, Prince Kassai of Tigre and Prince Menelek of Shoa were at each other's throats and it took all of Napier's skill to win passage from both without upsetting either! Napier conferred with Prince Kassai and his army of 4,000 warriors on 25 February and after two days talks and feasting they departed on mutual terms of endearment. Nonetheless two-thirds of Napier's army was prudently employed on garrison and line of advance protection duties, leaving but 5,000 men to make the actual assault.

The route chosen lay almost due south from the forward base, down past Undul Wells to Senafe, then on through Goona-Goona to Adigrat and Adabaji, with a camp established at Dolo, and then to Antolo. Crossing another range in the shadow of Mount Alaji, with a camp at Bulago, to Lake Ashangi their next stop was beyond Marawa and then through the defile at Dildi, with another intermediate camp, and then through the 10,500ft Wandach Pass across the headwaters of the river Takazze to the Wadela Plateau where two more camps were set up. The last stage was across the Djedda River (another camp) over the Talanta Plateau then on to the river Bascîlo the last barrier before the mountain range itself. Each river that had to be crossed wound through

its own gorge of about ten miles width and the column had to descend precipitous slopes into the troughs and then clamber up equally daunting heights on the far side.

The roads stopped beyond Antolo, about halfway between the coast and Magdala, and thus conventional transport for the two mortars and the Armstrongs was abandoned. Now the elephants came into their own. They had been used in India to haul guns, but now they were trained to carry these weapons on their backs. They knelt with the back legs out behind them and a strong platform was erected with heavy wooden spars forming a ramp. The dismounted guns and mortars were then manhandled with ropes up this ramp and secured atop the elephants' backs and covered to protect them from the elements. It was found that 23 of the beasts were needed to transport the various heavy components of the two mortars, four Armstrong guns, their carriages and ammunition boxes. Each beast carried up to 16½ cwt at a time. Under the command of Lt J. W. Ouchterlony, of the Commissariat Department, and formerly of the Madras Fusiliers, they left Senafe on 28 February and reached Antolo on 11 March escorted by 25 troopers of Native Cavalry and a company of Madras

Sappers. They certainly played a great role in the campaign and Napier recorded that: 'without them it would have been impossible to have taken the heavy guns and mortars to Magdala unless very considerable delay had taken place in making the roads fit for wheeled carriage'.

Napier of course could ill afford delay. With each day that passed, as the miles were painfully and laboriously counted, the unpredictable monarch, at this time still himself on the march through the interior towards his mountain fortress, might take it into his head to slaughter all the hostages outright, to take them deeper into the hinterland, or to keep constantly on the move and thus lead the column on a forlorn chase that would reduce the whole expedition to a laughing stock and a shambles. In fact he did no such thing but, in an epic journey of his own, led his 7,000 warriors, artillery, camp followers and prisoners on a nightmare march, pillaging, burning and slaughtering mercilessly on his way. He reached the heights of Magdala, where he encamped and mounted his heavy guns. Here he then spent the remaining days left to him in a torment of indecision. He brooded, got drunk, threw captives over the precipices, cried out to God for forgiveness, plotted and schemed in his final madness upon his mountain top as the thin scarlet and khaki line snaked its way slowly closer and closer to him and his destiny.

Conditions on the march progressively grew more difficult for Napier due both to terrain and weather conditions. At Wandach Pass on 20 March a heavy storm broke over the camp and it was bitterly cold. Both men and animals had clawed their way up 1,500ft from the previous stop and all were exhausted. So it continued throughout the final stages, hail and freezing rain lashed the men by night while a burning sun fried them during the day.

The rain had made the road so slippery that it was impossible on the steep parts for a man to walk without catching hold of the banks at the edge.

By 12 April the British Army had come within twelve miles of its final goal. Ahead lay the plain of Arogee and beyond, the looming mountains rising almost sheer and gaunt on the horizon. In front of them the track dignified by the name 'The King's Road' wound its way up past the jutting outcrop of Fallah mountain, with beyond and to the left, the flat top peak of Selassee. Just visible beyond was the fortress fastness of Magdala with vertical walls of rock dropping three hundred feet sloping terraces, stacking up in 600ft steps on the eastern face, dotted here and there with the conical, straw-roofed

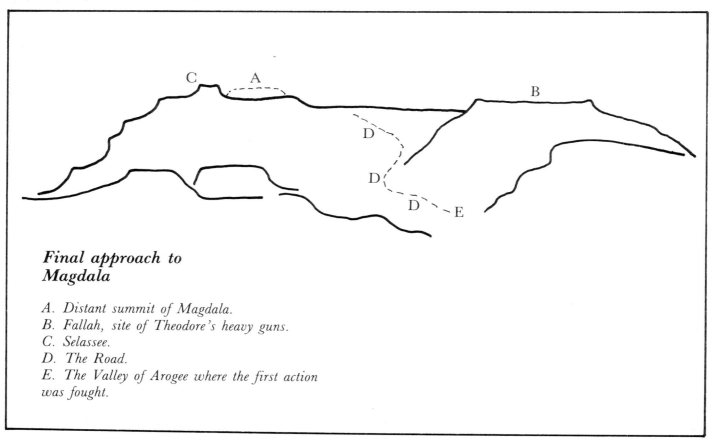

Final approach to Magdala

A. Distant summit of Magdala.
B. Fallah, site of Theodore's heavy guns.
C. Selassee.
D. The Road.
E. The Valley of Arogee where the first action was fought.

The great bulk of Magdala from the final plateau. Even close-up the brooding menace of this mountain fortress looks formidable. Note ruined native village in the foreground.

native huts and cut by deep ravines. Such a position seemed almost impregnable. Surveying it Napier was to state:

> 'If simply old women had been at the top and, hiding behind the brow, had thrown down stones, they would have caused any force a serious loss.'

Theodore however had placed his front line further down the mountain to protect the approaches and it was here, on the scrub-covered table of the Arogee plain, that the first battle was fought.

THE SETTING OF THE STAGE

Emperor Theodore, alternating between the hope-for peaceful negotiations and a fatalistic death wish for a show-down, watched the British column's final approach through a telescope and drew his battle plans accordingly. He was a warrior king and had not completely lost his soldier's touch even if the increasing bouts of madness negated much of his former wisdom for great periods. The bulk of his guns, including the

gigantic 21in brass mortar he had named *Sebastopol* (in deference to the siege weapons of the Crimea about which he had heard many stories) had been laboriously transported up to the lower slope of Islamgee, but he decided that a number of them should be sited further forward, on the flat top of Mount Fallah. This directly overlooked the 'King's Road' as it debouched from the ravine onto the Agoree plain. Here he had emplaced his seven heaviest guns, including a huge 56lb piece. His artisans readied the guns for the coming battle, under a heavy guard to ensure that they carried out their task efficiently. Around them were stacked the heavy cannon balls, including, from some obscure source, several rounds of chain shot used in naval battles to dismast ships.

A sizable battery was emplaced further up on Islamgee, in direct defence of the fortress. In all there were some thirteen heavy howitzers, nine mortars and no fewer than fifteen smooth-bore cannon, including three more massive 56pdrs. No wonder Theodore felt confident of holding the place.

On the night of 10 April he expressed his inmost fears. He clung to the hope that Christian Britain might be sending him help with which to crush the Moslem Gallas insurgents whose fortress Magdala had once been and who now surrounded it waiting with great glee for his fate to be decided. Dissuaded from such delusions Theodore determined to fight it out. He held the best ground; let the British come! The inhospitable terrain, his heavy guns, and the hard-core of 10,000 loyal hard-bitten soldiers gave him confidence. Much of his former great army had melted away, some in terror at his excesses and senseless slaughter, some lacking food or hope, some because of the hardness of their journeying and yet more for fear of impending retribution. Those who remained however were clearly those on whom he could rely utterly, his best chiefs and leaders, the toughest of their warriors, the most fanatical of his followers. He determined to use them against the British whom he was forced to accept not as his saviours against rebellious subjects but as bitter enemies.

His native soldiers were a ferocious bunch as their willing and enthusiastic perpetration of the atrocities ordered by Theodore had shown. Mercy they lacked but opportunism there certainly was. Their loyalty would be substantially reinforced and natural bravery equally enhanced by promises of loot and bounty. The emperor used the lure of both in planning his final battles to motivate his fierce warriors. If his artillery could not match the Armstrongs, or even the mountain guns, in efficiency they certainly created an impressive amount of noise which counted for a great deal to the Abyssinians. His foot soldiers were more indifferently equipped to tackle the regular troops, especially the European regiments armed with the breech-loading rifles. The Abyssinian soldiers were generally armed with long, curved swords, long stabbing spears and round leather shields some 3ft in diameter decorated with horse-hair. About half the soldiers had old muskets, flintlocks and matchlocks which were completely outclassed, although similar to those carried by the Indian regiments. However the Abyssinians lacked the skill and training of the Native regiments and generally tended to fire high thus negating their numbers.

A more serviceable weapon carried by many of Theodore's men in these final days was a fine piece, a double-barrelled percussion weapon imported from Europe. Again however it was a relatively close-in weapon, impressive enough when used against fellow natives but hopelessly outclassed when pitted against disciplined troops firing from beyond its best range. Other than a massed charge that would envelope and overwhelm any opponent the Abyssinians were short on tactics also. Perhaps their best bet would have been to withdraw every man to the fortress and contest every inch of the difficult approach. The cost of taking

Magdala might, in the long run, have proven too expensive and the exhibition forced to withdraw. It would have been a long shot, but better than the course that Theodore finally adopted. Still it was not taken.

This was due in part to a mistake by the British who, quite unintentionally, presented the Emperor with so tempting a bait that he could not refuse to take it. Disaster might have resulted had not quick reaction on the part of Napier turned a potential blunder of the greatest magnitude into a heaven-sent opportunity to deal the Abyssinian force a fatal blow.

There was never any question of a flanking attack and Napier could only make a frontal assault on each successive height as it loomed before him. However direct advance up the King's Road was putting one's head into the lion's mouth. Clearly the heavy equipment must follow such a course but it needed flanking protection along the route to prevent ambush. On 9 April therefore he directed that on the morrow, Good Friday, the 1st Brigade under Brig-Gen Schneider advance up to his right along the Affijo-Goomabgi spur and establish a forward camp there. The cavalry were not included in this force because of the terrain. When this was done Col Phayre was to push ahead as usual to scout out the approaches to Fallah and four companies of sappers were

to set to work to construct a passable track along the spur for the rest of the Brigade to advance along on the following day.

This was done and Phayre sent back word that the exit from the gorge onto the Arogee plain was secured and that the mountain guns and baggage train might therefore be sent forward immediately through the open gateway and deployed on the plain without further delay. Meanwhile the Brigade itself was toiling up the slope under a blistering sun, with the 23rd Punjab Pioneers in the lead followed by the Beloochees and the 4th Foot, the last having temporarily halted, sorely beset by thirst, sunstroke and exhaustion.

There was no reason to doubt the accuracy of Phayre's report and it was duly acted upon. However some hours later Theodore, watching intently from his position with his guns on Fallah, was delighted to see appear on the road before his eyes and heading directly toward his waiting guns, not a skirmishing line of advancing infantry but the mule trains and waggons of the baggage

The interior of the Emperor's stronghold of Magdala, pictured here after the last battle. The prisoners' huts are depicted but the occupants were in fact released before the last act of the drama took place.

column. Not waiting to see if such good fortune was not somewhat too heaven-sent to be true the Emperor, overjoyed at such an easy mark for his waiting warriors, sent for his chiefs. He sent them into action with the promise of an easy victory and mountains of loot. At the same time he ordered all his artillery to commence a covering barrage.

What the excited Emperor could not see from his lofty but limited vantage point was the almost simultaneous approach of the 1st Brigade over the spur. Fortunately General Napier himself had gone forward to view the situation and at once realised that far from sending his column into a secured position he was marching them to almost certain destruction! The relatively short journey time taken by the baggage train because of the easy road approach had caught the unprepared advance guard by surprise. Napier's amazement and chagrin can be imagined but he swallowed his wrath and acted with commendable speed to rectify this ghastly position.

First, he ordered that the Pioneers, just struggling into sight, take the place of the missing picquets and secure the mouth of the approach while his ADC, Capt Scott, was despatched at full gallop to bring the weary 4th up at once. They responded magnificently despite their fatigue and were soon on their way. As they emerged onto the plain it was clear that the situation was serious and that it would be touch and go to avert a disaster. The enemy guns were already shrouded in smoke and booming out across the plain. In the distance swarms of natives could be seen screaming and yelling as they erupted down the mountain and began racing towards them.

BATTLE IN THE VALLEY

At 16:00 on that humid afternoon the first Abyssinian volley roared out from the seven cannon atop Fallah Mountain. The range was extreme for those days, about 3,000 yards, but nonetheless, laid and trained by the Germans, the first salvo crashed into the ground disconcertingly close to the struggling 23rd Native Infantry who were leading the 1st Brigade's deployment. They also passed uncomfortably close to Napier and his staff officers. Such accuracy was unexpected and came as something of a surprise to the British. Lt William Scott recording how, as the heavy shot hissed over his head: 'I felt much inclined to duck my head down to the saddle. I, however, resisted the impulse.'

He was not alone in this reaction. However Theodore was soon beset by problems which impaired his apparently perfect positioning. The huge 70ton mortar.

Magdala

'Theodorus', his pride and joy, proved a very much overrated weapon, misfiring and bursting its enormous barrel on the very first shot, probably due to being loaded with excess powder. The rest of his cannon worked well but firing, as they were, from the top of Fallah down the valley onto the King's Road, necessarily involved complicated calculations and fine judgement of powder allocation to allow the plunging shot to fall accurately. The varying calibres of the guns did not make for easier calculations. The Emperor soon found, to his extreme vexation, that his gunners persistently overcompensated and all the heavy fire which they continued to direct was to passing noisily, impressively but, fortunately for the British, harmlessly above their deploying infantry.

The effect of this covering barrage was therefore to a large degree nullified once the British troops became used to the swish of the balls passing through the still air, realising that the enemy was miscalculating the range. There was little time for the advance units to mull over such matters for their immediate concern was to prepare themselves to receive the charging masses which were erupting out of the slopes that faced them and boiling down towards them.

On the right Maj-Gen Sir Charles Staveley gave the order, 'Fourth to the Front!' and the 1st Battalion King's Own Royal Regt under Major W. C. Cameron, went forward to the edge of the plain to be dressed into a thin khaki-clad line. To their rear the Madras Sappers took up position on the right with the 10th Company, Royal Engineers, under Capt G. D. Prichard holding the rear left. Between them were stationed the 27th Bombay Native Infantry (1st Beloochees). The baggage train and the guns were halted behind the ridge out of sight but the three companies of their escort, under the command of Lt Sweeny, were supported to their right by the 7pdrs of Colonel Milward's battery. These had been hastily unhitched from their mules and brought forward on the crest overlooking the road in front of the Warki Wawa rivulet that ran down into the river Bascilo to their rear. To protect the guns the 23rd Bengal Native Infantry (Punjabi Pioneers) under Major C. F. Chamberlain, took up position with their muzzle-loaders, having fixed bayonets.

The great Abyssinian attack was delivered by an estimated 6,500 men, their chiefs seated on their rearing and plunging ponies and mules urging on the wild warriors who came leaping and jumping down the mountain in a black torrent. They were led by one of Theodore's favourite chieftains, an ancient worthy named Fitaurari Gabi, and they were confident of an easy victory and limitless looting against the exposed

In the battle on the Agoree Plain the fanatical attack of the tribesmen broke under the steady fire of the British and Indian troops and a bayonet charge completed the rout of the Abyssinian forces.

baggage-train which they thought would be easy prey. But this great mile-wide crescent of humanity found itself confronted, not with a disintegrating and fearful caravan, but with three hundred well-positioned and evenly spaced regular troops in skirmishing order, firing steadily with breech-loading rifles at ranges from 250 yards in regular volleys. There was no pause between volleys with the new Sniders and row upon row of natives were mowed down steadily in front of the three hundred men of the British front line. These death-dealing individuals were backed by all manner of awesome weapons, including the rockets of the Naval Brigade, under Lt-Commander R. N. Fellowes. These unpredictable missiles had been hurried forward on Napier's orders and placed on the Affijo spur where they had a good view over the valley. Their spluttering trails and crashing detonations amidst the charging natives added a new and weird facet to the battle.

Despite their casualties the very momentum of this massive flood of men continued to carry them onward down the hills and towards the leading British line. The

rush might have been sufficient on its own to carry them through but the distance from which it was launched was too great and ensured that the British had ample time to ready themselves. As it was, the leading ranks came close before withering under the sustained and steady fire of the Snider-Enfields of the 4th Regt. As men and horses began to fall steadily the initial hysteria began to wane from Gabi's army, and he too was killed trying to rally them. He lay under the soaking sky, his crimson jacket and shirt stained darker with his blood, victim of many shots from soldiers who had taken him for the Emperor. More than five hundred of his warriors lay dead on the field. Independent fire was now ordered and at six rounds a minute the toll continued to be taken until the last desperate surge by three score natives was reduced to a twitching pile within 100 yards of the British Infantry. The best men slaughtered, the onrush was stopped and, after a while, a movement to the rear began, the natives taking cover among the ample places of concealment, ravines, boulders, large rock outcrops and bushes, from where they commenced sniping at the British line and this proved irksome and caused some casualties.

To counter this after the hour or so the British line was moved steadily forward, the 4th Regt and the Beloochees forming a line of advance that curved round

The 33rd Foot were in Napier's bad books because of their rowdy behaviour. He gave them the chance to redeem themselves by allowing them to lead the final attack and their audacity easily won the day.

to the right and enveloped the remaining enemy, the field artillery moving forward in conjunction. The British fire soon winkled out those hardy individuals still sniping at them and the Abyssinian musketry gradually faltered and died. As long as the light held the advancing British kept up a steady fire, while the Naval Brigade rockets switched their attack to the guns on Fallah itself, causing the hasty retirement of Theodore and his immediate retinue to Selassee in their rear. The Emperor's guns and their weary crews remained emplaced, but unsupported, in their original positions.

Meanwhile, although held and then broken in the centre, the mass of natives flowed out on either flank in an attempt to envelope Staveley's defence. One wing veered to the British right, under the very eyes of their Emperor on Fallah's peak, and threatened to encroach upon that side of the Affijo Plateau, where Napier and his staff were positioned. Their movements were quickly spotted and Napier pre-empted any such ideas by moving forward the rest of the Naval Brigade with two guns and a detachment of the Bombay Cavalry. The

Madras Sappers also shifted their position to take this enemy force with flanking fire and this wing of Theodore's charge melted away under his anguished gaze in much the same manner as the centre had done.

There remained the left wing and the tantalizing goal of the baggage train. This was still sufficiently tempting to bring another flank attack by a large group of the enemy which deployed under cover of the deep Dam Wanz ravine to the right of the main British firing line and threatened to reach its goal. 'A' Battery's mountain guns were early into action against this determined group but their salvoes of shrapnel, common and finally case shot failed to stem the rush and Milward for a time feared for the safety of the guns themselves.

The Punjabis gave them a volley at one hundred yards, then reloaded hastily and delivered another. It was the Indian's muzzle-loaders against the Abyssinians' swords, spears and percussion muskets for a while. However the 4th Regt detached two companies from the left of their line and these helped the Indian troops to hold their positions. In teeming rain the reinforced 23rd Punjabis then made a vigorous counter-attack with fixed bayonets and after intense hand-to-hand work, forced the enemy to fall back.

This was hot work as the long afternoon turned into evening and the heavens opened. But the enemy had still not completely shot their bolt. A wing of their force flowed on past the Punjabis and swarmed down towards the British rear. Capt Roberts hastily organised an impromptu firing line from the three companies of the 4th Regt under Lt Sweeny, who were part of the train's escort and moved them out in line. Once more the steady firing of the British regulars proved too much for the simple rush and stab tactics of the enemy and they were again stopped dead in their tracks and forced to retire with further heavy fire being poured into them by the 23rd Punjabis who could now take them in their flank. This bold group of Abyssinians suffered severely for their temerity, about one hundred corpses being counted in the ravine itself and many others littering the British left flank.

By dusk the ravine was clear of all the enemy save the dead and dying. Some 1,200 of Theodore's finest men lay dead along the valley, while scores more of dispirited troops crawled back up the pass to face the wrath of their leader and join with him in contemplating the failure of his 'tactics'. Twenty rounds per gun from the Sniders, with eight from the Punjabis' smooth-bores had sufficed to break the best that the Emperor could muster. Although initial reports of his army's casualties proved to be exaggerated they were nonetheless severe

and included the loss of many of his favourite chieftains. His losses were certainly enough for him to reconsider the opening of negotiations once more. This mood was soon to pass but for a while the representatives of the unpredictable Emperor and the resolute General had a parley. Meanwhile Theodore retired to drink himself into another sullen stupor while across the valley the British and Indian troops made bivouac in the cold rain under the same sodden sky as their opponents, without the benefit of either food or shelter. A poor reward for a decisive little victory. Three searchlights which had been brought all the way from England to this strange camp in the Ethiopian mountains, were set up around the perimeter, for dire warnings of night attacks had been received all along the route. None took place although darkness might have gone a long way to nullifying the British superiority in weapons. Instead the weeping relatives of the dead crept over the battlefield seeking out their loved-ones' bodies.

It was indeed a strange night, the thunder of the two sides' cannons being replaced by the thunder of the elements and the local wildlife also descending with the darkness to take advantage of the unexpected bounty provided by the human opponents, as the American journalist, Henry Stanley, recalled:

'In ravenous packs, the jackals and hyaenas had come to devour the abundant feast spread out by the ruthless hand of war'.

The dead Abyssinians numbered some seven hundred, in striking contrast to the British who had but two men die of their wounds. The wounded of both sides, twenty British and about 1,200 of the enemy, were duly treated by the British doctors and medical orderlies on the field of battle the following day.

CONVERSATIONS WITH A LUNATIC

Theodore III was now brought face-to-face with the results of his autocratic behaviour. He was strangely chary of putting his side of the story and sought every way possible to wriggle out of the final reckoning. His captives had early advised negotiation and he had scornfully rejected it. Now, in the desperate recognition of his impending doom, he was forced to re-consider this alternative. His feelings were perhaps characterised by the pensive but cruelly true statement attributed to him at this time:

'The British have destroyed my army with just their advance guard, what will they do with their main force?'

In his few rational moments he must have known the

he had Lt Prideaux (complete with monocle and gold-top cane), and the lay-preacher Mr Flad. Alami and his Abyssinian companions were taken and shown the British strength: the Armstrong guns, the two big mortars and the like, and when suitably cowed were informed that, should the Emperor fail to comply with the terms then being dictated by Napier, these powerful weapons would complete the job they begun the day before and there would be no escape.

Meanwhile the General had listened to the message conveyed to him by the two Britons, in effect that Theodore acknowledged himself defeated and did not wish to continue the fighting, and he also heard vivid accounts from the two men on the Emperor's mental state, the remaining strength of his army and the defences of Magdala. He wrote back a short reply. He too expressed the desire that the blood-letting cease, but in order for it to do so the Emperor must, '. . .submit to the Queen of England and bring all the Europeans in Your Majesty's hands and deliver them safely this day in the British camp'. If he complied he was guaranteed honourable treatment. The two reluctant envoys showed considerable courage in returning again to the fortress with this reply. They had seen enough of the Emperor's unpredictable outrages to be in fear of their lives in delivering it. Indeed Prideaux confided to another young officer that he doubted he would see the morrow.

Theodore was indeed deeply angered at what he took to be a rejection of his hand of friendship. He scornfully asked for the letter to be read to him as he refused to deal with any man who was subservient to a woman, even if she be the Ruler of the British Empire! He failed to understand that he must give himself up. He dictated another long letter to Napier, making this point clear and sent the two men back again while he retired to pray. Then another mood took him and he called a conference of his remaining loyal chiefs.

Most of these worthies, little better than brigands for the most part, counselled the slaughter of all the prisoners forthwith but Alami, aware of British might, gave the opposite advice. He saw their only hope was in releasing the prisoners in the hope that Napier would then be satisfied and take his terrible weapons and fearless soldiers away and leave them in peace. If they killed the Europeans who knew what revenge would be inflicted upon them all! Theodore reflected on all this and then sent for the prisoners. Before they could arrive his mind snapped again and he ranted and raged, even attempting to commit suicide by shooting himself in the mouth but the weapon misfired. In an instant his mood changed

Alternating hourly with plans to slaughter the prisoners or release them, Theodore finally let them go. He later changed his mind but by then it was too late to recall them.

answer to his own question. He despatched a delegation to General Napier's headquarters and included in their ranks two of his European hostages. The General was not to be swayed from his purpose at this late stage by meaningless promises from someone whose treachery and true nature had been only too clearly revealed by the trail of carnage he had left in his wake. Napier had been following Theodore's bloody spore with increasing horror during the latter days and what he found could have left him in no doubt as to the type of person with whom he was dealing. Indeed he gave a chilling description of the devastation Theodore's trail had left behind it:

'A bare plain, not a stick of food for man or beast within sight—nothing but the bare, undulating plain, old ploughed ground, and the remains of fields or what were once fields; a few piles of stones to show where a village had been razed to the ground.'
And again:

'. . . He has eaten up the land: and not content with that, he has burnt and destroyed the villages. There is hardly one stone left standing on another, and the people have all fled.'

At first light a small party of horsemen was observed wending its way down the defile under a white flag. It was led by Dejatch Alami, one of the Emperor's advisors clad in the traditional red coat of the leader. With him yet again and he decided on conciliation. Quickly, without bags or personal effects, all the Europeans were put upon mules and sent down the mountain, escorted by Alami himself.

They were received with great rejoicing in the British camp. All the struggles and efforts had been worthwhile and the main purpose of their mission had therefore been easily achieved. Despite so many years in captivity most of the prisoners appeared in reasonably good health and spirits. Just how close they had come to death at the very last minute they could but guess, they probably owed their final salvation not to Napier and his army but to the intervention of Alami. Later the Emperor sent down his European artisans as well, although these were his servants rather than his prisoners, but they would no doubt have all suffered the same fate. He also pulled back his guns from Fallah to defensive positions closer to his fortress and sent down gifts of cows along with yet another letter. In this remarkable missive the earlier bombast, declaring the support of the Holy Trinity and vowing to lead his victorious armies to Jerusalem and the like, were gone and replaced by a wheedling tone in which he describes his attempted suicide (which he claimed was prevented by the intervention of a miracle) and lamenting his previous rudeness to Napier and his envoys. By this epistle and his other gestures Theodore clearly thought he had bought himself peace but he was soon disillusioned! Napier now had to decide what to do next. He had already sent back the body of Gabri as his own gesture of goodwill but should he now leave the Emperor to his own devices or seek a final reckoning?

While the British general was pondering that night, Theodore suffered yet another change of mood. He became dejected on learning that his gifts had been refused and resolved to flee his mountain stronghold while he still had the chance. Some 2,000 warriors remained with him and these he assembled in readiness for a break-out to the south-east. But blocking that route were his old enemies the Gallas, just waiting their chance. Many of his men refused to go with him, preferring their chances behind Magdala's walls than out in the open beset by a totally hostile population.

So there was nothing else for the Emperor to do but to make a final defiant stand and he readied himself for the last battle. Napier had also come to the same conclusion. Word reached him that the Emperor's warriors were rallying to him once more and that the longer he delayed the final assault the harder it would be. At first light the British moved out in full battle order and headed up towards those forbidding walls on the distant summit.

THE STORMING OF THE FORTRESS

At 09:00 the 1st Division was early astir and was dressed on Arogee plain on the site of the earlier victory. Napier had decided on a methodical step-by-step clearing of the remaining heights between him and the fortress and this began with an advance by the 2nd Brigade with the 1st Brigade in direct support. First Fallah and then Selassee would have to be cleared and occupied. Then the troops could move against the great gun park on Islamgee, the last platform before the city gates. To prevent the Emperor and his remaining 700 followers slipping away a hotch-potch cavalry squadron was formed and sent out on the flank until the regulars could be moved up from the Bascilo river camp, the nearest water supply for men and horses.

The 10th Company of the Royal Engineers, acting as assault pioneers, led the initial advance up the King's Road together with the 33rd Foot (The Duke of Wellingtons Regt), a Yorkshire regiment but with many Irishmen and the aforementioned German contingent in their ranks. On the long march south they had disgraced themselves by their uncouth behaviour under pressure and had been sent to the rear of the column. Now Napier was giving them a chance to make amends and restore their name, which they did with a will. Accompanying them were the Mountain Batteries and the rest of the Brigade. With the enemy guns withdrawn from Fallah they were able to march in formation until they reached the connecting saddle that joined it to Selassee. Here three companies of the 33rd were detached and sent to occupy the summit of Fallah, while two more were similarly sent to Selassee, together with three of the 7pdrs. They were later supported by troops of the 1st Brigade as it came up from the rear.

Although vast throngs of Abyssinians were encountered on these hills they were all eager to surrender to the advancing British. Theodore had earlier given permission for all those who did not want to stand with him to flee and save themselves as best they could. Most needed no second bidding and some 20,000 warriors, women and children were thus herded down the mountains as the British columns tramped steadily upward. By midday both heights were occupied and fully secured and the elephants were brought up carrying with them three of the Armstrongs which Napier had placed on the leading edge of the saddle. From here their long-

Theodore's sickening slaughter of many of his own people by throwing them over the precipice hardened even the weakest British hearts against parleying with such a maniac.

range fire could reach the walls of the fortress some 2,700 yards distant up the mountain side. They soon began to make regular play at extreme elevation and before long their shells were bursting on the walls and inside the fortress, causing casualties among the remaining civilians inside.

The Emperor was now fearful of the loss of his precious cannon which were still positioned on Islamgee. Although, without his skilled European artisans, it is doubtful whether much real use could have been made of them, the Emperor was imbued with the tradition of not giving up the guns and rode forward with a large body of men to effect their rescue. He had however left it far too late for such heroics, since the largest of them could scarcely be manhandled by those men summoned at such short notice. They had to content themselves with two of the lighter guns but even here they were frustrated in the attempt by the bold attention of a squadron of Indian irregular horse, these being joined by an advance company of the 33rd Regt who opened a hot fire at long range and forced the Abyssinians to give up their efforts. It is said that the Emperor himself rode forward brandishing his sword and shouting for a champion to fight him for them, but he was not recognised and eventually he had to retire ignominiously back into the fortress, barring the heavy gates behind him and piling up huge stones to reinforce them. He was now finally trapped.

As the afternoon wore on regiment after regiment slogged up the steep approaches and was marshalled on the Islamgee plateau below the walls of the fortress. Here the British eventually came across the corpses of Theodore's earlier rage, chained and bound, some with hands and feet chopped off and all horribly mutilated by the prowling scavengers. If there still lurked in the heart of any of the officers or men of the British force a shred of pity for the madman they had cornered then it was instantly destroyed by such a ghastly scene. As Capt Henry Hozier noted:

> 'The sight of wholesale slaughter caused a deep feeling of hatred to Theodore among the British soldiery.'

Two sets of walls and two sets of gates now stood between the British and the fugitive tyrant. The outer, lower defence was the Kolkilbir Gate, twelve feet high and built of stone and wood composite with thorn bushes on top, all of which should easily have been demolished by even the small mountain guns once within range. Twelve were therefore brought forward to within 1,300 yards and were there joined by the indefatigable sailors with their remaining rockets. By 15:00 all these had joined in the general bombardment, along with the more

The last columns move up to storm the wall of Magdala. Initial resistance soon faded once the wall was breached and the troops inside.

distant Armstrongs, but although this fire was kept up for an hour it would appear to have achieved little positive result in knocking any substantial holes in the three-quarter-mile long bastion. About a score of the Abyssinian warriors manning the walls were killed and 120 wounded by the barrage. The defenders made no reply to all this sound and fury but waited patiently for the British infantry to move forward.

The final deployment now took place and order of battle for the 2nd Brigade was as follows:

In the van two companies of the 33rd Regt of Foot, in skirmishing order, to advance on either side of the final track up the cliff face and engage the defenders from cover to keep their heads down. Scaling ladders and blasting charges were then to be brought forward under cover of their rifles by 'K' company of the Madras Sappers and the 10th Company, Royal Engineers. Major Cooper would give them direct support with six

wave them once they were inside the enemy fortifications so that he might order the general advance.

At 16:00 Napier ordered them in and up they scrambled to be met by only intermittent musketry fire from walls and loopholes. Again, considering the restricted nature of the ground they had to cover, the casualties from this defensive fire were negligible. Perhaps the defenders' nerves had been shaken by the bombardment even if the walls had not! At any event few men fell, two officers and thirteen men were wounded in all, and the gates were reached in a rush. Here was an anti-climax for the Sappers, whose job it was to blow the gates. They had dropped their charges on the way up and likewise the scaling ladders were found not to be present. The reinforced doors were vigorously plied with crowbars and bare hands but little or no impression was made. The whole gallant assault seemed doomed to ignominious failure but the day was saved by the enterprise of the hitherto disgraced 33rd Regt.

The main gateway of the defensive wall around the fortress, which two privates of the 33rd stormed on their own, both winning the VC.

more companies of the 33rd Foot, with two more acting as support. Bringing up the rear of the storming party were two companies of the Bombay Sappers with yet more explosives.

Next the 45th Foot were dressed in line as the first reserve for the infantry assault and immediately behind them the 4th Regt and then the Beloochees were held ready, drawn up in column, if required, to move forward in order to exploit any breach made in the walls. Lt Reeve of the 45th, recorded his impression of Magdala just before the final attack:

'It was about three-quarters of a mile off, and standing completely by itself, appeared to be a massive lump of rock, and to the naked eye there was no apparent road to it. Down on the intervening plain we could see the 4th King's Own lying down and a battery joining in. The principal object of their aim was the gateway.'

In traditional style the Queen's and the Regimental Colours of the 33rd were carried into the assault by Ensigns Melliss and Wynter respectively and Sir Charles Stavely cantered forward and told the young men to

Magdala

The village and fortress were put to the torch by the British army, and were never rebuilt again. It remains today much as it did in 1868.

Three companies had been sent off from the main track to probe the strength of the walls on the right and see if they could effect an entrance somehow. Meanwhile two more companies had moved forward to continue the assault on the main gateway. Pte J. Bergin determined that, if he could not get *through* the wall then he would get *over* it. A tall man, he elected to try and to help him he asked one of the shortest men in the regiment, Drummer M. Magner. However the latter was unable to lift the big soldier so instead Bergin hoisted Magner aloft, helped by a strategically placed rifle butt and, once on top of the wall, the drummer leaned down and pulled Bergin to the top to join him amidst a hail of wild and ineffectually-directed musket fire. Once thus securely established Bergin opened fire with his Snider on the enemy and, under his covering fusilade, more and more of the 33rd's sweating and swearing infantrymen were hauled aloft by the strong arm of drummer Magner. Soon, enough were inside to cause the defenders to panic and beat a hasty retreat up the steep inner slopes toward the wide-open inner gate of the fortress. At the same time a second entry was afforded the stormers via the gate, and thus the outer defences were truly breached.

As if they had not contributed enough to the day's proceedings Magner and Bergin now joined in the general chase of the fleeing Abyssinians and reached the inner gate hard on their heels, thus preventing its being closed in their faces. In such simple and audacious fashion were the 'impregnable' walls of Magdala breached. Both privates received a well-deserved Victoria Cross for their remarkable exploits that day. Rarely if ever, have two unremarkable foot soldiers had such an effect on the outcome of a major battle as at Magdala.

Through the inner gates swarmed the cheering men of the 33rd, with Ensign Wynter still proudly clutching his Colour, well to the fore.

'I shall never forget the exhilaration of that moment', he later wrote, 'the men firing and shouting like madmen'.

Some forty-five enemy corpses were found after the 33rd's last charge, few of the enemy stayed to fight it out after that. Sadly observing his men breaking and fleeing at the first hint of an entry Theodore knew the game was finally up. He turned to his gun-bearer and released him from his service. Then he drew a pistol, ironically enough one of a pair presented to him by Queen Victoria years before the rift, and placed it to his mouth. This time there was no misfire and the Emperor fell dead. With his death all remaining resistance ceased and soon the two young officers of the 33rd were triumphantly waving the colours from the fortress.

As the British broke his final defences Theodore took his pistol, a present from Queen Victoria, and shot himself in the mouth.

END OF AN EPISODE

Little remained to be done. The guns of the fortress were destroyed, saved for *Sebastopol* which was so massive that all that could be done was to overturn it and leave it lying there. And there it lies to this day, a monument to one man's pride, folly and megalomania. The fortress itself such as would burn was put to the torch and was never rebuilt. That accomplished the Abyssinians, to their astonishment, and that of much of a jealous world outside were not subjugated by the victorious British, but left to get on with their lives and sort out their own troubles. The march back to the coast was as difficult, cold and tiring as the trek out, and the released captives did little to endear themselves to the rescuers.

The end of the story. The finding and identifying of Theodore's body brought Napier's remarkable little campaign to a satisfactory conclusion. The British immediately withdrew from Abyssinia.

By mid-June every man and animal was out of the country never to return. The Queen was delighted at the outcome and the small loss of life involved. It further raised the prestige of her beloved army in her eyes, and also restored it abroad after the Crimean fiasco. It served to show that victorious forays by the world's greatest power were not automatically expeditions of conquest but sometimes mere police actions. *Pax Britannica* had been honourably upheld and any similar despot hoping to twist the lion's tail was made to think twice and then forget it. The arm of the Queen was shown to be very long indeed. Napier received a thoroughly deserved peerage for this neat little job, as well as a KGCB and more usefully, was appointed Commander-in-Chief in India. He died a Field Marshal, honoured and respected, in 1890. He was one of the great Victorian generals, who thought before he acted and whose preparations served as a high model for the many campaigns, alas not all as successful, that were to follow in the next twenty years of the high tide of Empire.

Chapter Five

ULUNDI

4 July 1879

THE AMAZULU

'Whatever happens, we have got, the Gatling Gun, and they have not.' The might and technology of the European armies, when deployed against the primitive tribesmen of remote parts of the world must inevitably prevail or so legend would have us believe. We have already seen at Gujrat how the opposition was not only equal, but superior in terms of technology and its application. Adowa in Ethiopia firmly repudiated the assumed immutable outcome of a European versus a native army. For the British Army, Isandlwana taught a particularly bitter lesson of how contempt for one's opponent can lead to disaster.

The rise of the *amaZulu* was a remarkable example of how the will of one man could cause great waves on the sea of world history. In his own sphere of influence the unknown nephew of the chief of a little-known and unremarkable tribe, whose main achievements had been as tobacco growers, caused, as much upheaval and mayhem, both to the native populations and the encroaching white men, in his part of southern Africa as did Napoleon, or Hitler in their time. That man was Shaka ('Daybreak'—which probably signified his time of birth), known more widely to his people and his fearful

The left-hand edge of the main British square at Ulundi, with staff officers in the centre, and native troops in the centre with the waggons in the middle. Smoke from the steady volleys lies over the front lines.

Chief Shaka, who turned the ama Zulu from an insignificant Bantu band into the most feared warrior nation in southern Africa. He was a big man, but both shield and assegai are absurdly enlarged in this sketch.

enemies at the time, as Chaka. He was the illegitimate son of a daughter of the *eLangeni* clan and Senzangakona, chief of the *amaZulu*, a tribe of some 1,500 souls that had settled in the fertile plain between the Black and White Umfolozi rivers near what is now Mahlabanm in modern Natal.

The *amaZulu* were an insignificant clan descended from drifting nomads who had come down from the north at the turn of the century and had taken their name from the word Zulu, or 'The Heavens'. *AmaZulu* merely means 'the people of the Heavens' or more poetically, 'The Celestials'. They were typical of the Bantu tribes of that period and were initially under the sway of the military élite of the *Mtetwa* located to the south-east of their small territory. The clan's area had been turned

by their Chief, Dingiswayo, into a strong, little empire by force of arms, and the bonding of the groups of young men, the *iNtanga*, into identifiable military regiments had began to take place.

Shaka adopted and improved this set-up, becoming the archetype of what everybody now thinks of as a typical Zulu warrior. Six foot three inches in height and powerfully muscled, he was both strong and inventive. He was also embittered by his background and his social rejection, and used the most ruthless means to gain his revenge. Shaka saw strength and war as the best means of gaining sway over the smaller tribes in the region and fought numerous bloody campaigns of subjugation to concentrate all power in his own hands.

He led by example. A fearless and skilled warrior himself he emphasised the adoption of pride in the skills of combat in his young men and improved their means of achieving it. The traditional hunting and fighting weapon of the *amaZulu*, soon shortened to *Zulu*, was a light throwing spear, the *assegai*. This was a six-foot weapon which had a six-inch steel tip and, being lightly hafted, could be thrown by experienced warriors some sixty yards with considerable accuracy. Each man carried about half-a-dozen of these in battle. Although still principally a hunting spear the *assegai* was also to become a formidable close-range weapon, the last one of each man's armoury being retained as an over-hand stabbing weapon, although its length at first made it somewhat awkward for such use, even to such giants as Shaka.

The reason the Zulu depended on this weapon above all other was dictated by the region in which they lived. The coastal plains of Natal were scrub and bush country with few trees and therefore could not furnish enough raw materials to make large numbers of bows or arrows, the traditional long-range weapons of tribesmen elsewhere. They existed but in small numbers and had no great carrying power, and the hunters used poison tips to bring down the game.

The only other weapon used in warfare was the close-range *knobkerry*, a fearsome club made up of a long handle with a weighted burled head used as a pulverising mace in the general *mêlées* in which Bantu fighting had hitherto usually resulted. For protection the tribemen relied on a large oval shield, fronted with cowhide and a strong frame. Some three foot across at its widest point and tapering top and bottom, it was fitted with slots running vertically, into which leather thongs were woven together with a central stick for bracing. The shields were thus both light enough to be easily carried, and large and tough enough to offer considerable protection from spears thrown at good ranges. Close-in it could be used by skilful

Two of the short, stabbing, assegai, a knobkerry and full-length war shield. With such simple weapons the Zulu warrior became the disciplined scourge of the land, feared by whites and natives alike.

their leaders until the raising of a large force of fighting men from the various clans was ordered. This could be quickly achieved, creating an *Impi* which could be 20,000 strong and virtually unstoppable by other tribes. So the empire of the *Mtetwa* had gradually extended.

Eventually Shaka and the Zulus were to take over this ready-made elite technique and improve upon it in every way. A big man himself he was not content with the *assegai* as it stood. He was credited with shortening the long throwing handle and turning it into a pure hand-combat weapon for thrusting and stabbing underhand. The wider and heavier blade was balanced by the broader shorter handle and it was named *iKlwa* after the distinctive sound the blade made as it was withdrawn from the stomach of an opponent. After such a blow Shaka would shout 'Ngadla!' ('I have eaten') and the Zulu warriors continued this triumphant cry down the years, threatening to 'eat up' their enemies as an early method of pyschological warfare designed to soften them up prior to combat. The *iKlwa* did not completely replace the throwing *assegai* for both were carried, but the former now became the principal killing agent.

Such innovations, coupled with his fighting prowess, brought Shaka to the attention of Dingiswayo who made him commander of the *iziCwe* regiment. Shaka is also credited with imposing disciplined skills into the hitherto largely motley, if effective, formations of his warriors. They were instructed to organise themselves in four distinct groups, a central mass with a reserve and two flexible wings which approached the enemy in crescent formation. The central group was likened to the chest of a bull and the reserve as the loins. The wings were the bull's horns. The main group advanced under cover of their shields which protected them from traditional spear throwing until they could get close enough to make a final charge and then they set to work close-in with their *iKlwa*s. In the interim the two wings which had been deployed outflanked the opposing force on both sides and ultimately enveloped and surrounded them. There was no escape from the 'bull's horn' once those racing wings had closed the circle behind an enemy's exposed flanks. In the general confusion and panic the enemy would be slaughtered where they stood or cut down mercilessly as they tried to run. Nobody would be spared and the dead and wounded alike would be slit open lengthways. The reason for this was not purely bloodlust but superstition, as it was feared that the spirit of the slayer would be driven mad by his victims' spirits if they were not released from the bondage of the corpse.

Eventually Shaka assumed leadership of the whole Zulu clan and imparted all these lessons to them while

warriors as another clubbing weapon. As with most shields used in warfare, decoration was later to form part of the identification process. At first though, no special markings were used but the hair of the cowhide was left on the shield to give it added strength and the colouring of the covering gave each unit, *Impi*, a rallying and identification motif.

These weapons were all the Zulu soldier had needed. With a minimum of clothing, a loin cloth, headband and oxhide sandals to protect his feet from the thorny scrub, he was able to travel swiftly and silently on foot, living off the land. Hardy and tough with few physical needs and a fierce loyalty (backed up by fearsome penalties for any lapse), he was a resiliant and awesome opponent. They were organised in their loose-knit groups under

improving them still further. He forced them to go bare-
footed and executed those who felt reluctant to do so.
So toughened did they eventually become that the Zulu
Impi could move through the thorn bush at up to fifty
miles a day with silent and steady trotting thus giving
them unprecedented manoeuvrability at a time when
the average European army, weighed down with baggage
trains and the like, could manage fewer than twenty miles
a day. The Zulu supply train consisted of the young
children, normally herdboys who, loaded with food and
water spare weapons and cooking utensils, followed the
warriors. This human supply train could be raised at
short notice and in large numbers. Some cattle would
be driven out initially but these did not last long and
slowed down movement anyway. Nonetheless a large
Impi on the move was restricted in campaigning time
to what it could forage or be supplied with, which meant
that most wars were of short duration. As the Zulu
Empire expanded it failed to encounter any opponent
that called for a long campaign!

Shaka recognised fully the value of regimental *élan* and
encouraged it as much as any European Commander-
in-Chief using similar methods. Each regiment was given
its own distinctive shield pattern decorated with pigments
and designs. The designs of headbands, skirts, amulets
and anklets of feathers and fur were made unique to each
unit. Moreover every regiment adopted its own battle
song and war cry and was endlessly drilled.

The achievements of this leader were awesome. He
had started out with fewer than 400 warriors, but so
disciplined were they that, from this tiny cadre, by 1830
he had gone on to create the mighty Zulu Empire
embracing more than two million subjects. Its boundaries
encompassed most of the land north to the Pongola
River, west to the Drakensberg mountain ranges, east
to the sea and south into central Natal. Their military
skills were at the core of the new nation, and were
essentially part-and-parcel of it, rather than being
something separate, and existing for one purpose only
as in Europe. The very structure of the *amaZulu* rested
on a series of strictly controlled groups which together
made an easily managed and formidable machine.

Shaka's rule however grew more despotic and he was
eventually murdered by his younger half-brother
Dingane in September 1828. This worthy ('Poor
Creature') was in turn overthrown in 1840 by his
younger brother, Mpande with the aid and collusion of
the Boers who proclaimed him King while at the same
time claiming Natal for themselves, a claim which the
British gave but short shrift to before occupying it two
years later. This contact with the white man did not

*King Cetawayo, who gained the throne by dubious dealings
and murderous schemes. He was nonetheless shrewd and
unless forced to, had no great wish to take on the British
army.*

lessen the Zulu's power or confidence in themselves to
any great degree. Although his influence was gone, the
nation Shaka had created out of nothing remained all-
powerful. Several generations had passed but although
many of Shaka's firm strictures had become watered-
down the basis of a unique fighting organisation
remained. By 1872 when Mpande died his successor,
Cetawayo kaMpande, after killing his own brother
Mbulazi at the battle of Ndondakusaka in 1856, inherited
a still powerful state and a still formidable army.

What of Cetawayo himself? Contemporary descriptions
of him, not surprisingly, depicted him as a bloody tyrant,
insolent and contemptuous of Great Britain, the Queen
Empress and her emissaries, eager only to extend the
boundaries of his own little empire which had been built
on the blood of fellow natives. Typical of how he and
his motives were seen at the time is the brief dismissal
of him by General Sir Bindon Blood:

'. . .before long it became evident that he had made

up his mind to try conclusions with the white men, and that his army and most of his subjects were at one with him about this.'

Certainly the British High Commissioner, Sir Bartle Frere, steadfastly believed he was dealing with nothing more than a bloodthirsty tyrant hell-bent on slaughter. Of course no sooner was the war over than the opposite viewpoint held sway and continues to do so in both book and on film, that Cetawayo was a simple and misunderstood chieftain, eager to keep the peace, who was tricked into a war he did not want by devious colonists looking for further expansion.

Cetawayo was probably, like most absolute rulers, a cynical opportunist who had no reservations about shedding blood if it aided his policy and he was not particular whose blood it was, fellow Zulu or Redcoat. Certainly the temptation to show the increasingly interfering British just what his warriors were capable of proved a temptation, which was at first resoundingly vindicated. But he never completely despised the white man, nor did he fully understand the nature of the power he was challenging. By western standards he was a bloody despot while in the eyes of his people, his behaviour was the norm for their leaders. Their nation had been born out of, and fed by deceit, murder, death and destruction and reached maturity on the same diet. They did not regard it as strange to be ordered to slaughter invaders of any kind and they knew less of the British than did their leader. Finally, even if he was a tyrant, he commanded unflinching loyalty from most of his subjects who, to a man, and woman, followed him to war with considerable enthusiasm and, even after the

A typical Zulu warrior equipped with all his weapons, stands outside a kraal. Note headband, arm and chest bands and size of assegai (which the Zulus themselves called umkonto) *and shield.*

tide turned against him, remained considerably devoted to him.

Before recounting the events which led to the inevitable clash between the Empire of Cetawayo and the Empire of Victoria mention must be made of one baleful influence which contact with the white man had brought. This was the introduction of firearms into Zululand. Although much was made of it at the time to explain both the war and the early results of it, and certainly a good number of firearms did find their way to the warriors, there was no great adoption of it by the *Impi* who retained their faith in the old skills, kept finely honed down the decades. John Dunn, the eccentric trader, was credited with bringing in some 250 rifles but several thousand more (some estimates give as high as ten thousand, though mainly obsolete) found their way into native hands via Portuguese traders landing consignments on the coast at Delagoa Bay. Against other tribesmen these rifles posed a threat and a menace, but

Sir Bartle Frere. His great vision was of a peaceful federation for all the people of South Africa.

the Zulu never became a very proficient marksman. More valuable were the hundreds of modern Martini-Henry rifles gathered from the British dead on the field at Isandlwana.

On the eve of the war Cetawayo's standing army was based on the considerable manpower of twenty-seven *amakhanda*, the *kraals* set up for the fighting men, half of them concentrated on the Mahlabathini plain close to the head *kraal* of Ulundi itself. Here the core of the fighting force, young unmarried warriors, the *amabutho* lived in enforced celibacy for most of the year. Not until they reached the stage of *iKhehla* could they seek out young brides and adopt the head ring to denote their new status. Here they trained and drilled and, occasionally sortied out to kill at their king's command. They were becoming increasingly unruly and fretful but the declining state of the Zulu economy, centred as it was on cattle, forebade any demobilisation of these vast numbers of surplus young men because of the destabilising effect it would have throughout the nation.

In all some 50,000 men could answer Cetawayo's summons. Regimental organisation remained much as in Shaka's day. Each *ibutho* was composed of sections of about fifty warriors called *amaviyo*. Most of the thirty-five regiments, and about one sixth of the warriors themselves, dated back to the days of Shaka and Mpande. Many of these old men had little fighting value, but a hard-core of 40,000 men of military age remained organised into twenty-six corps, each commanded by an *Induna* and several sub-officers. Thus the regiments were for the most part made up of well-trained, strong, resilient and confident men, sure of their power and boastful with youth, eager for battle. To underestimate what such a force could do, even against a modern European army of the period, was to tempt Providence. That temptation came in 1879.

The British presence in southern Africa had been long established, the usurping of the Dutch East India Company from New Holland undertaken in 1795 having been followed by complete sovereity over Cape Colony within another decade. Further inland British rule was progressively extended north to Natal and then to the Orange River and up to the Vaal. The discontented Dutch descendants of the original colonists, the Boers, retreated steadily up-country to find their own living space and eventually began crowding the already established tribes who were on the move south. On the eastern coast, British influence spread to Durban itself and in order to hem in the Boers in the then independent Transvaal with pro-British 'allies', Cetawayo was 'crowned' king of Zululand, in the name of Queen

Sir Theophilus Shepstone. His early awe and admiration for the Zulu race later turned to intense dislike and the urge to curb their military power.

Victoria by Sir Theophilus Shepstone. Many of his subjects thought this was condescending as the title was not Her Majesty's to convey but already Cetawayo's by right. However at the time he was glad to play along as there were, as always, other pretenders to the throne and some dispute among his people. Once established however Cetawayo determined to go his own way again, as he had every right to. Puritanical wagging of fingers at the old Zulu ways and his own solemn agreement to end death as the normal punishment for a whole range of offences had no meaning once the British representative had returned to Natal. While the Zulu king may have been contemptuous of British diplomacy, Shepstone returned proclaiming that the new ruler of Zululand was intelligent, sophisticated and, most important, respectful.

The honeymoon did not last long. The establishment of the diamond fields brought about demands for native labour which were unsettling. There were uprisings in Cape Colony which, rumour said, the Zulu king had inspired. Other tribes rose against the Boers. Drought struck Zululand and cattle-sickness, introduced from the south, was soon reducing its once mighty herds of cattle to a pitiful remnant and for the first time showing the face of poverty to its proud people. On its western borders the Zulus had many grievances against Transvaal but hardly any such disputes with the British. However when the British annexed Transvaal in April 1877 the Boer/Zulu claims and counter-claims became a British problem and Shepstone's former admiration and friendship turned to hostility.

In March of the following year, in an attempt to heal the rift, a boundary commission arrived at Rorke's Drift to discuss these issues with the Zulus at the urging of Natal's Lt-Governor, Sir Henry Bulwer. This was complicated by the call for confederation to unite all the various South African provinces and kingdoms to keep other continental powers out while at the same time disassociating Britain from further rampant imperialism. A new Governor of Cape Colony, Sir Bartle Frere, was appointed in 1877, with this overall policy in mind, and he had the additional title of High Commissioner for South Africa. His first task was to settle the uprisings which he quickly did the following year in the Ninth Frontier War, in which the British and colonial forces were commanded by General Frederick Augustus Thesiger.

However, partly in pursuance of the confederation ideal, partly through the inevitable conflict of an advancing civilisation pre-empting a potential threat to its progress, and partly because of the inability of men of so widely differing cultures to compromise, the obstacle of a free and independent Zululand could no longer be tolerated, if only for the overall good of southern Africa as a whole. Much to the frustration of Sir Bartle Frere's hopes however, the boundary dispute was settled largely in the Zulu's favour. He suppressed these hopes but what he could not supress however were the many, relatively trivial confrontations that continully arise in such circumstances. Incursion over the border by Zulus and inter-tribal rows were blown-up off all proportion and relayed to London, along with highly alarming reports on Cetawayo's conduct and ambitions.

The British Government had no desire for any such complications at this juncture. The rabid aggression and continued coveting of Afghanistan by the Russians, and the threat to India that such a policy alway constituted, was yet again preoccupying Her Majesty's ministers. They had little time, or troops, to spare for native unrest on the borders of Natal, especially since one such revolt had only just been put down. Also they knew that to tackle the Zulu armies would require more than just a token force. No telegraph as yet connected London with the Cape and so specific instructions to parley and at all cost to refrain from war with the Zulu arrived too late, by which time the machinations at local level had taken on a momentum of their own which Whitehall was powerless to check until too late.

In July 1878 came the final justification for armed intervention against Cetawayo and his kingdom. A party of Zulus in search of women who had fled across the frontier with their younger lovers to take refuge from their husbands and vengeful relatives, violated the border in kidnapping the fugitives. In accordance with Zulu law, they executed them. Even the ever patient and conciliatory Bulwer was forced to demand an explanation of Cetawayo. The King replied with soft enough words and all could have been patched up if Frere had not been so determined to seek an issue. A fine of cattle was being contemplated for this incident when an even smaller one, involving two surveyors who came to no harm, took place.

In July, General Thesiger had reported back to the Commander-in-Chief, Victoria's well-trusted but hopeless, hidebound Duke of Cambridge, on the successful outcome of the latest Kaffir War, but, after consultation with Sir Bartle Frere, had added a footnote with a request to hold the bulk of the Imperial troops because: 'It is still, however, more than probable that active steps will have to be taken to check the arrogance of Cetawayo, Chief of the Zulus'.

Frere believed that war was imminent. He was convinced that to leave such a potentially hostile, fully-armed power unquelled on the borders of the new confederation threatened its very existence. Therefore Zululand must join the confederation and, since such a proud nation would not willingly submit to such a notion, war was unavoidable. The right provocation was easy enough to find with such a martial and proud people. The campaign should be conducted swiftly and decisively, preferably while seasoned Imperial troops were available and in close proximity to the enemy. He therefore despatched General Thesiger to carry out a survey of Natal's defences against a possible Zulu incursion while sending the boundary report to London to keep it 'on ice'.

The General found the colony's defences against a theoretical Zulu attack almost non-existent. He immediately recommended that further reinforcements be made available should it be necessary to invade Zululand to bring the enemy to pitch battle before they took the initiative. Frere duly forwarded this request to London in September. He later added that the Zulus were 'out of hand' but nothing Cetawayo had done justified such alarmist talk. Indeed the Zulu chief was being as co-operative as his status, and nature, would allow and for the previous five years had done nothing but reside relatively peacefully in his kraal at Ulundi. Sir Bartle Frere chose to interpret this scene of almost unrecognisable domesticity on the part of the Zulu nation as a critical situation in the neighbouring Natal colony. He insisted that peace rested by a hairspring on, '. . .the caprice of an ignorant and bloodthirsty despot, with an organized force of at least 40,000 armed men at his absolute command'.

On 11 December Frere delivered the boundary report but attached to it his own ultimatum to Cetawayo. It included demands that the four Zulus who had killed the unfaithful wives be surrendered for trial under Natal, not Zulu, law; that a fine of 500 cattle be paid for the incursion and the King's delay in replying and that another fine of 100 cattle paid for the affair over the two surveyors. Ten more demands were added. These included a call for the complete disbanding of the Zulu Army, the disarming of warriors and the establishing of a British resident with powers of diplomacy that superseded the King's authority completely in several matters. Cetawayo was given thirty days to comply.

The ultimatum was similar to those European powers used to issue to smaller European nations prior to absorbing or annihilating them and, although Frere was by no stretch of the imagination a dictator, his method of diplomacy and his style of backing his potential victim into an impossible corner was on this occasion, identical with those to which the world was to become accustomed in the 1930s. Frere was far exceeding the authority of his office in making such demands and was clearly obsessed. When a copy of this document reached the Colonial Office the path to confrontation was set. Frere got his war and on 11 January 1879 the invasion of Zululand commenced under the command of General Thesiger by now, following the death of his father, the Second Baron, the Lord Chelmsford.

What sort of soldier was Chelmsford? Edward McCourt dismissed him as he did almost every other Victorian general as an 'earnest, slow-witted and unimaginative veteran of the Crimean War'. A contemporary of Chelmsford, Bindon Blood, described him thus:

'Lord Chelmsford was originally a Guardsman, and in the days of the 'extra rank', when captains in the Guards ranked as lieut-colonels and lieutenants as captains, he exchanged while comparatively a young man to command a line battaliion. He was Adjutant-

General in India when I first met him, being universally liked and respected, and considered one of the best Adjutant-Generals there had ever been.'

He had certainly seen service in the Crimea, being promoted from captain to brevet-major in November 1855. He had saw the edges of war as a lieutenant-colonel

Lord Chelmsford, a sketch by a fellow officer, just before Ulundi. His first disastrous under-estimation of his foe made him cautious in the extreme when undertaking the second invasion of Zululand.

in the Indian Mutiny and learned about campaigning in rough country from the master, being part of Napier's epic campaign to Magdala. Donald Morris described him as competent, reliable and tactful. He was not a political animal but applied himself to the task at hand to the best of his ability and earned the loyalty of his subordinates.

He was a thoughtful man but rather overwhelmed by the magnitude of the task in hand. This was to be no re-run of the Kaffir skirmish. He faced hazardous transport difficulties and also decided to split his forces, for which he received most criticism. Ox instead of mule, a divided force not a concentrated one, these were charges which were to be levelled at him frequently, but his men retained their affection for him despite the early disasters, although the Government never forgave him.

Lord Chelmsford had scouted the terrain before the war, at least that area close to the border and he made his dispositions on the judgement of what he found and knew of his opponent. He initially had 5,600 British infantry, 750 cavalry and over 9,000 native troops under his command and he decided to deploy them in five columns for the war against the Zulu. The massed charge of the *Impi* might be a fearsome sight but would surely melt before the discipline and steady, long-range fire of regular troops drawn up in good time ready to receive them.

The Zulu, Chelmsford reasoned, must realise this and would therefore avoid such actions as long as his force was strong enough, and could be correctly deployed for battle. If they did attack any of his columns during the advance they would be repulsed, considerably reducing their numbers, and once he had concentrated all his forces in the vicinity of Ulundi, Cetawayo would finally be brought to battle.

The columns were formed-up in a wide arc on the borders of Zulu territory. Two were to remain on the frontier, one at Middle Drift on the Tugela River to block any Zulu incursion south and the other in the north at Lunebeg on the Pongola River in the Transvaal to keep watch on northern Zululand, but also to guard against the chance of a Boer uprising while the British were otherwise occupied.

Of the three columns tasked with invading Zulu country, the first was headquartered at the mouth of the Tugela River in the south, with orders to move cautiously north toward Ulundi. The third column was based in the north-west at Utrecht under the command of Col E. Wood of the 90th Regt. His orders were to cross the Blood River and advance on Ulundi by way of Khambula Hill. The second, or central, column under the 24th Regt's Col R. Glyn, and to which Chelmsford

Isandlwana. Poor scouting, deployment and distribution of reserves of ammunition led to the greatest defeat of British arms in Africa up to that time.

had attached himself, was positioned at Helpmekaar to the west of the Buffalo River.

On 9 January, hostilities commenced and the central column crossed the river at Rorke's Drift and moved eastwards towards Ulundi via the mountain at Isandlwana. Here, on 22 January 1879, it was largely destroyed.

The Zulu king planned to fight a defensive war to protect his land but his scouts were more efficient than those of Chelmsford, who was manouvering largely in the dark. Cetawayo knew the exact location of the British columns. That Chelmsford's dispostions contributed to the massacre at Isandlwana cannot be denied, since he had chosen Isandlwana himself during one of his pre-war scouting missions, though he had always intended that the camp be placed in state of defence and that the second column under Col Durnford should reinforce the third column. He failed, however to make clear his orders to his sub-ordinates and the Zulu attack took them by surprise. To add to the overall confusion and lack of proper deployment there was a fatal breakdown in the supply of ammunition from the waggons to the firing line. Although heavy casualties were initially inflicted on the charging *impi*, firing dropped away and the troops who stood their ground were wiped out. The native contingent largely fled in disorder but most of these were also cut down by the horns that closed in behind them along the river bank. As Major C. F. Clery, the principal staff officer of the centre column, wrote to Sir Archibald Alison, Head of Army Intelligence in London, on 1 February:

'Every officer of the 24th, and with a couple of exceptions every man of the regiment left in camp, died there. Besides these were a number of stray officers left in camp for one reason or another, so that including the native contingent, 46 officers and about 750 British soldiers died on the ground. Five companies of the 1st Bttn 24th Regt had been totally destroyed both officers and men, together with one company of the 2nd Bttn 24th Regt which happened to be coming off outpost duty that morning.'

THE SECOND INVASION

After this disaster, redeemed somewhat by the gallant stand at Rorke's Drift, the first invasion of Zululand was terminated. It should be remembered however that an attack by an *Impi* on the first column commanded by Col Pearson of the Buffs, which had crossed the Tugela lower down near the coast and which was making its laborious way toward Etshowe, was repulsed near the Inyezane River on the same day as Isandhlwana. Over 350 Zulu were killed out a force of 6,000, for a British loss of ten men killed and sixteen wounded, which showed what a properly prepared Imperial force could do. Pearson reached Etshowe, constructed a fort there and was besieged until relieved on 3 April. The Zulus were again beaten off, at the battle of Ginginhlovo, by the 6,000-strong British relief column which Lord Chelmsford had ordered entrenched. Heavy Zulu losses were inflicted for the loss of two British officers and eleven men killed and 48 wounded, it being estimated that about 1,500 of the enemy were killed. Etshowe was nonetheless abandoned by the British after this battle. In the north the 4th column similarly repulsed an attack by 20,000 Zulu on their entrenched position at Khambula Hill on 29 March where, suffering the loss of twenty-nine dead, they killed about 2,000 Zulus.

All these actions merely confirmed Chelmsford in the correctness of his original reasoning, that the Zulu masses could not prevail against modern weapons. But is was not sufficient to go on inflicting defeats on such an enemy from behind embattled defence works and waggon laagers. To show the young warriors that they could be defeated in a 'fair' stand-up and out-in-the-open fight was the only way to convince them to give in. Chelmsford was determined to do this. He was also determined to demonstrate finally to the other natives in South Africa that the white soldiers were able to win on their feet. Finally he needed to demonstrate the same point to the British public back home, to his Queen and also to himself. He must burn Ulundi and bring Cetawayo back in chains and that quickly to salvage his own honour.

By the end of May, Sir Garnet Wolseley was

summoned from his enforced idleness on Cyprus to assume command of the British army in the field and to retrieve a desperate situation. Only primitive communications and the state of the surf at Port Durnford where he attempted to come ashore, prevented his doing so before the final reckoning! He issued a stream of orders to Chelmsford in anticipation of his arrival, but the latter set his face steadfastly against altering his own plans. This took time and the mustering of considerable forces but, on 4 July, Lord Chelmsford finally gained the victory that he planned for six months earlier. However Sir Garnet had no faith in him to bring this second campaign to any more successful a conclusion than he had the first. His opinion of Lord Chelmsford was crisp, 'He is a gentleman and a very nice fellow but the Lord forbid that he should ever command troops in the field'. Wolseley might rail from afar. Chelmsford's two new columns were by now deep in hostile territory, beyond communication with the outside world, and rarely in contact with each other.

By the end of April reinforcements had poured into Natal from Britain and were assembled into a new invasion force, reaching some 22,500 men by the end of June. These forces Chelmsford organised into two

Lieutenant-Colonel J North Crealock, CB.

Major-General E Newdigate.

While the Zulu warriors moved swiftly with the minimum of supplies, the British army made ponderous progress accompanied by its elaborate provisions train which turned the ground into a quagmire.

divisions, the 1st under Maj-Gen H. H. Crealock at Fort Pearson on the coast with 9,000 men, and the 2nd under Maj-Gen Newdigate at Landsmann's Drift on the Buffalo River with some 10,000 men, as well as the 'Flying Column' commanded by Colonel Evelyn Wood. While the 1st Division, pressed in from the east and served to protect Natal from a flanking movement, Chelmsford had chosen to mount his main attack from the west, with the 2nd Division, in connection with Wood's men. This time it was to be launched some distance further north from the central column's earlier, ill-fated advance so that the long straggling force would have easier going across the headwaters of the Buffalo and Blood rivers before turning down to the east of the Nqutu mountains. Then passing through the gap between Isipezi Hill and Babanango Mountain, it would leave Isandlwana far to the rear before striking up through Mtonjaneni and across the White Umfolozi to Ulundi itself.

The new British army had a long road to travel to reach the start line on the Buffalo River and Landmann's Drift east of Dundee. Fresh from England and full of confidence the troops tramped the 200 miles toward Zululand. The route was recorded by one private of the 58th in detail thus: Durban, Enshange, Camperdown, Pieter-maritzburg (the capital of Natal), Howick, Lidget Town, Kark Loof River, Weston, Mooi River, Eastcourt, Blaaun Krunty Coleno, Rovet Spriti, Ladysmith, Welsh's Stables, Sunday River, Commissariat Depot, Dundee and Landmanns's Drift. Having landed at Port Natal on 4 April, 1879, Pte T. T. Tuck of the 58th Foot recorded that they spent four days in Durban, then:

'All preparations being now made for advance we left

one Company of our Regiment behind to guard this Station and the remainder of the Regiment, numbering over 700 men under command of Colonel Whitehead, left Durban on the 7 April, 1879, to proceed up-country to Zululand. Our marching in the boiling hot sun was fatiguing every day and we averaged 12 miles per day. We encamped in the vicinity of several little towns inhabited by Europeans and kaffirs, but the land between these towns is very barren and mountainous, in fact the country at large is very mountainous and rocky, the highest point being in Natal and is called the Cathkin Peak which is over 10,000 feet high.

The roads are also very wearisome for marching especially in wet weather when they are so muddy. We have now marched up country over 200 miles and have come to a place called Landsmann's Drift and on our arrival we found part of the Force encamped on the borders and we pitched tents and received orders to make a stand for one month to make time for the whole of the column to mobilize before advancing into the enemy's country. During this period we are making complete preparations and are doing night outpost duty all round the camp in event of the enemy making a night attack, and during this stay we captured many Zulu spies and they were made prisoners and escorted down country for punishments; we are also cutting wood every day, packing up provisions and communication with other garrisons relative to the enemy's movements etc.'

The spies were much more likely to be semi-official emissaries sent by Cetawayo to try to get further attacks called off and negotiations commenced. The king was a realist. Over 10,000 of his finest young warriors had been killed or severely wounded in the various battles around the frontier and, Isandlwana apart, he had only a few isolated skirmishing victories and the withdrawal of the first British invasion to show for these terrible casualties. His young men were as sure of themselves as ever but the warriors were not conditioned for long campaigns. He knew that whatever had come his way previously would be as nothing to the force that was being assembled against his people now and that he could not hope ultimately to prevail. However all his attempts at a peaceful conclusion were rejected or ignored. Too many white soldiers had been killed and mutilated to now countenance any other solution but force. The preparations proceeded steadily, with, if anything, an over-preponderance of troops and corresponding increases in difficulties of supply and transportation. During this long waiting period tempers began to fray,

Capt J. MacSwiney of the 94th for example writing, 'Everyone is still crying out, "Whence the delay?". All the troops on the border of the Blood River ready to cross for the last three weeks'.

Eventually the advance was made with slow, steady progress marred only by the needless loss of the Prince Imperial, (ambushed while out with a small party on 1 June) and Lt Frith of the 17th Lancers (shot while on reconnaissance on the 5th). The combined forces of Newdigate's Division 3,600 infantry, 1,300 cavalry, 300 artillerymen and 48 engineers and Wood's 'Flying Column' comprising 2,300 infantry, 800 cavalry, 194 artillerymen and 95 engineers totalled some 8,500 white troops plus the Natal Native Contingent. By 27 June they had reached Mtonjaneni and paused there for two days building laagers for the bulk of the supplies and equipment pending the final 'dash' to Ulundi itself. In the heavy heat they moved out from this camp on 30 June through the thick scrub and thorn bushes carrying ten days' provisions. They had word that at least 15,000 warriors had gathered at the Nodwengu military kraal and that others were on their way. This was good news for Chelmsford; the last thing he wished was for the Zulu army to melt away intact when he had staked all on one last battle before he handed over his command.

Although there were seasoned veterans fighting in the column, there were also of course a larger number of men fresh out from England and they were jittery. On the night of the 5/6 June for example there was panic when a picquet of the 58th opened fire at a shadow taken to be a Zulu. The company then formed up and fired three volleys. Pte Tuck described the utter confusion of this panic, for there were no Zulus within miles of the camp.

'...If you could imagine yourself in a tent with 16 men all with their arms and belts under their heads. The alarm shots are heard from the outpost, every man is in the tent, and it is in pitch darkness, then comes the scramble for rifles, belts and other thing, no one can see his fingers before his face and in the darkness everything seems to be suddenly animated with life eluding your hands as you grope for them. Outside some of the fortunate one having arms and belts are shouting "down with the tents", the men inside shouting "Stop a minute where's my rifle?" everyone around cursing and swearing, when at last you manage to get hold of a rifle and now you wonder what keeps the gun as firm, little thinking in the darkness that another man has hold of the same gun as yourself...'

By 2 July the force had reached the right bank of the

White Umfolozi River and had Cetawayo's capital in striking distance. A temporary cease-fire had been arranged while, what Bindon Blood derisively termed, '..futile negotiations..' took place. Chelmsford had only late in the day been recognised by the Zulu king as the man with the power to stop the war. He certainly could not hold his own warriors back while the kraals were being burnt down but he hoped to buy off an enemy he recognised was too strong for him. Chelmsford pitched his demands high, impossibly high. All the captured arms had to be surrendered at once, selected Zulu regiments had to approach within one thousand yards and lay down their arms and so on. Talks dragged on, Chelmsford not being influenced by gifts of elephants' trunks and the like, but the Zulu King's logic made him pause and he finally agreed to less harsh terms, the surrender of just one regiment, the confiscations of the cattle at Ulundi and so on. J. N. Crealock, Chelmsford's assistant military secretary, recorded what this involved in a letter to Sir Archibald:

> 'We are in the midst of a virtual cessation of hostilities up to noon tomorrow, supposing the Zulus do not fire. If they comply with the General's demands of giving up 1,000 rifles, the two 7pdr guns (which had been captured at Isandlwana) and an *induna* comes in, we are bound to order a cessation of hostilities, until negotiations can be placed in train.'

Futile negotiations they were and on expiry of the cease-fire work was put in hand for the final manouvres. A strong defensive laager was thrown up on the banks of the White Umfolozi based on the 96 waggons detached from the 600 of the main force left behind at Magnum Bonum Hill. On 3 July Col R. H. Buller's irregular

Lord Chelmsford and his staff, with the help of a white irregular, scouting the final advance on Ulundi. After his earlier impetuousness every step of the army's march towards Cetawayo's kraal was methodically reconnoitred.

cavalry (the Frontier Light Horse) were sent forward to make a reconnaissance in force of the Mahlabatini plain with a staff officer, Lord William Beresford. They stumbled on more than they bargained for, an *Impi* of 3,000 warriors which suddenly burst out of the long grass in a hollow some 150 yards to their front. They were forced to beat an undignified retreat back across the river with the loss of several men. This proved to be the Zulus' last victory.

Next day the whole of the column came out of laager at 04:30 and by 06:00 crossed the river at daybreak. The only exceptions were the 1st Company of the 24th Regt, whose ranks were filled with boy recruits whom Chelmsford was loath to expose again, (although Clery, in a letter to Alison, stated that this was a 'punishment' for another night panic in their ranks and 'low morale of our young soldiers and all those in the new regiments out here.'). The indignant officers of the 24th Regt were thus thwarted in their oft-expressed hope that they be allowed to avenge their slaughtered comrades and were very angry at the decision. The negotiated time limit having expired the whole force was formed up in one large square, four men deep, with the cavalry and other mounted men extended to the front. The line was dressed in perfect order in the old style and then the whole massive formation started forward towards the distant *kraals* on the open rolling depression of the Mahlabatini. The moment of truth had come for the Zulu nation.

THE BATTLE

The British infantry advanced in their traditional red serge tunics and blue trousers under the baking African sky. 'You will know the soldiers by their red jackets' their King had told the Zulu warriors. The traditional uniforms continued to be used despite attempts by some officers to have more suitable clothing introduced for hot weather fighting. The only concession was the white pith helmets, extended to cover the back of the neck, each with the regimental badge emblazoned on the front. But soldiering in the ranks still remained an uncomfortable profession under the baking African sky.

The standard British infantry weapon was the Martini-Henry .450 single-shot rifle which had first been introduced in 1871. It was almost 122cm long and weighed just under 4kg and its most effective killing distance was just short of 400 metres. It was considered the best rifle in service with any army in the world at the time. Well-trained British infantrymen could squeeze off twelve rounds a minute with this weapon. The 45cm bayonet, still the British foot soldier's best friend, could naturally be affixed to this weapon for close-in work.

The Natal Native Contingents' 2nd Btn was also present, under the command of Maj H. M. Bengough. They were confined to the centre of the square surrounded by the ox and mule carts, with medical supplies, ammuntions and engineering equipment. A company of Royal Engineers commanded by Major John R. M. Chard, of Rorke's Drift fame, was also present in the square.

Also included in the ranks of the irregular cavalry were units such as Capt Watt Whalley's Natal Light Horse. Whalley was himself a former veteran of the 17th Lancers who had served in the Mutiny, Abyssinia and the Ninth Kaffir War among numerous other campaigns and he had 130 riders with his unit. The Transvaal Rangers were another hard-bitten bunch of Boer rough-riders under Commandant Pieter Raaf. There were also mounted natives of the Edendale contingent, so-called because they originated at the Edendale Mission, who were led by Theophilus Shepstone Jr.

The square was formed on the high ground, with Wood's column forming the front half with the 80th, 90th and 13th Regiments. The rear comprised the 2nd Battalion 21st (2 companies) 58th (4 companies) and 94th

The final march down onto the plain to offer battle. The various scattered kraals can be seen while the distant hills and scrub-covered slopes gave the Zulu army ample cover to prepare their ambush.

(six companies), with the guns being distributed at the angles and faces (12 guns and 2 Gatlings). Cavalry was placed outside at first, native contingent inside. The square was faced outwards, formed four-deep. A short drill was held to practise the form-up and then the square marched forward en-bloc. The 2nd Battalion of the Royal Scots Fusiliers marched with their Regiment's colours proudly uncased, the last regiment ever to do so. The 1st Battalion of the 13th Foot (Prince Albert's Light Infantry) had their bandsmen playing the regimental marches. After about two miles had been covered, distant and scattered bands of Zulus began to appear on all the surrounding hills, but they were still out of range. The kraal at Nodwengu on the line of march was burnt and the smoke rose into the baking morning air as if to announce the coming doom of Ulundi itself.

Tuck wrote: 'I must first say that the Zulus thought the White man could not fight except in laager, and that if they got us on a plain they would eat us up in no time. On the morning of the 4 July 1879 at daybreak the whole of the column (except the 24th Regt) crossed the river and formed up in one large square four deep, the rear being so that we could not be surrounded to any effect by the Zulus. After advancing about three miles (during which time our mounted men were out in front and on our flanks burning some of the large Zulu military kraals), the enemy was seen approaching from all sides in immense numbers. I should estimate their number

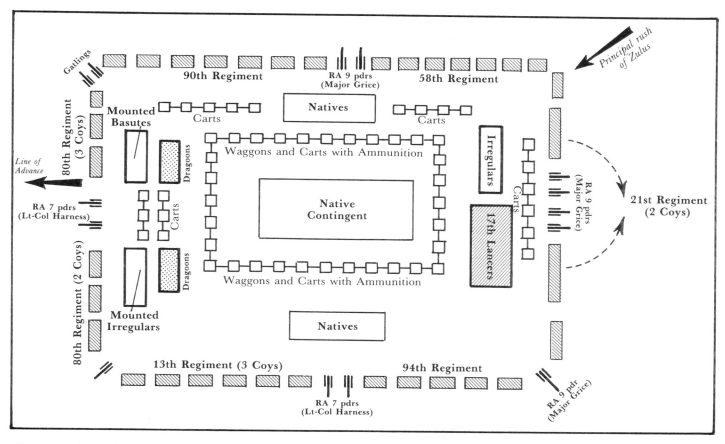

Gatlings

90th Regiment

RA 9 pdrs
(Major Grice)

58th Regiment

Principal rush of Zulus

80th Regiment
(3 Coys)

**Mounted
Basutes**

Carts

Natives

Carts

Irregulars

*Line of
Advance*

Dragoons

Waggons and Carts with Ammunition

**Native
Contingent**

Carts

17th Lancers

RA 9 pdrs
(Major Grice)

21st Regiment
(2 Coys)

RA 7 pdrs
(Lt-Col Harness)

Carts

80th Regiment (2 Coys)

Dragoons

Waggons and Carts with Ammunition

**Mounted
Irregulars**

Natives

13th Regiment (3 Coys)

RA 7 pdrs
(Lt-Col Harness)

94th Regiment

RA 9 pdr
(Major Grice)

*The composition of the square at Ulundi showing natives
and cavalry safely protected inside.*

at 20,000'.

Tuck listed the troops engaged as:
1st King's Dragoon Guards; 17th Lancers; 3 Batteries of Artillery; 2nd Battalion, 3rd Buffs; 2nd Battalion, 4th King's Own; 1st Battalion, 13th Regt; 2nd Battalion, 21st Regiment; 1st and 2nd Battalions, 24th Regiment; 57th Regiment; 58th Regiment; 3rd Battalion, 60th Rifles; 80th Regiment; 88th Regiment; 90th Regiment; 91st Regiment; 94th Regiment; 99th Regiment.

Major Charles Robinson, Assistant Adjutant-General of the 2nd Division, recalled:

'We marched on, and wheeled a little in the direction which led best to Ulundi. Then we saw they meant to attack us, so we halted and faced outwards again. The irregular cavalry then skirmished and were driven back, and with the Lancers all entered the square. It was like a picture battle. You can't imagine anything prettier than the surrounding green hills, and the skirmishing cavalry and the red square and the black Zulus. A slight trench was thrown up by Wood's column but none by ours outside the battle formation'.

There were two Gatlings, a hand-cranked, ten-barrelled machine gun which was mounted on a light artillery carriage. They had been developed in America but the Zulu war was their first outing with the British

135

The aim was to smash the Zulu army by controlled rifle fire, but the cavalry was eager for action and here General Newdigate is seen addressing the Lancers, assuring them their chance would come.

Army. They were in the charge of a section of Royal Marine gunners and bluejacket personnel from the Naval Brigade. Like all the weapons they had a reputation for unreliability and sticking, the bases of the rolled-brass cartridges tending to be torn off by the extractors thus jamming the guns at crucial moments. The Gatling gun was also rather heavy but on this occasion at least did not prove as unreliable as expected. It had done good work earlier in the campaign.

Chelmsford was much criticised for lack of heavy artillery, having only twelve guns with his force on this occasion 'N' Battery 5th Brigade; 'M' Battery 6th Brigade and 'O' Battery 5th Brigade. Moreover the two of Lt-Col Arthur Harness's three batteries, 'O' commanded by Major Edmund Tremlett, RA and 'M' commanded by Major Willoughby Hamond Sandham, RA, were equipped with only the smaller 7lb mountain guns on light carriages. However 'N' Battery 6th Brigade, commanded by Major Frederick Swain Le Grice was equipped with 9lb guns, which General Newdigate considered far more serviceable weapons. Blood, an artillery officer stated that in his view this was due, '...to remarkable ignorance'. Lord Chelmsford however believed that long-range shelling would only scare off the *Impi*, quite the reverse of what was required which was to bring them into the massed rifle and Gatling fire. There was also the difficulty of transportation which always weighed heavily on every commander's mind during this period.

As for cavalry, pride of place went to the 17th Lancers, 'Bingham's Dandies' who had been renamed in 1876 as The Duke of Cambridge's Own, he having served in their ranks. They were proudly clad in dark blue jackets, with white facings and with white plumes and their Death's Head badges on their helmets. Col Drury Lowe had been brought back to serve as commander. Their high-spirited and temperamental mounts found conditions in South Africa trying after the long sea voyage from England and initially they could only manage ten miles a day on their journey up-country from the disembarkation ports. As each horse was carrying about 260lb with rider and equipment a considerable period was required for them to settle down in the new environment. There was much complaint that the views of the cavalry were little sought but Chelmsford used them in their traditional role well on this occasion and certainly gave the 'Death or Glory Boys' their chance for both this day. A squadron of the 1st (The King's) Dragoon Guards, commanded by Col Henry Alexander, completed the regular cavalry. They also wore blue velvet uniforms with red head plumes and we met them last in China at the Taku Forts.

The cavalry was superbly supplemented by Col

The irregular cavalry served with distinction in the final advance. Here are two typical officers serving with the Frontier Light Horse.

Redvers Henry Buller's irregulars. The Frontier Light Horse, now under Capt Parminter, numbered about ten score riders who wore their slouch hats with a red puggree wound around them and either the original black corduroy uniforms with twin red stripes down the breeches or their usual hard-wearing drills. They looked, and were, tough locals going about their business in a professional, workmanlike way.

All were astounded that the Zulus allowed them to cross the river at all, let alone form up as they wished with no hindrance. On the high ground between Nodwengu and Ulundi, which was described as perfectly open and free from bush, the clumsy square could manoeuvre without losing its essential cohesion which favoured the British force. It was believed that the enemy also favoured combat here for the Zulus, having suffered heavily in their attacks on laagered formations, actually wanted the battle to take place on an open plain. Cetawayo reputedly told his warriors that if they could catch the red-coated invaders in the open they were certain to destroy them. A Zulu prisoner later stated that they thought the British 'moonstruck' when they observed them advancing in the open, thus inviting the *Impi* to 'eat them up' in the classic manner. They were to be rapidly disillusioned. The native troops in the British force shared the conviction that to meet the Zulu warriors in the open was suicidal and they were kept firmly inside the square until British victory was obvious. Not until their Dutch courage had been boosted were they released.

What of the Zulu Army? Many of their finest fighting formations had already seen hard service at earlier battles and had taken heavy casualties. Even their greatest victory at Isandhlwana had cost them dear, in its earlier stages before the redcoats' ammunition ran out. Subsequent reverses against the various columns had always resulted in large numbers of dead and wounded, the latter tending to drift back to their home kraals having contributed all they could to the war. Even so the Zulus managed to assemble an imposing force to defend their 'capital'.

Their regiments moved silently down from the hills to the north and through the long grass in perfect alignment to meet the British square. They fanned out to east and west as the horns started to envelope the British force. A large group closed round behind the square at Nodwengu. Here were famous Zulu units,

gathered for the last defence of their old ways, the *isaNgqu*, the *uDududu* both of the *uNodwengu* Corps, the *umXapho* and the *inTsukamngeni*, veterans of Majia's Hill, the *uDloko*, from Isandhlwana and Rorke's Drift, the *amaKwenkwe*, the *unCijo*. Beating their shields and initially moving in slowly, lured on by the irregular cavalry Chelmsford had sent out for just such a purpose, the massed and purposeful Zulu warriors closed in. There was a leavening of old warriors in their ranks, men who had witnessed at first hand the destructive power and stopping effect of massed Martini-Henrys who still trotted on to give their lives for their king. Among those regiments decimated in earlier encounters the ranks contained fresh-faced youths, confident in their own strength and power, urged on by their leaders and ignorant of what they were to face. They had been chanting and singing all night working themselves up in readiness for a great battle. Twenty thousand pairs of unshod feet gradually built up a steady drumming on the ground as they advanced, that famous and feared sound of the South African veldt. Gradually the tempo increased as the extended lines started to trot and then run, seeking the weakest points in the massed ranks before them.

En Masse there were fewer more intimidating sights than the great black waves sweeping forward unafraid and confident. The Zulu ranks were not initially massed as they closed in, rather they advanced carefully in extended line, prior to the main rush. Nor was every Zulu warrior a Shaka in stature, even though this was how they were always depicted. Bindon Blood made one of the very rare comments on this aspect of the presentation of the war in his later recollections of the campaign:

'I remember that on this and other similar occasions I was much struck with the superiority of our men to the Zulus, and all other natives, in muscular and physical development generally. Owing to the eugenic and other special arrangements in Zululand, the Zulus were taller, better-looking and better made generally than ordinary negroes; but even they did not compare well with our men in muscular development. All the black men were smooth-bodied, like women; whereas our men made a very fine show! This was curious, as in our illustrated papers and books we had been accustomed to see African natives, and especially Zulus, depicted as of Herculean proportions!'

From the distant British laager the advancing Zulu army was being watched through telescopes and some excitement was felt when a wing was thought to be heading for them, but this proved a false alarm. 'For the first half hour all seemed quiet, then gradually we saw thick lines of black men advancing rapidly down the opposite hills and out of the bush on our right, moving in splendid order just like the skirmishing waves of modern tactics.'

Major C. F. Clery, from within the square remembered: 'It was a curious sight to see the Zulu army quietly moving down to surround us in the centre of the Ulundi basin. They began closing in on us in a circle of about three miles from where our battle formation halted to receive them. But our position was a good one except that the grass was rather long, and as the leading line advanced they concealed themselves wonderfully.'

Chelmsford and his army were ready. The square itself had wheeled slightly to the right as it crossed the Mahlabatini and then advanced up the slight incline that rose before finally descending to Ulundi itself on the far side of a small rivulet, the Mbilane. This marked the boundary of the King's kraal and their final objective. He had not expected to get this far and, as the long grass parted in front of the mounted men revealing the

The Battle of Ulundi
– the Advance of the British Square

1	Bonampie
2	Nodwengu
3	Bilawayo
4	Kandampempi
5	Meityo
6	Zuegazi
7	Ndabakaembi
A	Square first formed
B	Square during burning of Ulundi

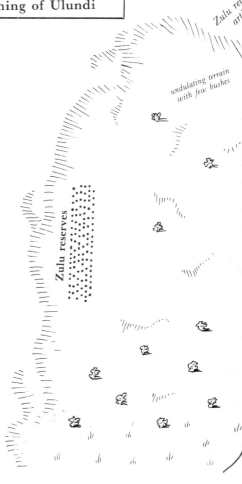

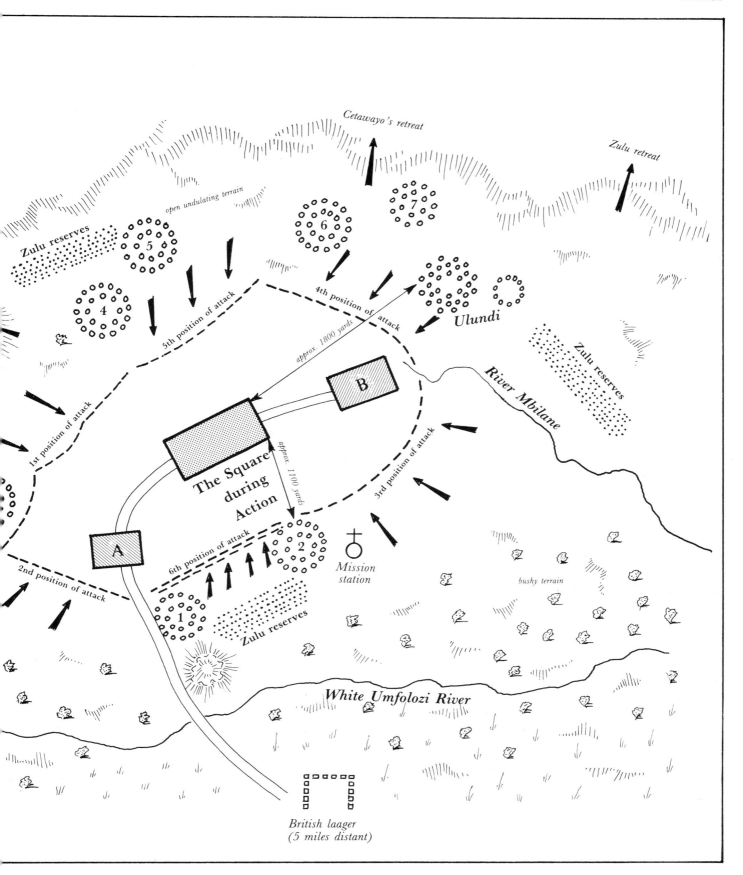

Cetawayo's retreat

Zulu retreat

open undulating terrain

Zulu reserves

5

4

6

7

4th position of attack

Ulundi

Zulu reserves

5th position of attack

approx. 1800 yards

River Mbilane

B

The Square
during
Action

approx. 1100 yards

1st position of attack

A

3rd position of attack

6th position of attack

2

Mission
station

bushy terrain

2nd position of attack

1

Zulu reserves

White Umfolozi River

British laager
(5 miles distant)

Ulundi

advancing ranks of the leading *Impi*, the general brought the square to a halt on level ground and put his final orders into effect.

The troops faced out and closed ranks shoulder to shoulder. The two front ranks knelt, the two rear ranks stood, all watching the oncoming enemy. For perhaps one hundred yards all around the silent and expectant square the ground had been trampled flat. Beyond that was long grass on the hillocks about them. On command the infantry opened their ammunition pouches, loaded and fixed their bayonets. Ammunition boxes, their brass bands already loosened to prevent any repeat of the earlier tragedy at Isandlwana, were passed down from the waggons and the regimental bandsmen went round behind the front lines distributing cartridge packets. The Native troops and cavalry were mustered in the centre on the high ground to await their chance. A gap was briefly opened to let in the retiring horsemen and then closed again. All the officers remained mounted on their chargers following the example set by Lord Chelmsford who disdained to dismount.

The British square is formed. The ranks of the infantry pour volley after volley into the Zulus as their initial rush is broken and the remnants of once-proud impi seek cover in the long grass and scrub.

The artillery then opened fire with shells at the distant lines, but the Zulus were too widely spread for great execution and the lines came steadily forward, the explosions cutting holes here and there which were soon filled. As the speed of the charge increased the Gatlings at the corners of the squares and the four lines of infantry began firing steady, measured volleys into the now compressed ranks of the enemy. Trench's two guns switched to case shot and fired seven rounds each which tore great gaps in the Zulu lines and soon the effect of the deliberate rifle fire began to take effect.

Some shooting was initially high, due to the grass, but this soon settled down and rank after rank of Zulu bodies began to crash to the ground. The initial rush continued with its own momentum despite the casualties and it appeared that the onrush must carry them into the square

140

itself. Officers drew swords and revolvers in readiness for hand-to-hand fighting. It never came to that, not even when the massive Zulu reserve held behind them was unleashed and made a final mass charge toward the rear, right-hand corner of the square. Here it was met by canister and steady volleying and stuttered to a halt like all the others without a single Zulu getting within thirty yards of the square. Bindon Blood wrote: 'The Zulus advanced to within 70 yard of the British square, which must have shot badly...'

By contrast Pte Tuck in the front rank, noted carefully: '...a hot engagement ensued for one hour and a half inflicting severe loss on the enemy's side but few on the British. Our cavalry was surrounded by them, we standing perfectly steady, until the enemy coming too close, when the cavalry retired into the square, and then the Infantry and artillery commenced such a fire that no living being could possibly come within a hundred yards of us as shells and volleys went into their midst. Still, on they came with great determination but they could not stand against our fire and advance, so they turned and ran. No sooner had they turned to flee then out of our square popped the 17th Lancers, Mounted Volunteers and all mounted men cutting the enemy down like grass

The scene inside the square with Lord Chelmsford and his fellow officers disdaining to dismount and the wounded being tended, as all around the Zulu warriors are shot-down well out of range of their own weapons.

before the scythe.' He added; 'Our Regiment got great praise from both Lord Chelmsford and General Newdigate for our steady behaviour in the field under their command during such trying circumstances which was gone through. I am only too proud to bear the name and title of Bandsman M. Tuck (An Old Steel Back)'.

Massed in such a compact formation, the British troops should have presented an easy target to all those thousands of rifles in the Zulu Army, but most of the shots whistled high over their heads and casualties were few. No warrior ever got the chance to use his *assegai*.

As the Zulu onrush was broken and the attack faltered under the disciplined and steady firing, they began first to waver and then retreat. Many had known their cause was hopeless from the first, others had been long in the field and had seen enough fighting, many fledglings were shaken that the redcoats had no flanks to be turned. The charges had been eddying round the smoke-wreathed square searching for an opening but there was none and

141

The Lancers are unleashed in typical fashion 'go at it' to complete the rout of Cetawayo's last regiments of defeated Zulus.

the bodies piled up as the minutes passed. Soon, enough was enough and general retreat commenced. Lord Chelmsford had been waiting the moment. Now he shouted to Drury Lowe who had been patiently waiting his turn, to 'Go at them'.

A gap was again opened in the British square, the 2nd battalion of the 21st Foot and the 94th making way and through the sudden break in the solid red ranks trotted the squadrons of the Lancers and Dragoons, lances bedecked with fluttering red and white pennons in the grand old style. They wheeled from the rear of the square to the front where Drury Lowe formed them up in two lines, with the irregular horse behind them facing the stream and the straggling columns of retreating warriors. Lowe then ordered the charge and the whole splendid formation moved off down the gentle slope quickly overtaking the Zulus, spitting them expertly and harrying them mercilessly. Lowe himself was hit by a bullet as was Lt H. Jenkins but both kept going. The rout was temporarily halted at the stream and a ragged volley fired by the Zulus killed Capt Wyatt-Edgell but soon a new charge was made across the Donga and this last resistance broken. As the Zulu streamed back over the brow of the

hills from which they had so confidently descended a scant half-hour before, the artillery helped them on their way with well-placed salvoes while the Native contingent was released to hunt out any armed combatants among the hundreds of wounded in the surrounding long grass.

Major Frank Russell described events from his distant viewpoint thus:

'...At 8.35 musketry began, and up till 9.15 the action appeared most sharp and well contested, a nervous moment for us all. At 9.20 I was able to send down to Colonel Bellairs news that the enemy were in disorderly retreat. Then we saw them squatting down on the hilltop and shells admirably directed by the artillery bursting among them.'

Thus was Ulundi fought and won and the power of the Zulu nation broken.

AFTERMATH

Bindon Blood estimated that the Zulu casualties were about 1,000 killed. The British casualties were 12 killed and 70 wounded. From the ranks, Tuck estimated the enemy loss at between 3,000 to 4,000 killed and wounded.

On Sunday 6 July shortly after Divine Service the column was formed up at the camp and General Newdigate made a speech. He said (in Tuck's version at any event), 'I have come here today to thank you and from the bottom of my heart I thank you for your gallant conduct in the battle of the day before yesterday, July 4th 1879, and for your coolness and bravery. Seldom as it been the lot of a General Officer to witness such behaviour as yours. Your firing was most effective and your coolness under fire could not be surpassed. I noticed one and all doing their duty well, both Regimental and Company officers, and in fact all ranks, and you won a most decisive victory against great odds. You have taught the enemy a terrible lesson which will never be forgotten by the Zulu nation. I was the more especially pleased to see the way you cleared your front and repulsed the enemy with such a small expenditure of ammunition. (Each man had averaged seven rounds apiece). You waited until the smoke of your firing had cleared away and then your well-directed volleys mowed the enemy down like grass before the scythe. Once more I thank you for you good conduct, one and all, of which I shall make the most favourable positive reports in my despatch'.

Many considered Chelmsford's abrupt withdrawal from the field of victory, without taking final steps to finish off a beaten foe and bring Cetawayo to justice, highly premature and somewhat unprofessional.

Clery wrote: 'We had a good position on the Umfolozi River, plenty of wood (a rarity in this country), plenty of capital water, six days' supplies with us the day after Ulundi, fifteen days' supplies one day's march back, and sufficient supplies *somewhere* along our line of advance to keep us where we were. Yet strange to say we fell back from this position this morning after our victory when it would apear as if every muscle should be strained to keep us there'.

Robinson also stated that:

'The king has, I dare say, gone back to the bush-kraal of Amazikanzi with his guns captured at Isandlwana. The prisoners say be watched the battle from a hill and was in Ulundi the night before. We ought (to complete the war) to turn him out of this also, but the road is, they say, very bad—too much so for a horse to go over it in many parts and we had too many wounded and our provisions were not sufficient for us to face with prudence. In the meantime our having gone out and fought and beaten the Zulus (20,000 and all the best regiments were there) fairly in the open, has had an immense effect on our natives and morally has done 10 times as much good for our prestige with them as a victory from a laager would have.'

Butler commented scathingly that: 'When the pursuit was over the mounted troops were sent to destroy the Ulundi kraals, which they burnt, and, later in the day, the British army returned to camp without making any attempt or arrangement to follow up their victory, or to capture the King. Stranger still, they commenced at once a retrograde march on Natal, Lord Chelmsford resigning his command and proceeding with a large staff direct to Pietermaritzburg. Thus was the bubble of the Zulu military power burst! The Zulus made no visible attempt at a rally, although thanks to Lord Chelmsford's arrangements, or rather to his neglect of obviously advisable precautions, there was nothing to prevent such an attempt.'

But Chelmsford had already been relieved. He had made his point and now he saw no reason to continue. It was left to his successor to finish the war, and the pursuit and final capture of Cetawayo and his surviving chiefs occupied Wolseley for more months and involved not much glory or satisfaction either. When the Zulu King was brought to England he was treated more as a novelty and a victim than the bloodstained fanatical leader of a crazed nation of killer-warriors which the British public had gone to war to erase.

Lord Chelmsford vindicated himself at Ulundi and the most savage warrior tribe in the whole of Africa had

A ZULU REBUS.—" CIGAR. NET-WOOL. SEE."

Despite the smug self-satisfaction of the Victorian cartoonist's portrayal of Wolseley capturing Cetawayo, the Zulus had initially shaken the world's greatest empire badly.

been defeated by the British soldier, almost without loss in a stand-up, face-to-face battle. That was the military significance of the battle. In Queen Victoria's eyes this was important also. She wrote to Sir Bartle Frere on 21 August 1879:

'The news of the victory at Ulundi was received by herself and the whole country with the greatest satisfaction and gratitude. And there was but one feeling of pleasure, that this great success should have been achieved by Lord Chelmsford after so much anxiety.'

Was there a sting in the tail? Whatever pleasure she felt at the final outcome of the battle was tempered by the ghastly butcher's bill of Isandlwana and her personal distress at the death of the Prince Imperial and the suffering this caused her friend, the Empress Eugenie. Prime Minister Disraeli was not so pleased with the conduct of the campaign and although awarded a GCB Lord Chelmsford himself was never given another field command. As for Sir Garnet Wolseley he had been thwarted, which pleased the establishment. However they had been forced to send for him, and he was not long in finding another chance to prove his ability and worth, also in Africa, but this time at the northern end of the Black Continent.

Chapter Six

TEL-EL-KEBIR

13 September 1882

PRELUDE

The still night air of the Egyptian desert, between the banks of the Suez Canal in the east and the great river Nile to the west, was disturbed on the night of 12/13 September, 1882. Two great armies stood poised for battle to the north of a stagnant ditch, christened by some forgotten humorist 'The Sweetwater Canal'. Its sluggish and vile water-course linked Cairo, the humid Egyptian Canal capital at the head of the Nile's delta, with Ismalia, at the head of Lake Timsak. Along the raised, northern bank of the canal ran the tracks of the railway connecting these two centres of population via the junction of Zagazig and small towns such as Abu Hammad and Masama. Other little halts on the railway had recently become known the world over through the preliminary skirmishes that had taken place there: Mahuta, Kassassin, and now, Tel-el-Kebir. On either side of the track and waterway the desert stretched away to the north and south, a featureless wasteland.

Strangely the very barrenness of the desert had resulted in its being selected as a battleground, because, although the twenty-five mile stretch between the Suez Canal and the fortifications at Tel-el-Kebir offered nothing in the way of cover for any army, the smooth gravel surface

A Royal Horse Artillery battery crashes into the Egyptian trenches after they had been stormed at bayonet point by the British infantry.

The defender of Tel-el-Kebir, Arabi Pasha, Military Dictator of Egypt at the height of his power. Arabi was of the Army and their loyalty to his cause was never in doubt.

was firm enough for an army to move over with reasonable ease. The terrain was ideal for horse-drawn artillery and certainly also the cavalry formations of an army would find the firm surface, in the main, most suitable for enveloping and flanking movements.

The desert's lack of suitable cover and openness was the main reason why it was also, conversely, ideal for a static defence. Behind strong earth-works and in deep, interlocking trenches, a reasonably equipped and well-directed army, heavily supported by dug-in artillery which had completely unrestricted and well-sited fields of fire, should, in theory, have very little difficulty in inflicting wholly disproportionate and unacceptable casualties on any enemy advancing towards it. Thus both defence and offence found common ground in the wilderness of sand, rock and scrub.

At Tel-el-Kebir lay the defending army of Egypt, an Egypt under the control of a military dictatorship led by Colonel Arabi Pasha. To the east that night, advancing steadily towards the strong fortifications of the Egyptians, came the attackers, the British Expeditionary Force, skilfully led by Sir Garnet Wolseley, one of the most outstanding campaigners and original military thinkers of Victorian Britain.

The well-equipped defenders lay in their splendid fortifications awaiting the blow which they knew must come soon but not, they judged, without their being duly warned. This warning Wolseley was determined to deny them. Against them, as one officer wrote at the time, 'there was to be launched out into the night a gigantic bolt of flesh, steel and iron shot, westward into the darkness'.

Both sides had much to ponder on that final, fateful night as this mass of men started its march across the silent and moonless desert. For Arabi Pasha this was his moment of truth. His future was staked on the defences at Tel-el-Kebir and on the ability of European-trained troops to hold their own in their first real test against an enemy of quality. For Wolseley, his brilliant reputation, greatly enhanced by the sureness and swiftness of every one of the opening moves he had so far made in this campaign, depended on the ability of his army to cover the six miles from the start line at Kassassin to the Egyptian trenches and fire pits in pitch blackness.

Further, his army must also arrive at first light in correct fighting order and alignment ready for the assault. The risks he ran should not be underestimated. No commanding officer had previously staked so much on a night march, an operation which was recognised in itself as one of the most hazardous of military operations, so very much could go wrong.

The British force that moved on that night consisted of some 20,000 men organised into two brigades and supported by artillery units and a cavalry brigade. This great mass of men and *matériel*, in full combat order, would have to cover those fateful six miles in precise formation at a pre-arranged pace and conform precisely to a detailed timetable. One wild shot from any soldier in that great force, a lapse in position-keeping or the falling behind of any unit, would result in the whole carefully planned advance floundering in a confused mass of disorganised regiments. Should that occur then the rising of the sun in the morning would expose the unprotected British troops to the 26,000 defending Egyptian troops and their 75 heavy guns. A frightful massacre could then well result. General Wolseley, however, was not the type of man to give any hint of self-doubt, quite the contrary, for on his appointment to the command of the British force on 3 July 1882, he gave the confident prediction that the Egyptian army would be finally and totally defeated, and at Tel-el-Kebir! Before he even embarked for Egypt from England he approaching its climax on an autumn night of 1882, could be traced back still further than this. Back in fact to 1863 when the appointment of Khedive Ismail as Viceroy of Egypt was a fateful step. He instituted drastic reforms in order to drag the nation into the 19th century. On the face of it his achievements were immense; railways were introduced, Cairo was largely re-built in modern style, the Civil Service was re-modelled on European lines. To all this the opening of the Suez Canal was a crowning achievement.

To complement this modernisation of the Egyptian state Ismail had also trained and re-organised his standing army on European lines, brought in British officers, and had lavishly equipped it. This new army was intended to lend weight to his next stage of planning, the spread and consolidation of Egyptian power southward into the Soudan, the Red Sea and to the sources of the Nile's rivers.

Unfortunately his 'Grand Design', like so many others before and since, had somehow to be financed and his mammoth adoption of credit had, by 1879, bankrupted Egypt to the tune of one hundred million pounds. One result of this was that Disraeli, at the time Premier of Great Britain, and always a first-class patriot with an eye for the main chance as well, was able to purchase the Egyptian Government's shares in the canal for a mere one million pounds. Henceforth Britain was to be even more closely tied up with Egypt's destiny. In June, 1879, Ismail Pasha was deposed by the Sultan of Turkey in a belated effort to undo some of the harm he had done. However this gesture was somewhat marred by the fact that he appointed as successor, Ismail's son, Tewfik. He, no matter how well-intentioned, was unable to withstand the popular revulsion of the ordinary people of Egypt against exploitation and heavy taxation.

As usual it was the army which provided the real power and which gave vent to public wrath at their rulers. Colonel Ahmed Arabi Bey was able to direct, with considerable gusto, this frustration in the customary manner, against the European advisers and businessmen, rather than the Pashas, the Turkish ruling class.

Under the mindless chant of 'Egypt for the Egyptians' a group of army officers managed to pressure Tewfik, at the point of 4,000 bayonets, into accepting a ministry totally subservient to the army and, in 1881, Arabi himself entered this assembly and soon became War Minister, and, in effect, virtual dictator.

By April, 1882, the British Consul-General was reporting that: 'The country will soon be governed by none but officers'.

Despite this, and the continuing exhortations for the

A contemporary viewpoint on the cringing and ambivalent attitude of de Lesseps towards the British initiative on the Suez Canal purchase.

further predicted that the battle would be fought on 15 September—he was two days early!

But why had the two armies come into conflict in the first place? Had not Britain, above all nations, aided and assisted Egypt during the previous century and helped rid it of French conquerors? The country was still, of course, nominally under Turkish rule, and, of all the foreign influences therein, it was the Greek moneylender and the French trader who predominated rather than the English advisers. However for Great Britain, at that period approaching the zenith of her power and influence, Egypt held one treasure above all else. This was a very key of such enormous importance that this country could not stand aside from involvement, no matter how much it wished to do so. This vital factor was of course the Suez Canal which had been constructed in 1869 by the French engineer de Lesseps, with French interests at heart. However, once complete, it was such a vital strategic artery to the Indian and growing Asian Empire of Great Britain, that it dominated Imperial policy.

The complicated train of events, which was rapidly

populace to throw out all foreigners from Egypt, Britain, under the radical leadership of Gladstone's Liberal Party, was more concerned, as always, with such matters as the Irish question and social reform. Sympathetic to the basic ideas of Egyptian nationalists, and tending to overlook their violent expressions of hatred, they were extremely reluctant to become involved.

However, matters were taken out of their control by a series of violent anti-European riots in Alexandria that June, fermented by Arabi. On the 11th and 12th of that month a massacre of more than fifty helpless Europeans took place in that city, despite the presence of an Anglo-French Naval Squadron in the harbour. The decision to send in a British force to protect both nationals and vital interests by deposing the virulent nationalists now gained Gladstone's reluctant approval. His fellow Liberals were persuaded that a swift, clean-cut operation would purge the evil from Egypt and that it was also

The Turkish Government was reluctant to commit itself to grasping the nettle of Arabi's seizure of power, until far too late. It remained for Britain to send its troops to crush the dictator.

PUNCH, OR THE LONDON CHARIVARI.—AUGUST 5, 1882.

THE LION AND THE FOX.

British Lion. "GOING TO HELP ME, ARE YOU? THANK YOU FOR NOTHING, MASTER FOX. I BEGAN THE WORK ALONE, AND I MEAN TO FINISH IT!!!"

in that nation's ultimate best interests if this were done and done quickly.

Further emphasis was given to this decision when Admiral Seymour over-reacted to the strengthening of the Egyptian shore batteries around Alexandria harbour. He took this act as a direct threat to his squadron, despite the fact that it comprised the most powerful warships then afloat in the world. The resulting British Naval bombardment completely wrecked the force and sailors and Royal Marines were landed and cleared the town. But the overall result was the closing of Egyptian ranks around Arabi. The Khedive sought the protection of the British occupation forces in Alexandria, his power finally being usurped by Arabi after this incident.

Britain was now left in the lurch by the French and forced to act alone instead of in concert with that nation and Turkey. Scorning to desert her obligations in a like manner Britain went ahead on her own and planning was implemented to carry out a 'policing action' under the command of the Empire's 'Only General', Wolseley.

The strictly military preparations that followed were an impressive example of Victorian efficiency and organisation and completely refute all the hoary legends that have been planted in recent years by sensation-seeking historians, most of whom seem to be trying only to degenerate everything British as either immoral if successful, or hopelessly inefficient if a temporary failure.

aid of the Mediterranean Fleet. Hoodwinking the numerous journalists and Arabi's spies alike, his main force sailed as if bound for Aboukir but by-passed it and, by dawn on 20 August, disembarked at Ismailia. One daring move and the whole of the Suez Canal was taken intact, despite the vehement protests of de Lesseps, who despised the British. His main dispositions outflanked, Arabi had hastily to transfer troops to his threatened eastern front. The defence works at Tel-el-Kebir were hastily improved.

In the intense heat of that summer the British army moved step by step westward along the Sweetwater Canal until they held the locks at Kassassin and had repulsed a sortie led by Arabi himself. This repulse turned into a rout but Wolseley stayed his hand from pursuit until his main force was ready to deliver a decisive blow against an enemy prepared to stay and fight it out. By 12 September all was prepared.

The approaches to Tel-el-Kebir lay due west across the desert following the route of the ill-named 'Sweetwater Canal' and the rail link. Here a patrol pushes forward to test Arabi's strength.

General Wolseley surprised the Egyptians (and, to their fury, the Press) by landing his main force at Ismailia thus outflanking the coastal defences.

As Wolseley was to term it later, with undisputed accuracy and conciseness of phrase, the Egyptian Campaign of 1882 was, 'the tidiest war in British history'. Wolseley was appointed to command the Expeditionary Force on 20 July and, by the middle of August, 20,000 men had arrived in Egypt from units based in England and India. There was much concern in British Government circles that this force would prove insufficient but the General was sure it was ample.

It was widely expected, by both Egyptians and British observers alike, that, in order to capture Cairo quickly (and thus ensure that Arabi was deposed before he could fulfil his threat to destroy the city rather than surrender), the British Army would have to follow Napoleon's invasion route straight up the Nile valley. Certainly the Egyptian army at first deployed its main force on this assumption. Wolseley however was not the man to do the obvious. For one thing the sprawling delta with the myriad water courses and irrigation ditches was easily defended terrain and certainly not suitable for a modern army to manoeuvre or fight in. Artillery would be bogged down and cavalry would lose their mobility.

Instead Sir Garnet made an elaborate feint with the

THE DEFENDERS

Arabi at the head of his troops.

Arabi himself had arrived at Tel-el-Kebir to supervise the defence leaving a strong holding force at Kafr-ed-Dawar in the north to cover Alexandria. At Tel-el-Kebir his Eastern Army was under the command of General Ali Fehmy, one of Arabi's most loyal supporters. However Fehmy, and Rashid Pasha at Ismailia, had been completely outwitted by the British thrust down the canal. Initial British estimates put the Egyptian Army's strength in the east at about 12,000 troops backed by by 3,000 Bedouins, but further reinforcements of the best regular units soon swelled this total considerably. British Intelligence reports were never very precise when it came to head counting.

By the eve of the battle Wolseley was estimating his opponent's numbers at some 30,000 regulars and reservists, 60-70 guns and 3,000 Bedouins. Perhaps 25,000 was a closer figure but the General was little concerned with mere numbers anyway. As he wrote at the time, '. . . many of the regulars are old men recalled who know nothing of rifles and new drill. We have taken some of these poor old creatures prisoner and they can be of no use to Arabi whatsoever'.

In the event Wolseley was confident in the superior qualities of the British soldier. Whether Arabi had on hand, 'A mob of 30,000 or 100,000 is really of little consequence to us,' he wrote. 'With our two divisions and the Indian contingent the whole of Egypt assembled at Tel-el-Kebir would be made short work of; please believe this if any croakers try to frighten the Government.'

So much for Wolseley's opinion of his foe. The defence works themselves however certainly gave him greater cause for reflection.

More correctly written as 'El-Tel-el-Kebir', 'The

Great Hill', the position chosen by Arabi to make his decisive stand was the strongest one possible against an advance from the east. The village itself lay between the railway to the north and the Sweetwater Canal to the south. For many years the heights above this village had been utilised as a military encampment and base for the Egyptian army and, indeed, Arabi himself had undergone a brief period of exile there in the autumn of 1881. Charles Royale described the position thus:

'Near the station at Tel-el-Kebir there is a general and gradual rise of the ground towards the west, culminating in a range of hills that stretch from a point on the railway about a mile and a half east of this station, northward to Salaheih. Roughly parallel to the canal is a second series of hills intersecting the first about two miles distant from the railway. Viewed from the railway this east and west range appears as a moderate hill. Its real character however is that of a table-land sloping away to the northward with a rather steep descent towards the south. The ground is generally even, and barren almost to desolation, the soil consisting of sand and rock, producing only small scrub. To the eastward of the lines and in the direction of Kassassin was a tolerably level desert with small sand and pebbles.'

As soon as it was known that the main British strike was to come across this desert from the east considerable work was put in hand to enlarge the fortifications and entrenchments on this natural barrier. The ultimate plans of the defenders called for no less than the construction in the virgin desert of a complete network of continuous entrenchments, intially from Es-Salihiyeh to Tel-el-Kebir, a distance of twenty miles, and then this system would have been still further extended for a further thirty miles south, towards Dar-el-Beida. The Egyptian plans also included a series of dams across the Sweetwater Canal itself to deny it water to the British Army.

As Colonel T. F. Maurice, RA, was to write later:

'The whole mass of the people are labourers trained in one particular class of work. Thus the ruling council had at its command, in the then excited condition of the peasantry, an unlimited supply of skilled labour which they resolved to turn to the utmost account'.

The trenches of this gigantic plan were, of course, never completed, but what was achieved at Tel-el-Kebir itself was sufficiently daunting and gave some idea of the potential and formidable defence such a scheme would have presented had it been carried through. The ghastly carnage of trench warfare of the First World War was still over thirty years ahead but, in 1882, the indications were all there.

The completed trenches ran up from the Sweetwater Canal northward for some four miles, although those in the extreme north were largely incomplete at the time the battle took place. From the centre of the main line a supporting system ran back at right-angles towards the old army camp where the HQ was established. Laid out along the crests of the hills the main trench lines were between five and nine feet in depth, eight to twelve feet wide, with a four to six feet high breastwork. Along the length of this system were a few salients with strong redoubts giving a wide field of fire across their flanks.

Behind this main line were constructed shelter trenches and elaborate rifle pits with further artillery positions on high elevations. Passages were cut through in places for field-pieces and these were guarded by breastworks and traverses. South of the main switch line was established a telegraph station and here also were located camel enclosures and the like.

The artillery was placed as follows: at the extreme south of the line were two redoubts abutting either side of the canal, each mounting three guns. A dam was constructed across the canal at this point linking them. Three single gun positions straddled the railway line immediately above these first emplacements.

Two large salients, with one gun and four guns respectively, were fronted at a distance of some 1,100 yards to the east by an advanced redoubt. This formidable outwork was built on rising ground and polygon-shaped with eight guns. From the east it tended to merge into the lines and works behind it and in fact was not marked on the British assault maps. Only a stroke of luck prevented this forward position from having a decisive effect on the battle.

This forward work was flanked by the telegraph site, and where the east-west lines intersected the south-north line was located the largest and most powerful redoubt in the system, mounting four guns. Above this was the last of the fully completed fortifications terminating in a five-gun redoubt, also of extremely strong construction and design. Further north, the line was being extended and was continuous for some distance but not fully completed, with the partially-built redoubts designed to mount three and four guns respectively. The east-west switch lines were designed to protect the main rallying point of the Egyptian army and reserves and were to form a secondary defence assembly should the main line be breached with effect either north or south of the most powerful redoubt. However, as it in fact played no part in the battle, being outflanked on both sides, it needs no further description or elaboration here.

The actual pieces that the Egyptian artillery mounted numbered 75. All were either 8cm or 6cm, breech-loading Krupps guns of 1868 pattern mounted on field carriages. Most of the shells they fired were fitted with percussion fuses which tended to bury themselves in the desert ground and were thus effectively muffled by the sand before bursting. This obviously much reduced their effectiveness in action although little opportunity was to be given to the Egyptian gunners, generally acknowledged as their best arm, to make the planned leisurely play upon the advancing infantry.

The Egyptian infantry were deployed on the night of the attack as follows: there were a total of 25,000 regular troops and 5,000 Bedouins at Tel-el-Kebir according to the most quoted figures and this is generally acknowledged as accurate by the ration issue on the eve of the battle.

A single battalion manned the advance redoubt while a further two battalions, together with 2,000 Bedouins and 300 cavalry, were positioned on the desert's edge at Abu Nishaba. The dams constructed to the rear of the main line were defended by a further three battalions, while one more battalion was placed south of the canal, a little to the east of the main force.

The bulk of the Egyptian troops were in the main a defensive line, some ten battalions in all, with 54 guns. In reserve Arabi had three battalions, five guns and 1,700 cavalry, all he had. The ten battalions in the line, on whom the brunt of the attack was to fall, were distributed with six of them along the southern sector, below 'K', three battalions between 'K' and 'M', with the last to the extreme north of the uncompleted works. The regimental officers were with their men in the line, with the senior officers close behind them.

The equipment of the Egyptian soldier was, in the main, the Remington breech-loading rifle and the supply of ammunition was enormous. At three to four yard intervals along the length of the line boxes of 1,050 cartridges were subsequently found, the majority of them little-used when it came to it. Certainly there was no need to despise in any way the equipment of Arabi's men.

On morale there seems a general divergence of opinion and the comparison of the officers with the men, and of the Soudanese troops with the Egyptian, merits some consideration. Certainly, as we have already noted, the calibre of their opponents was not rated very highly by

Simplified map of the Egyptian defences at Tel-el-Kebir. The Great Hill gave the defence dominance over the featureless desert while the canal protectected their flanks.

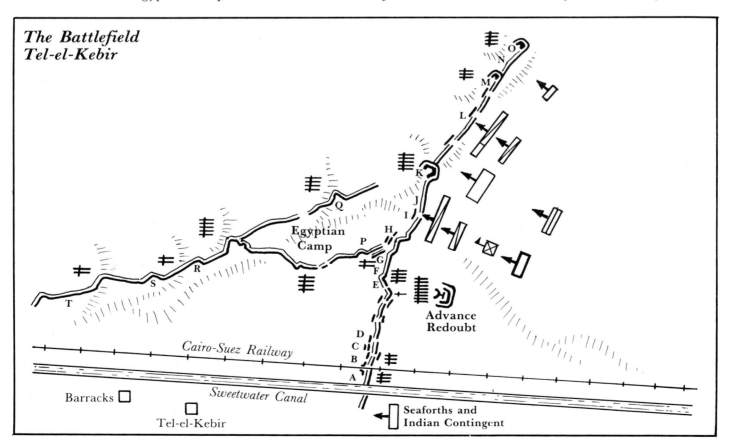

The Battlefield Tel-el-Kebir

Egyptian Camp

Advance Redoubt

Cairo-Suez Railway

Barracks ▢

Tel-el-Kebir ▢

Sweetwater Canal

Seaforths and Indian Contingent

the British on the spot. This was particularly the case of the officers whose subsequent casualties were minimal compared with the troops they were supposed to have led. As Royale quoted, the popular conception of Egyptian officer was that:

'It has been both humorously and truthfully remarked that each officer knew that *he* would run, but hoped his *neighbour* might stay.'

He concludes that there appeared no doubt that proper leaders were wanting in the Egyptian army.

On the other hand he is quite clear on the quality of the soldier in the line. 'The Egyptian soldier displayed real courage. The black regiments, composed of negroes from the Soudan, were especially noticeable for their pluck, fighting bravely hand-to-hand with their assailants.' He concludes, 'it has been well observed that more intelligence and less downright cowardice on the part of their officers might have converted these men into a formidable army'.

Subsequent fighting in the Soudan against these warriors and their kinsmen did much to confirm these conclusions.

Butler of course heaped praise upon his defeated foe in the usual manner, although on this occasion it was probably, to some extent, justified. He wrote that the Egyptians: '...fought with the greatest determination and gallantry against overwhelming odds'. The latter point is a moot one, but no one would deny the lowly fellaheen credit for more stomach than his officers.

Arabi was quite confident that, behind his formidable defence works, his modernly equipped army, of equal or greater size than his opponent's, and with the cards seemingly on his side, could hold out forever.

What of Arabi himself in whose hands the destiny of Egypt was held? He was the son of a sheik born near Zagazig close to Tel-el-Kebir in 1840. He studied at Cairo university until he was fourteen when he was conscripted into the army. Under the patronage of the Viceroy, Said Pasha, who backed the fellaheen against their Turkish rulers at every opportunity, he was ensured of privileged treatment and by the age of twenty he was Lieutenant-Colonel. The dizzy ascent was halted in 1860 with the arrival of the Khedive Ismail with the opposite policy and from this stemmed most of Arabi's hatred for the ruling caste.

This hatred endured for twenty years until Ismail was removed when his star again began to rise. Tewfik appointed him as his Colonel of the Guard, but this was not enough. His ambition thus whetted he rode the feelings of his countrymen as described, until he held ultimate power. But this position was granted to him,

as to so many dictators, for only the briefest of periods.

As nemesis approached he slept in his camp to the rear of the lines soundly and confidently. Close by, the Commandant of Tel-el-Kebir, Ali Rubi Pasha, also slept undisturbed.

THE ATTACKERS

The man who was to be responsible for Arabi's rude awakening that coming dawn was perhaps the most outstanding of the late-Victorian generals. His rise had been a spectacular one and he was at the peak of his fame in 1882.

As a young ensign Wolseley had come to early prominence leading a suicidal attack during the final Burmese War and this early promise had been ably fulfilled during the Crimea War, at the siege of Sebastapol, and also during the Indian Mutiny. The Red River Expedition in Canada had shown him to be a master of organisation and detail which he later put to

'All Sir Garnet'. When General Wolseley was in charge campaigns tended to be quick and decisive. The public loved him, the establishment did not!

use in his successful campaigns against the Ashanti and in South Africa. So outstanding a general was he at this time that the saying 'All Sir Garnet' had become the cockney slang for everything's being in order and correct.

Over the years he had gathered around himself a band of officers equally as efficient in their own spheres as he, and this happy brotherhood, which included such famous soldiers as Colley, Butler and Buller, became known as the 'Wolseley Ring' because of its exclusiveness to only his favourites. He was a great reformer, determined to shake the army into acceptance of modern methods and equipment and he was largely instrumental in bringing about the reform of the old long-service system and the abolition of the old numbered regiments, for which he earned for himself the intense dislike of both the Duke of Cambridge and Queen Victoria.

The 'Ring' was again in evidence during this campaign and the brilliance of their planning and methods was ably demonstrated, as was the justification of the reforms he had fought for for so long.

The force he commanded was the largest Expeditionary Force that had left British shores since the Napoleonic wars and was probably the fittest ever to campaign abroad up to that time. Thanks to the care and foresight of their leaders their health was reported as being better under the scorching Egyptian summer sun that it had been back home in barracks!

It was an army of confident, able men. Joseph Lehmann describes them thus: 'Most of the soldiers marched dressed in red tunics and Indian mud-coloured helmets, stained to prevent them becoming conspicuous under the bright sun. Every man had his hair cut as short as possible before landing and most were issued with a pair of dark spectacles and green or blue veils, though many refused to wear them. The troopers had their swords ground onboard, hilt and scabbard were browned by burning to prevent their glaring in the desert.'

Wolseley himself, by contrast, was attired in a blue tunic, brown boots, with gauntlets and he also sported a solar topee and huge black goggles. He was much concerned by the fact that his fine soldiers had to fight under the boiling sun dressed in their traditional red serge jackets, flannel shirts and woollen trousers.

In the main though he was happy for he was among friends. Among the members of the 'Ring' present, other than those mentioned, were Baker Russell, Evelyn Wood VC, Herbert Stewart and McCalmont', with the faithful Maurice, who later became the campaign's official historian. Maj-Gen Gerald Graham was a sturdy veteran who had served with Wolseley in China many years before and Bindon Blood was another Anglo-Irish soldier

The 1st Life Guards. Wolseley was not enamoured of the Queen's 'toy soldiers' but in fact they redeemed themselves in his eyes in this battle.

on the scene with the Engineers.

The General was, however, much irritated by a certain number of less welcome 'guests' who had been forced upon him, such as the Duke of Connaught, Queen Victoria's favourite son acting as a Brigade Commander, the Duke of Teck, a nephew of the monarch and, as a further sop to Her Majesty, the only 'long-service force in the army', the Household Cavalry. All these royal associations, from a ruler who had not hitherto been a very enthusiastic admirer of his, made Wolseley squirm but he endured it all with a brave face.

The British infantry were armed with the splendid breech-loading Martini-Henry rifle which had a good loading and firing rate but also had a vicious kick and tended to jam in the sand. For the main attack however, it was the bayonet, that ultimate friend of the British soldier, which was to form the main weapon on which the mettle of the Egyptian army was to be put to the test. The type of bayonet used with the Martini-Henry rifle was of the old, socket type, one-foot ten-inches in length, triangular with three channelled-out sides, a formidable close-range tool in experienced hands.

For the night march prior to the engagement each man was allocated 100 rounds of ammunition although every effort was made to ensure that these were carried in the

As always the Naval Brigade were much in evidence and their Gatlings, seen here at Port Said, were moved forward with the British advance.

men's pouches and not loaded in their rifles, lest a stray shot ruin the element of surprise. Many men naturally objected to this, feeling that a soldier needed 'one up the spout' to protect himself in an emergency during a direct assault. A notable feature of this campaign was the employment of mounted infantry, an arm for which Wolseley had long asked, and their conduct to date had justified their inclusion.

For heavy metal the British force was not over-equipped. The two divisions of the Royal Artillery had forty-two guns, 9-, 13- and 16pdrs, with which to oppose Arabi's heavy guns. In addition the Naval Brigade would take into action a single 40pdr and there were the Horse Artillery batteries to take the total to 61 guns, with six Naval Gatling guns.

For cavalry Wolseley could call on an arm in which he had great confidence through their commander, Drury Lowe. The Household Cavalry had redeemed themselves in his eyes by their dashing conduct in the early skirmishes and, despite himself, the General was taken by these vast men mounted on their huge horses, who, '...with their heavy swords cut men from head to waistbelt'. He had the 4th and 7th Dragoon Guards and the 19th Hussars in line as well and their main duties would be to conduct an enveloping movement to cut off

the enemy retreat as well as perform a swift follow-up to prevent the army's reforming later.

Again, the Commander-in-Chief was not initially enamoured, of the Indian Army contingent which was added to his force, having a limited opinion as to its value, although he was delighted when his brother George turned up at Ismailia with them. However the work of the turbaned and bearded Bengal Lancers in skewering the fleeing fellaheen in their hundreds won him round later.

All in all the total British strength on the eve of the battle was as follows:

Infantry: 422 officers, 11,702 NCO's and men
Cavalry: 125 officers, 2,660 NCO's and men
Artillery: 87 officers, 2,405 NCO's and men

For several days General Wolseley and his brother had ridden out over the nine miles of wilderness before dawn to survey the Egyptian lines. Observing them with his one good eye through a brass telescope the General noted how, with strict punctuality unusual for them, the first mounted sentinels left the Egyptian trenches for forward observation just after dawn every day. There were apparently no outriders at night. The determination to attack just before this hour grew on him for, in addition to the surprise it would give him and his own men, it would also give his mounted forces the maximum time to get behind the enemy ere he could retire towards Cairo itself.

Wolseley confirmed his plan on the morning of 12 September when, on this occasion in company with all his generals, he surveyed Tel-el-Kebir for the final time in this manner. At 05:45, as the dawn broke in the east behind him, Wolseley told them:

'Note the time! Our attack must be delivered this hour tomorrow morning, otherwise those vedettes will detect our presence.'

He then explained his plan to his officers and if there were any who had qualms none expressed them at this time. There was no discussion anyway. Dismissed, the generals rode off to set in motion his orders without alteration. Wolseley, as usual, was supremely confident. He told Herbert Stewart:

'I know what the best troops feel and do when suddenly surprised at night; a surprise means panic, and a panic under such circumstances means a general stampede, and the side which is sufficiently well-drilled, disciplined and handled to enable it to make an attack at night will generally succeed, whether the enemy be surprised or not.'

Prophetic words.

To help the troops form up in correct position that

night a line of telegraph poles to act as guide posts had been erected by the Engineering officers. These posts ran west for 1,000 yards from 'Ninth Hill', just above Kassassin camp. Previous reconnaissance had also charted the star sights necessary for Lt Rawson, the RN *Aide-de-camp,* who was well used to guiding his way by such methods, to plot the course of the whole army across this strange sea of sand. The night of attack was blacker than usual and some difficulty was found in fact in locating these posts initially, although eventually all was smoothed out satisfactorily, ready for the off.

Right: *Lieutenant Wyatt Rawson, RN, was one of the heroes of the night march. He took star-sights to keep the 20,000 men aligned. He died in the assault knowing he had 'led them true'.*

Below: *Schematic and simplified diagram showing the disposition of the advancing British forces on the eve of the battle. In fact the night march meant that this plan went slightly awry but it was nonetheless successful.*

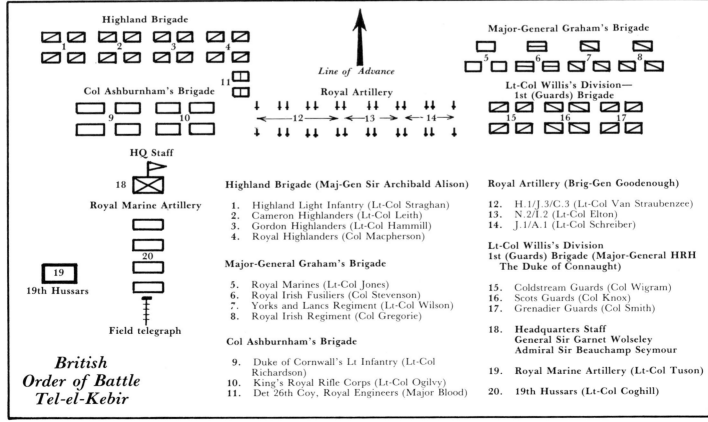

British Order of Battle Tel-el-Kebir

Highland Brigade (Maj-Gen Sir Archibald Alison)

1. Highland Light Infantry (Lt-Col Straghan)
2. Cameron Highlanders (Lt-Col Leith)
3. Gordon Highlanders (Lt-Col Hammill)
4. Royal Highlanders (Col Macpherson)

Major-General Graham's Brigade

5. Royal Marines (Lt-Col Jones)
6. Royal Irish Fusiliers (Col Stevenson)
7. Yorks and Lancs Regiment (Lt-Col Wilson)
8. Royal Irish Regiment (Col Gregorie)

Col Ashburnham's Brigade

9. Duke of Cornwall's Lt Infantry (Lt-Col Richardson)
10. King's Royal Rifle Corps (Lt-Col Ogilvy)
11. Det 26th Coy, Royal Engineers (Major Blood)

Royal Artillery (Brig-Gen Goodenough)

12. H.1/J.3/C.3 (Lt-Col Van Straubenzee)
13. N.2/I.2 (Lt-Col Elton)
14. J.1/A.1 (Lt-Col Schreiber)

Lt-Col Willis's Division
1st (Guards) Brigade (Major-General HRH The Duke of Connaught)

15. Coldstream Guards (Col Wigram)
16. Scots Guards (Col Knox)
17. Grenadier Guards (Col Smith)

18. **Headquarters Staff**
    General Sir Garnet Wolseley
    Admiral Sir Beauchamp Seymour

19. **Royal Marine Artillery (Lt-Col Tuson)**

20. **19th Hussars (Lt-Col Coghill)**

THE NIGHT MARCH

At dusk on the evening of 12 September the camp at Kassassin was struck, the troops moving silently and quickly, and all the tents and similar encumbrances were piled up alongside the railway line. However, in order to deceive any distant watchers, the camp fires were left ablaze as the troops formed up in order of advance along Ninth Hill. Here no fires at all were permitted, nor was any soldier allowed to smoke despite the mounting tension as the hours ticked away. The strictest silence was insisted upon and when any loose cartridges were found they were immediately confiscated.

In their ordered ranks the British force lay, fitfully sleeping or resting, awaiting the word to move off. Most men tried to sleep, most tried not to think of what awaited them at dawn. Each man had two days' rations issued to him, rifles were emptied. Thus the long, silent lines of men lay waiting after a last brief inspection by the C-in-C.

Extreme Left — South of the Sweetwater Canal:
    Indian Contingent (Maj-Gen Sir H. Macpherson)
    1st Battalion Seaforth Highlanders (Lt-Col C. M. Stockwell CB)
    7th Bengal Native Infantry (Col H. R. Worsley)
    20th Punjab Native Infantry (Brevet-Col. R. G. Rogers CB)
    Mountain Battery (Major J. F. Free)
    Sappers and Miners (Col J. Browne, CSI, RE)
    6th Bengal Cavalry (Major R. M. Jennings)
Left Flanking Force:
    The Naval Brigade (Capt Fitzroy RN)
    17th Company Royal Engineers (Capt E. Wood)
    Gatling Gun Battery
    Pontoon Troop Royal Engineers (Major R. J. Bond)
Main Attack — Left Flank:
    2nd Division (Lt-Gen Sir E. Hamley)
    Front: 3rd (Highland) (Brigade Maj-Gen Sir Archibald Alison)
    Highland Light Infantry (Lt-Col A. Straghan)
    Queen's Own Cameron Highlanders (Lt-Col J. M. Leith)
    Gordon Highlanders (Lt-Col D. Hammill)
    Royal Highlanders (Black Watch) (Lt-Col D. Macpherson)
    Rear: 4th Brigade (Col C. Ashburnham)
    Duke of Cornwall's Light Infantry (Lt-Col W. S. Richardson)
    King's Royal Rifle Corps (Lt-Col W. L. K. Ogilvy)
    26th Company Royal Engineers (Major B. Blood)
    General Sir Garnet Wolseley and HQ Staff
    Admiral Sir Beauchamp Seymour
    Royal Marine Artillery (Lt-Col H. B. Tuson)
    19th Hussars (Lt-Col K. J. W. Coghill)
Main Attack—Centre Front:
    Royal Artillery (Brig-Gen W. H. Goodenough)
     9pdrs H1 Battery (Major C. Crosthwaite)
     13pdrs, J3 Battery (Major L. F. Perry)
     13pdrs, C3 Battery (Major E. R. Cottingham, Lt-Col Van Straubenzee)
     16pdrs, N2 Battery (Lt-Col W. G. Brancker)
     16pdrs, N2 Battery (Major W. Ward, Lt-Col Elton)
     16pdrs, N2 Battery (Major T. J. Jones)
     16pdrs, A1 Battery (Major P. Taylor, Lt-Col Schreiber)

Main Attack—Centre Rear:
> One company Royal West Kents
> Reserve ammunition column and transport (Major W. S. Herbert)

Main Attack—Right Flank:
> *1st Division (Lt-Gen G. H. S. Willis)*
> *Front: 2nd Brigade (Maj-Gen G. Graham RE)*
> Royal Marines Light Infantry (Lt-Col H. S. Jones)
> Royal Irish Fusiliers (Col T. R. Stevenson)
> York & Lancaster Regiment (Lt-Col F. E. Wilson)
> Royal Irish Regiment (Col D. G. Gregorie)
> *Rear: 1st (Guards) Brigade (Maj-Gen HRH Duke of Connaught)*
> Coldstream Guards (Col P. Smith)

Extreme Right:
> *Cavalry Division (Maj-Gen D. C. Drury Lowe CB)*
> *Indian Cavalry Brigade (Brigadier General H. Wilkinson, HP)*
> 13th Bengal Lancers
> 2nd Bengal Cavalry
> 6th Bengal Cavalry
> *The Royal Horse Artillery (Colonel C. E. Nairne)*
> N/A Battery RHA (Lt-Col Borradaile, RHA)
> G/B Battery RHA (Lt-Col W. M. B. Walton)
> *The Heavy Brigade and Mounted Infantry (Sir B. Russell, KCMG, CB)*
> 4th Dragoon Guards (Lt-Col J. B. Shaw Hellier)
> 7th Dragoon Guards (Lt-Col C. Campbell)
> 19th Hussars (Lt-Col K. J. W. Coghill)
> Household Cavalry and Life Guards, Royal Horse Guards (Col H. P. Ewart)
> Mounted Infantry (Capt R. C. B. Lawrence, King's Royal Rifles)

The short respite that the troops received at Ninth Hill was terminated at 01:30 when they received the order to move off westward by muffled vocal commands up and down the line. In order that the silently-moving columns could maintain constant touch with each other a series of connecting files were established between the brigades at the head of each division and those following behind them.

As the army moved out there was one notable inconsistency in their overall deployment between the two divisions. The original orders had not laid down a precise formation to be adopted for the night march towards the final deployment line which was to be reached just before dawn. Therefore each Divisional Commander interpreted it in his own fashion. General Willis advanced his men in the orthodox drill-book formation of 'columns of half-battalions at deploying intervals'. In this formation the 1st Division advanced until their deployment line was reached and this necessitated their dressing into line.

General Hamley however advanced the 2nd Division in half-battalions in double company columns at deploying intervals. The two lines thus formed consisted of a front rank of two companies of the right and two of the left-hand battalions and the second rank was of the same composition. Perhaps this is best illustrated thus:

2nd Division				1st Division	
XXXXX	XXXXX	XXXXX	XXXXX	XXXXX	XXXXX
XXXXX	XXXXX	XXXXX	XXXXX	XXXXX	XXXXX
				XXXXX	XXXXX
				XXXXX	XXXXX

Both divisions moved off together on time but, south of the Sweetwater Canal, the Indian contingent was held back one hour after the main force had started. On this southern bank the land was fertile, cultivated and fairly well populated. The disturbance of domestic or farm animals around the hamlets on the line of advance by the troops was thus a risk that had to be minimised and for this reason an hour's delay was decided upon. General Maurice recorded:

'It is impossible adequately to convey an impression of the absolute silence which prevailed, and of the entire absence of any indications of the existence of the columns. Sound or sight at one hundred yards from any column there was none, save of the desert and the stars.'

Colonel Field of the Royal Marine Light Infantry wrote:

'My recollections of the march itself are very like those of the monotonous and unending journeys one takes in dreamland. We halted more than once, but there was nothing to differentiate one halt from the other, always the same shadowy battalions to our right and left, the gravelly ground underfoot, and the enclosing night.'

The night was in fact pitch black, and, despite the care of the preparations of the plan, disaster almost overtook the Highland Brigade once when a warning of advancing horsemen caused the centre to hold back while the wing columns, who did not receive the same whispered information, continued to advance and, in keeping their contact with the centre, performed a wheeling movement.

The two wings after a short time were thus almost face to face in the darkness. Here the wisdom of carrying unloaded rifles was borne out for in such circumstance one stray shot would have been the undoing of the whole expedition. As it was, the columns were halted and redirected by alert officers almost without a sound and no such tragedy took place.

It was thought that the sound of the staff officer' horses moving up the columns had been mistaken for the advance of an Egyptian scouting force. Colonel Maurice in the official history discounts any such presence of enemy forces during the night, or of any mounted *picquets* being out. The Egyptian soldiers who were detailed off for the defence of their parapets this night, as well as their artillery, were all lying in their trenches with their weapons at hand beside them ready for instant use, together with an ample supply of ammunition as has been already noted.

Although some Bedouin tribesmen had been told off for advance patrol work, together with some Egyptian cavalry on the right, Maurice concluded that none of these horsemen moved from the near neighbourhood of the trenches and that they made no report. Although the latter point is true the first point is often disputed and we shall record one such notable exception to this in due course.

The forty-two guns of the artillery moved equally and carefully, pacing the two divisions on their flanks between the Brigade of Guards and Colonel Ashburnham's brigade, with Colonel Goodenough himself aligning their forward movement by the North Star.

The Cavalry Division had moved off separately and kept itself well clear of the infantry formations in order to minimise confusion. They gathered at a marker post, a flagstaff located a mile above the camps, and here they were held back to await events before taking their places on the extreme right of the British formation.

General Wolseley also kept constant check on the march, especially giving attention to its strict timing, on which so much depended. He used a repeater watch which had been presented to him by Lord Airy. Butler rode at his side and recalled how the constant striking of the ever-longer numbers of this watch screwed up the tension inside him. It '...seemed to draw into tight twists all the strands of our expectations' he later wrote.

The last halt that night was made around 03:00 for a final check and make-ready. When the army moved off tension had reached a new peak and this was reflected by one Highlander, who, having filled his flask with rum, a somewhat stronger beverage than the recommended cold tea, broke out in a wild peal of laughter that echoed through the still night air. He was quickly over-powered and silenced by his comrades and taken to the rear to sober up. The ever poetical Butler mused on this event, likening it, this solitary cry, to mocking laughter of the very desert itself, which had seen many a proud army advance across its wastes and fade into time, forgotten, during Egypt's long and bloody history.

The correspondent of *The Times* wrote of this final hour:

'There was no moon and thus, almost within cannon shot, the two armies were resting peacefully, the one side dreaming probably little of the terrible scenes of the awakening, when, their rest at length rudely disturbed, they awoke to see swiftly advancing upon every side an endless line of the dreaded red coats, broken by the even more fearful blue of the marines.'

As the troops formed up for the final dressing of the line the distant horizon was, at 04:50, lit up in the eastern sky although it still wanted some time before sunrise. It was impossible to see watches and thus there was great anxiety that the attack was going in vital minutes too late, despite all the precautions. However this gleam soon died away to everyone's great relief.

It was in fact a false dawn caused by the passing tail of a comet that same day was first sighted in Europe. It was a strange omen.

It was at this time, just before the attack was mounted, that Colonel Field witnessed the following comedy which marked the first contact with the enemy that fateful day.

'About this time,' he wrote, 'the battalion next on our right seemed to be thrown into some confusion by the sudden appearance of an Arab horseman slowly coming over the rise in front of us. A cry or two were raised, and I saw some of its men bring their rifles to the 'ready' but they were prevented from firing. As the newcomer approached I could distinguish that he was mounted on a wretched pony, and was half-crazed with fear at so unexpectedly happening on a hostile army which extended beyond his vision to the right and left, and was topped with a glittering line of bayonets. Powerless to turn and fly, he dropped his reins and wrung his hands as he was carried towards us by his Rosinante, who on her part did not seem in the least put out by the encounter. He passed through the lines close to me calling out as he came, ''Me Christian, me Christian''. He was pulled off by the supernumerary rank, and that was the last I ever saw of this warrior.'

At this point in time the British army had moved into position in irregular echelon due to some inevitable difficulties during the long approach and thus lay in relation to each other before the Egyptian trenches:

Highland			
Brigade	Artillery		
		Second	
		Brigade	
			Cavalry

Thus, as the first shots rang out from the startled Egyptian sentries, as an Egyptian bugle blared out warning of the attack and as the click of several thousand British bayonets vibrated through the desert air as they were locked home, it was upon the Highland Brigade that the first burden was, perforce, to be thrust. The time was 04:55.

THE ASSAULT

It had been the movement of the stars, as they set to the north-west, that had unwittingly led the advancing British forces to follow a similar course and which resulted in the loss of alignment. This was, however to have one happy result, for, although it meant that the Highland Brigade initially assaulted in advance of Graham's men, they unknowingly by-passed the formidable outwork of the big redoubt on the left of their advance. Thus its prime purpose was nullified by the merest chance and the Egyptians received no warning, nor any support, from this powerful work.

The signal to advance was received with a rousing

cheer as the two lines of Highlanders moved off into the fast-dispersing morning mist, towards the awakening ramparts that loomed high before them. No traditional skirl of bagpipes stirred their blood as they stormed forward because the bags of the pipes had not been inflated as yet, another precautionary measure. Determined efforts by the pipers later resulted in their first stirring clarions being heard soon after the first assault had gone in.

At a steady trot the Highlanders advanced, '. . . in the good old style', Cameron, Gordon Highlander, Black Watch, HLI, charged towards the distant earthworks which now lit up with a continuous sheet of flame as the dazed defenders poured out their first ragged volleys. The distance that the Highlanders had to cover under this fire was 150 yards, but, such was the frenzied response of the defenders, most of that initial salvo, and those which followed it, went high over the two long lines of the advancing redcoats. Only 200 men fell as they crossed that potentially murderous open stretch of ground, and they fired no shot in reply but the glistening lines of bayonets advanced remorselessly onward without a check.

the parapet. The first of the Gordon Highlanders to reach the crest was Lt H. G. Brooks. A concentrated burst of fire hit him and he fell dead with four bullets in his head and upper body. A similar fate befell Pte Donald Cameron of the Cameron Highlanders, the first man to mount the parapet, who was shot through the head as he reached the summit.

But gradually their momentum carried more and more redcoats over that crest and then the British bayonet went to work with deadly effect in the close, desperate hand-to-hand conflict that ensued. The Soudanese and Egyptian troops at this point, one of the strongest parts of the work, fought with bravery and tenacity backed up by desperation. In the face of this, several isolated groups of Highlanders who had forced the parapet found themselves surrounded and heavily outnumbered. Exposed to withering and merciless fire many such groups were forced back from their hard-won toe-holds in the defences. Among them was Sir Archibald Alison, who had advanced in the thick of the fight with his men but had to retire to regroup. Crossing a second time his horse was shot from under him but he continued fighting on foot.

It was here that Lt Edwards was awarded the only Victoria Cross of the battle and the first to be awarded to his battalion, the Second Battalion Highland Light Infantry. Storming one big redoubt, Lt Edwards, who was in advance of his party, with great gallantry rushed alone into the enemy battery and killed the Egytian Artillery officer in charge. He was knocked down by a gunner with a ramrod but was rescued by the arrival of three men of his own regiment.

What, at this point, could have been a very decisive moment of crisis, was relieved by Sir Edward Hamley. He had formed a supporting force for just such an emergency from the second line, and these hastily collected groups he led in close formation through the leading line, rallying men to him and pressing forward. The mixed groups from all battalions gradually mopped up the centres of resistance in the frontal defences and cleared their objective of all organised resistance between 'H' and 'K' redoubts. The Highland Light Infantry to their left had, if anything, an even tougher fight on their hands. The work here was itself formidable in its construction, the ditch was deeper, the earthworks higher and steeper, than any other part of the line. Moreover it was manned by fanatical Nubian troops who gave no quarter and asked for none.

Under officers who were unique in their intelligence in the Egyptian army, and who had not allowed themselves to become rattled by the surprise, like many

The final advance of the Highland Brigade. At first light they still had a good distance to cover.

The Egyptian gunners let loose a torrent of shot and shell also but they likewise appeared to have had their guns sighted on far behind the oncoming infantry. The first shot indeed pitched into the sand close by General Wolseley and his brother, who had dismounted and were using their field glasses in an effort to make out how the infantry were faring. Fortunately for them this shell, like so many others, did not explode. Further shells from the startled Egyptian gunners screamed overhead to land close to the following brigades of Ashburnham and the Duke of Connaught.

The half-battalions, double columns had gradually merged in the approach and the two lines were both continuous and close in upon each other as the final rush took place.

'The Highlanders,' wrote Lehmann, 'tumbled into the deep trench and scrambled for the fiery top pushing, pulling, cursing, as they slipped in the soft sand and tried to mount each other's shoulders'.

It took a little while before they could struggle up to

*Once into the entrenchments the HLI set to work with a
will and routed the Egyptian defenders.*

of their Egyptian comrades, these units deliberately held
their fire until the light had strengthened and the HLI
line had become broken up into panting struggling
groups of men trying to gain a foothold on the steep glacis
of the trenches' forward face. Then, and with
deliberation and steadiness, these defenders poured down
a hail of bullets into the scarlet tunics massed below them.
Their artillery also fired a lethal salvo and then the black
troops surged forward in a well-led counter-attack which
momentarily swept the British assailants away before
them and cleared part of the trench.

The Black Watch also failed to carry their objectives
in the first rush. This resulted in the Highland Brigade's
gains taking the form of a thin wedge into the defence
works, severely hemmed in on either flank by stubbornly
fighting defenders who were far from broken. Such a
situation was later to become the standard formula for
the failure of the countless trench battles of the Great
War thirty years later. Even now the situation was grim
enough.

Meanwhile, over to their right, the men of General
Graham's battalions had formed up under fire and
rushed the line ahead of them, led by the General himself.
They were fortunate in that the trenches and redoubts
at this part of the line were much less well constructed
than those struck by the Highlanders. All the same it
was no walk-over. Not only were the Egyptian and
Soudanese already fully alerted by the fighting on their
flank, but the British troops of the 2nd Brigade had a
far wider field of open ground to cover before they
reached the first trenches, some 900 yards in all.
Changing front forward on the left company they went
in, adopting the regular attack formation at 300 yards,
firing a volley, rushing in 150 yards and firing a second
volley, before entering the ditch.

Again Colonel Field gives a vivid account:

'It seemed to me that the Egyptian lines were 800
to 1,000 yards distant, and this being the case, we were
ordered to lie down and fix bayonets. Four companies
were then extended as a firing line, followed by the
remaining four as supports. We advanced by rushes,
lying down to fire. The enemy's bullets were still
falling thickly and the entrenchments, and our own

The Royal Irish gain the firing step with dash and courage.

firing line still blurred with smoke, when the bugles, to the relief I think, of everybody, sounded the charge. The whole line, every man burning to get at the Egyptians, rushed forward at the double with a continuous shout or roar rather than a cheer. As we approached the misty outline of the parapet at a few yards distance there was a slackening of fire — our firing line had at that moment rushed it, followed closely by the supports, and after a minute or two's play ''with butt and baynit'' that part of the work was ours.'

The pipes of the Royal Irish now skirled out as that battalion moved forward on the right flank in a series of steady rushes taking advantage of what cover they could find. Soon they were in among the Egyptians doing great execution among them as the white-clad defenders briefly stood and fought.

Likewise the York and Lancasters moved forward as one man to take 'M' reboubt in a single rush and join hands with the fighting Irishmen. Here also the defenders held for a short while in new positions some sixty yards further back. The decisive point of the battle had now been reached.

The British artillery in the centre had resumed their advance and then again halted at 04:50 to find that the advancing Highlanders were overlapping their field of fire. One reason why the artillery was placed in the centre was to prevent the soldiers firing upon each other (presumably the artillerymen were considered expendable in such an eventuality!). Anyway the drivers were

dismounted to await better light and in the interim the Egyptian artillery salvoes crashed harmlessly over their heads unanswered.

Then General Goodenough resumed his advance once more, in echelon of brigades divisions from the centre, so that Lt-Col Branckner's battery was the first to cross the gap into the Egyptian lines. The position here had meantime fallen at last to the Black Watch at 05:25. One gun broke its wheels crossing the guarding ditch but was soon dug out and raced into line with its companions. The whole battery came into action against the Egyptian guns and infantry at close range.

Colonel Scheiber's battery also came into action at this time, sending shell after shell into the Egyptian lines where they were still unassaulted by the British infantry formations. Close-range firing was also commenced upon the defenders as they began to break in large groups and

Once the strong lines had broken the defeat was turned into a rout by the British and Indian cavalry.

some canister-shot did enormous execution in this period, which further accentuated the Egyptians' discomforture and hastened the disintegration now beginning to take place.

The British cavalry, on the extreme right, advanced at 04:40 at a slow walk and then at a trot. As the first infantry assaults commenced they were some 2,000 yards from the entrenchments and were soon under fire. The Egyptian guns were soon brought under return fire from the Royal Horse Artillery and the position was quickly silenced. Led by the Indian Brigade the cavalry then further increased their pace and, in line of squadron columns, they swept forward over the shallow trenches at the northern end of the line and began swiftly to encircle the Egyptian battalions on the left rear of their holding positions.

At this time the defenders, north of 'K' redoubt, cracked and then began to flee. With British guns in action on both sides of their flanks, the deadly lances of the British cavalry fast approaching their rear and with General Graham's battalions, now fully supported by the Guards, resuming their remorseless advance in line, the fight went out of the Egyptians in a rush. Soon their carefully organised defences were dissolving into a panic-stricken stream of fugitives flying to the rear.

These fleeing masses presented closely-packed and open targets to all three arms of the British army in this sector. Many Egyptians got under the hoofs of the galloping Bengal Lancers and were skewered on their lances. Others were mown down by canister shot in untidy bunches, while huge numbers fell, many facing their enemy and firing back, to the carefully aimed volleys of the Royal Irish, Duke of York and Lancasters, and Royal Marine Light Infantry as they streamed across their sights at point-blank range.

The rout continued with men flinging down their arms as they ran or surrendering in large bodies. The inner works were thickly covered with the fallen. One eyewitness described the scene of carnage here as the sun rose in the sky:

'The day was now fast lightening and looking back we could see the earthworks we had won standing darkly against the orange dawn. Smoke and dust hung around in ragged strands, and here and there arose heavenward in slender columns. All the brown gravelly soil between us and the trenches was scattered

The fierce Bengal Lancers spread terror among the ranks of the fleeing Egyptians and won the admiration of Sir Garnet himself.

thickly with white-clad bodies, the once snowy linen of their uniforms now disfigured by ugly patches matching the hue of their fezzes, while rifles, ammunition boxes, and every kind of military debris lay in all directions.'

From the Egyptian viewpoint the situation was now grievous. Arabi himself was awoken from his slumbers by the sound of the first gunfire and by the time he arrived on the scene he found his northern flank crushed and his troops in full flight.

He still had all his cavalry, three infantry battalions and five guns in reserve for him to plug the gap. True, his right was holding for the moment but the breach in his left was irretrievable. It is interesting to note that in his own accout of the battle Arabi held firmly to the the conviction that it was against his right flank that the British assault had gone in first, where his entrenchments were weakest, when in fact the reverse had been the case. Such an impression is perfectly understandable as he saw it in the first light of that day, for his Soudanese battalions were still holding out against the Scots, although beginning now to crumble at last.

Within a short time even this respite had been taken from him and he was left with no alternative but speedy flight. It was the remorseless advance across the flanks by the British cavalry and the equally steady advance of the First Division that caused what reserves he still could muster to join in the general exodus without contributing more than a token resistance to the flow of the battle.

We must now return to the grim struggles of the Highland Division as they inched their way forward in small storming parties against fierce resistance.

By 05:25 the guns of Lt-Col Branckner's battery which had done so much to relieve the Highlander's uncertain position, were able to take advantage of the early morning sunlight now breaking over the battlefield, to shift their fire to the railway line in the rear of the Egyptian positions. Arabi himself went there in an attempt to extradite himself and his staff as soon as possible.

General Willis joined Brig-Gen Goodenough at the battery just before 06:00 and witnessed the escape of two fully-laden trains containing many Egyptian troops leading the retirement. However a direct hit on the third train blocked this escape route completely to the many thousands now trying to follow their leaders to safety.

At the same time the advance party of the Highlanders had finally broken through the last resistance and, only some 200 strong, had gained the prominence overlooking

Having survived all the shot-and-shell Arabi's gunners could deliver the Black Watch were in no mood to parley once inside the gunpits.

Arabi's now deserted camp.

Instead of halting until Graham's men could come up in support as originally planned, General Hamley decided to continue the pursuit without more ado and press home his advantage. Re-formed afresh the Highlanders therefore moved out again and pushed forward, all resistance crumbling fast. Soon they had taken the Egyptian main camp with its enormous booty of stores, tents, baggage and ammunition. They also carried the railway station at Tel-el-Kebir, some one hundred fully laden railway coaches falling into their hands at this time.

Meanwhile the unsuspected advance redoubt of the Egyptian fortifications had sprung into belated life at long last. It opened fire on Sir Garnet and his staff, who were the closest and most obvious targets. The Egyptian cavalry also made a brief appearance, but as soon as a squadron of the 19th Hussars cantered out to meet them,

Wolseley and his staff gain the Tel-el-Kebir bridge early in the morning with the victory already complete.

the Egyptians immediately made about and vanished over the sky-line.

Lt-Col Scheiber's battery moved in subsequently and, after their first shots had detonated the Egyptian magazine, silenced this redoubt, whose own shelling had caused no damage and very little incovenience. With the fall of this work the whole of the Egyptian line north of the canal was in British hands.

General Wolseley then rode forward over the field of battle and reached the bridge at Tel-el-Kebir just as the Highlanders arrived there at the end of their final advance. Here the General was joined, one by one, by the commanding officers of his divisions and they made their reports.

Behind him, in the distance, fled a disorganised rabble, all that remained of Arabi's proud army. It was Wolseley's most overwhelming victory and one that was achieved at the remarkably low cost of only 480 British dead and wounded. The RMLI suffered the most on the right for they took sixty casualties, the Highland Brigade in all lost 45 killed and 188 wounded and missing. In the defence works lay the bodies of 2,000 Egyptian dead, while innumerable wounded lay gasping their lives away in the hot sun. All that remained of Arabi's force was far in the distance beyond recall, a disillusioned rabble, being hunted down in scores as they ran.

South of the canal the day had also gone well for the

British and their Indian allies. Here, the Indian contingent under General Macpherson, advanced in fours, due to the restricted nature of the ground, supported by a mountain gun battery and the guns and Gatlings of the Naval Brigade, with the cavalry to the rear.

Some fifteen minutes after the first shots had been heard from the north bank the Egyptian defenders on the south opened fire on this column. Immediately the 680 men of the Seaforth Highlanders, under Lt-Col Stockwell, advanced against these guns and the 400 Egyptian infantry waiting for them in fire trenches protecting the gun positions. At the same time the 20th Native Infantry moved to outflank this position from the south and these two advance formations were backed by the 7th and 29th Native Infantry respectively. The mountain battery opened fire on the Egyptian guns themselves, aiming at the enemy gun flashes with good effect.

But it was the Seaforth Highlanders who carried the morning here. Their leading company was commanded by an ex-Musketry instructor who controlled all the volleys personally. Advancing in rushes, and firing volleys at intervals, they soon covered the intervening ground. At 06:00 Colonel Stockwell halted his men in line and ordered 'Fix bayonets'. The attack then was delivered smartly and with dash against little real resistance and, within a few minutes with little loss of life, the Egyptian trenches along with their four guns, were all captured intact.

The 20th Bengal Infantry had, at the same time, taken the fortified village at bayonet point with similar panache and, with the whole of the south bank defences fully cleared, the Bengal Cavalry were unleashed to cut off the escape of the fleeing Egyptians who were pouring across the bridge from the debacle in the north and fly-ing panic-stricken towards the dubious safety of Cairo. Many were slaughtered as the fled.

The British victory was now complete. Lighting a cigar Sir Garnet sat down and wrote out a telegraphic despatch to the British Government giving word of this event (which the edgy and vacillating Gladstone received with tears of relief) and also issued order for the follow-up operations.

Drury Lowe was ordered to continue to harass the fleeing enemy right into the streets of Cairo if this were possible, and Macpherson was to move at once to Zagazig, the next likely place for the Egyptians to make a stand if they were going to. Arabi was to be allowed no time whatsoever to regroup his battered and shaken army.

The follow-up operations were both swift and audacious. Arabi was given no chance to make a stand and Cairo was quickly occupied by a small force of British cavalry.

THE PURSUIT

Thwarted in his attempt to escape by the railway (he later complained that the British did not even give him a chance, to get his boots on!) Arabi made off by horse, with his Second-in-Command, and reached Belbeis. Here they found a train which took them, weeping and broken back to Cairo. His army took a different route back to safety but their mood was equally despondent.

'More like a hunt than a pursuit,' was how Macpherson described the next two days. Overcoming fatigue and taking great chances amidst the hordes of Egyptian infantry, the British cavalry pushed on at breakneck speed. Led by the 6th Bengal Lancers they passed streams of men who had thrown away their arms and encountered only slight, sporadic resistance along their path. They arrived at Belbeis around midday on the 13th, and there Capt Watson, RE accompanying General Wilkinson's force, seized the telegraph office, intercepting a frantic call from Arabi for his northern armies to come to his aid. Here the Indian Cavalry Brigade rested overnight and were joined by Drury Lowe and Sir Baker Russell with the 4th Dragoon Guards.

Encountering some difficulties in traversing the narrow bridges over the numerous small water-courses along the route the Horse Artillery were delayed but Stewart scorned any further dalliance and, casting caution aside, the mounted troops moved out again before first light, unsupported, to continue the rout alone.

It was forty miles to the capital and heat was intense along the rim of the desert. Nonetheless the cavalry maintained a good pace being met not with bullets but with crowds of fawning natives crying 'Peace, peace' while every village was bedecked with white flags from every house.

On reaching the region of Abbassiyeh barracks on the eastern outskirts of Cairo itself, Drury Lowe halted his breathless advance to take stock. He was now far in advance of any infantry or artillery support, while the state and quantity of the defences that Arabi might have mustered was still not known.

Lt-Col Stewart was therefore sent forward, with a mere fifty lancers, to investigate, taking with him an interpreter and two Egyptian officers. It was the supreme bluff.

While this party advanced the remaining British troopers stayed out of sight in the desert so that their actual numbers could not be guessed. It was enough. The mere fact that the British cavalry had appeared before the gates of Cairo so soon convinced the Egyptian commander on the spot that resistance was futile on their part.

From the ranks of several thousand Egyptian troops a mounted party detached itself and rode to meet the fifty British horsemen. They approached under a white flag. Stewart accepted the surrender of the Abbassiyeh garrison and then sent for Cairo's Governor, the Chief of Police and the Citadel Commander. These worthies asked for time to organise a surrender on the condition that the British remained out of the city that night.

However at 20:00 that evening Capt Watson, RE, with 150 men, set off for the Citadel which they reached undetected at 21:45. The Citadel was held by 5,000 Egyptian soldiers, but, nothing daunted, Watson rode up and demanded its immediate evacuation. The Commander complied immediately and his men marched out in file by the Bab-el-Ayab gate to the Kasr-en-Nil barracks where they lay down their arms. By midnight some 10,000 Egyptian soldiers from the Cairo area had been so treated and sent home.

Thus, at dawn on the 15th Arabi awoke at his home to find himself alone and deserted. He had no option but to surrender himself, which he did, at 10:45 that morning, with quiet dignity.

Meanwhile Macpherson had become so embarrassed at the huge numbers of survivors from the battle wishing to surrender to him that he was forced to allow them to continue in without guards while he pressed on with his own small force. They were joined at Zagazig on the 14th by the first trainloads of British infantry moving up from Tel-el-Kebir.

Here they received a telegram thanking them on behalf of the Egyptian nation for freeing them from Arabi's rule and requesting that the British halt any further action until notified by the Khedive. However a squadron of the 6th Bengal Lancers and the 13th Bengal Lancers pushed on and, by the 15th, had taken over the Cairo Railway Station and the telegraph office. At 09:45 General Wolseley arrived in Cairo by special train with an escort of Scots Guards.

It was all over

FINALE

Tel-el-Kebir was perhaps the most complete and decisive British victory of the Victorian era. The very speed with which the operation was completed, and the efficiency with which it was carried out, mark it out as almost the perfect military operation of any period. The night march crowned the other British military tactics and Wolseley's planning and confidence were vindicated absolutely.

Even Queen Victoria was pleased. She felt, 'unbounded joy and gratitude for God's great goodness and mercy,' and even began to comment on Wolseley himself in a more favourable tone.

Arabi himself went into exile and Tewfik was restored. In Parliament Gladstone promised that all British troops would be out of Egypt by Christmas. But it was not until the Suez fiasco of 1956 that the British presence in Egypt, so easily established in 1882 but so humiliatingly terminated seventy-four years later, finally came to an end.

One man felt no great elation as the whole Empire celebrated. Butler felt that the whole campaign had been conducted against the wrong people, for the wrong reasons. As he saw it the poor, exploited Egyptian peasants had been sacrificed and used yet again and the restoration of the old Egyptian officials he saw as a scandal rather than as a cause for rejoicing.

He paid tribute to the ordinary Egyptian soldier, who had fought and died under British bayonets for a cause they had believed was right for their people.

'Peace be to them,' he wrote, 'lying under those big mounds on the lone desert. . . No words should soldier utter against them; let that be left to the money-changers. They died a good death. Dust to dust. They did not desert the desert, and Egypt will not forget them'.

Chapter Seven

TAMAII

13 March 1884

MASSACRE AT THE WELLS

The British Prime Minister, informed the House '. . . we are not at war with Egypt'. British troops would be quickly out of that land, but of course they were not. The British *de facto* take-over of the administration of Egypt's affairs inescapably followed Tel-el-Kebir and so did the British Empire's even more reluctant entanglement with Egypt's vast and unruly neighbour to the south, the Soudan. The Khedive had ruled that unfortunate nation, inefficiently and corruptly, from Egypt on behalf of the Turkish Sultan. To the long-suffering Soudanese of course, all foreign officials were 'Turks', who cared nothing for the Soudan or her people other than what could be wrung from them both.

Consequently, when Wolseley so briskly routed the only efficient fighting force Egypt possessed, there was little left to hold in check the seething resentment which had been fermenting in the Soudan from time immemorial. With the gatekeeper locked up it only needed a catalyst to unleash the pent-up Soudanese hatred for their masters. That catalyst was the erstwhile carpenter's son turned mystic and *fakir*, Mohammed Ahmad. He proclaimed himself 'Mahdi,' or 'Chosen of God,' long ago predicted by Mohammed himself, as he who would come to cleanse and purge his homeland to

The fierce Dervish charge sweeps down on the British square at Tamaii. Despite measured volley firing of the ranked infantry, courage and weight of numbers took the tribesman through and into the front ranks.

171

The Mahdi. This portrait shows him in a noble and awesome light as becomes one who called himself the 'Chosen of God', come to rid his land of the barbarians.

reclaim it for Allah. Any who stood in his way were to be put to the sword, a promise that, although initially greeted with ridicule by the Governor-General, was soon made manifest. Preaching his own violent fire-and-death brand of religion in much the same style as the present Ayatollah in Iran, the Mahdi soon used this message to kindle the flame of rebellion and, once aroused, it spread like wildfire across the land.

Egyptian expeditions, always too small and too late, were despatched to crush the rebels. Each, in turn, was massacred and with each Mahdi victory new converts flocked to his banner. By the end of October the Governor-General was appealing for an army of 10,000 men to be sent from Cairo to restore order. Britain made it clear she had no wish to become embroiled in all this and so the Egytians hastily re-enlisted the survivors of their shattered army and urgently despatched them south under the leadership of a former British officer, Colonel W. Hicks. Hicks *Pasha,* as he became, had served in the Indian Mutiny and we have met him earlier with Napier in Abyssinia. His first skirmish was a small victory and,

thus braced, and after some squabbling with his Egyptian and Soudanese employers, Hicks set off to finish the job with his motley crew of 10,000 men and a few European officers. The Mahdi led him a merry dance through the backlands of Kordofan and, on 5 November 1883, when the struggling column was hopelessly lost, wandering in swamp and jungle near Sheikan south of El Obeid, his army fell upon it mercilessly. The Egyptians were reduced to sheer panic and most fled or fell on their knees instead of fighting. It availed them naught. They, along with the few that stood with the British officers, were wiped off the face of the earth.

This massacre led to serious misgivings in London, and also to a great upsurge to the Mahdi's cause all over the Soudan, not least among the wild tribes of the burning Nubian deserts between the Nile below Berber and the Red Sea coast. Here the fiasco was repeated and another former British officer, Valentine Baker *Pasha,* led a second Egyptian army, even more of a shambles than the first, ('the sweepings of the Cairo streets') to another crushing defeat at the hands of these warriors. The battle, such as it was, took place at an unheard-of place called El Teb, south of the main Red Sea port of Suakin and en route to the threatened town of Tokar. These two disasters finally led to British intervention in the Soudan and the beginning of a long and frustrating series of campaigns, not finally resolved until the 20th century, when Queen Victoria's reign was nearly ended.

The Royal Navy's C-in-C in the East Indies, Admiral Sir William Hewett, (who had won his Victoria Cross fighting ashore in the Crimea and had served in the Naval Brigade during the Ashanti War), was also nominated as Governor of Suakin and thus, being on the spot, was the first British commander to react. It soon became clear that a far more substantial force than a few sailors and Royal Marines was required to hold onto what remained of Egypt's power in the eastern Soudanese provinces.

One man's name was soon ringing round this barren wilderness and carrying with it almost as much terror as the Mahdi's itself. That name was Osman Digna .

Soon only Suakin, Trinkitat and Tokar on the shore of the Red Sea remained free of his bloody touch and to prevent the former being put to the sword Admiral Hewett landed a strong naval brigade to reinforce the cowering Egyptian garrison. Even the Gladstone administration could not allow the over-running of a port on the main line of communication through the Suez Canal to India, for which they had just fought a war to keep open. An Expeditionary Force was hastily assembled and despatched to also try to save Tokar.

DIGNA'S DERVISHES

The Mahdi proclaimed himself chosen of God, but others who embraced his cause were motivated more from opportunism than religion! One such was Osman Digna, who elevated himself to *Emir*. Time and again he suffered defeat at the hands of the British only to slip quietly away from the battlefield and re-appear later as cocksure and spry as ever! He was described by one admirer as one who, '. . . certainly deemed it wise to live in order to fight another day'. He developed elusiveness to a fine art and no matter how many Arabs might die for the faith, Digna himself made certain he was never among them. He boasted later of his wars with the British, '. . . they cannot be defeated without deceit!'. Truly these were heartfelt words from the master of such tactics. Each time he had hastily to explain away his army's defeat and enormous losses he did so by convincing his gullible followers that he had, by mistake, given them the wrong fetish against steel and lead. Why he was not dismembered on the spot by the bloody and battered survivors for such a costly and elementary blunder is not explained. Instead they went again to their deaths at Tamaii, apparently believing the same pack of lies from the 'Holy Man'.

He must also have possessed a remarkably persuasive tongue, for his talents and his blandishments persuaded the fanatical Soudanese warriors he led to fling themselves onto the muzzles and bayonets of the British infantry, not once, but time and again. Each time thousands of them died, but always Digna managed to rally them anew for fresh sacrifice. How he managed to explain away so many defeats and still remain a credible lieutenant also remains a mystery. Certainly the Mahdi and his successor, Abdullahi, the *Khalifa,* seemed remarkably tolerant of a deputy who led his men so consistently to defeat at the hands of British 'Turks'.

Digna might have been elusive and silver-tongued, but his position became increasingly shaky as the year went by. He probably survived on the reputation of earlier victories over the Egyptian rabble of Baker *Pasha* and similar massacres, while relying on his undoubted quick wits and the ability to deliver fresh men whenever required, for his survival in the frenetic world of the Dervishes, especially as there was considerable hatred between him and the *Khalifa's* other supporters. True to his nature Digna was always careful to be reticent and self-effacing in that worthy's presence, however much he might rail against him in private. In the last campaigns he constantly urged caution and care when tackling the British, but he was confronted by the

Osman Digna. 'Osman the Ugly' as he was known to friend and foe alike. He outlived all his contemporaries, and died peacefully having outwitted them all!

younger fighting men who scornfully remarked that his long experience had taught him only how to avoid destruction and not how to achieve victory. This, coming from his own kind, is probably a most accurate summary of his war leadership abilities. The British viewpoint was crystallised by Lord Cromer who wrote: 'The Dervishes were themselves devoid of all military qualities with the exception of undaunted courage'.

Digna himself was of mixed blood, having Hadendowa/Turkish ancestors, another fact which he no doubt did not dwell upon. The majority of his followers were of the *Beja* people of the great arid Nubian desert whose piled up, buttered frizzle-hair and generally wild appearance soon brought about their nickname of 'Fuzzy-Wuzzy' from the British soldier. The *Beja* were a composite of several of the eastern Soudanese tribes, the Amarar, Bisharin and Hadendowa though occasionally reinforcements came from further afield (for his later assaults on Suakin in December, 1888) when he was joined by Baggara and Jaalin tribesmen. However he usually managed to persuade the locals, they were after all 'family', to rise-up periodically, after they had drifted away and brooded for a few months following his latest defeat or costly victory.

Between battles, Digna waxed rich on the slave trade. Indeed the British Government's conscience was only pricked from time to time (as in the campaign against Tokar in 1891) because of his notorious activities in this field and his outstanding success at it! Those who objected to British intervention because of their opposition to Imperialism and Jingoism must have found it difficult to justify the toleration of such blatant slave trading on the very borders of British-occupied Egypt.

In defeat he was remarkably resilient, in victory he was ruthless. When he occupied the southern town of Kassala he ordered the wholesale slaughter of leading dignitaries including an innocent Greek merchant, in revenge for yet another defeat, this time by the Abyssinians at Ras Alula. He was no more bloody than his men, whose common practice was to mutilate the dead and torture to death the wounded. This remarkable survivor evaded even the eventual smashing of Mahdiism but was finally hunted down and caught in 1900, most appropriately by the commander of the Suakin police, whose town and population had been for so long under threat of extermination at Digna's hands. He was imprisoned in Egypt but, in deference to his years with the usual show of British weakness to one's enemy, was released in 1908. He lived quietly at Wadi Halfa until his death in 1926, no doubt laughing up his sleeve the whole time. One of his last acts was to visit Mecca no doubt to offer up a prayer of thanks for the gullibility of his enemies!

General Graham posted this proclamation, addressed to Dinga's followers after the battle of El Teb in 1884:

'You trusted the notorious scoundrel Osman Digna who is well-known to you as a bad man. He has led you astray with the foolish idea that the Mahdi has come to earth. We tell you that the Great God that rules over the universe does not allow scoundrels such as Osman Digna to rule over men.'

The General also slapped a price on the *Emir's* head, but all to no avail.

Recent British historians have praised Digna; as 'clever' '. . . one of the ablest of the Khalifa's lieutenants . . .', possessing, '. . . military wisdom and tactical skill'. He was an Arab slaver, when the principal ecomomic mainstay of the Soudan at this period of history was slavery. While the Royal Navy had stamped out this trade out along most of the sea routes to the Middle East,

'Colonialism' is today a bitter rebuke for White rule in Africa but it was Arab power that waxed fat on African slaves in the late 19th century and it was the Royal Navy at sea and British bayonets ashore that finally put a stop to it. Osman Digna was a well-known slave dealer and his use of religion to rouse the tribes was very much a suitable cover for his more lucrative activities.

the inland desert trails and huge rivers were safe from their incursions, and up these long, hot tracks or along the wide tributaries of the Nile came caravans of Arabs leading chained negroes from the rich southern lands for sale in the Turkish outposts of the Gulf and beyond. Osman Digna had a large and lucrative slice of this very profitable action. His 'conversion' to Mahdiism came late, but after the defeat of Hicks *Pasha*, he no doubt considered it both prudent and politic to jump on the band-waggon of the new faith and he quickly raised the Eastern Soudan under his banner and led it off to war, plunder and pillage, all under the convenient guise of spreading the word of the prophet. However it is on record that before the battle of Tamaii, Osman Digna

Captured muskets and rifles were plentiful, but like most primitive tribes, training was rudimentary and hampered by lack of ammunition. They tended to fire from great range in night ambushes and caused the British few losses. Their long, hacking spears and broad, curved swords were another thing altogether! Sturdily built and lovingly honed to an unbelievable sharpness, once the Dervishes could close to hand-to-hand range these vicious weapons were plied with dedicated, deadly skill. An eyewitness account describing a 'Fuzzy-Wuzzy' attack mounted on a British square stated:

'The practice of the Arabs, both at El Teb and Tamaii, was to rush down upon us with a thick, round cow or rhinocerous-hide shield in their left hands, grasping in the same hand a sword or spear. In their right hands they generally carried a short, bent stick like what is used in the Scotch game of 'shinty' or Irish 'hurly'. When within ten paces of the soldiers, without pausing, they would throw the piece of wood violently in our men's faces; then, seizing the weapon from their left hand, charge full at us. Upon their feet they wore a kind of sandal. It was merely a leather sole, tied round the great toe and ankle with a piece of thong. Many men received slight wounds and contusions, of which no report was made. The latter caused chiefly by the thick, bent sticks which the Arabs threw into the soldiers' ranks as they charged, and by pieces of stone.'

The courage of such warriors was never disputed.

took himself off twenty miles into the hills to some holy spot in order to pray for a victory, so it would seem his religion was not entirely hypocritical.

The *Ansar,* led by Digna in his fierce clashes with the British over several decades, were a primitive people. Ferocious in the extreme and utterly without pity, they were a close-knit series of communities who, like most such peoples, tended to allow themselves to be worked up for short periods of intense effort and then to drift back to their homes again if the going got altogether too bad and they could see no future in it. Thus they could be recruited or pressed into service but often needed cajoling with promises of booty.

The primitive tactics of their infantry, with whom we are principally concerned here, consisted only of the massed attack delivered with wide, double-edged 'Crusader' swords, spears and knives by huge numbers of men at lightning speed. This did not require much sub-division other than for laying their ambushes. For such control their armies were divided into *rubs* (or quarters) of up to 2,000 men apiece, led by their own tribal chiefs. These *rubs* were in turn further sub-divided.

A Soudanese hippo-hide shield. It could not stop a bullet but at close quarters was capable of turning a poor quality British bayonet point.

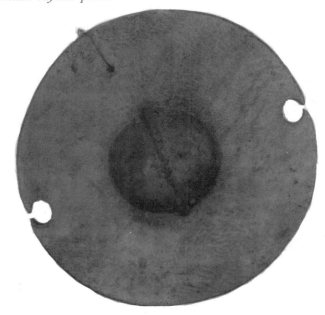

After the battle of El Teb for example, Sgt William Darby of the 10th Hussars wrote home that:

'Without a doubt these Arabs are the most fierce, brave, daring and unmerciful race of men in the world. They fear nothing, give and expect no mercy and they are indeed skilled with their knives and spears, swords and clubs.'

And again an eyewitness at Tamaii wrote:

'Fearless and daring, they ran amuck, so to speak, at our men, hitting right and left even when themselves badly wounded. It was this very recklessness of death on their part which made them so dreaded.'

Many of these fierce warriors carried into battle with them a last prayer written on a sheet to remind them that they were dying for immortality.

Even in death or defeat they remained arrogant and fanatical. To walk among their wounded after a battle, said one observer, is like:

'treading through a nest of vipers. Dying natives would be seen crawling on towards the British line in a desperate attempt to kill with their last gasp in order to die a warrior's death and so enter the concubine-stocked heaven promised them by their leaders. Even medical parties tending the wounded were at great risk, several Marines being slaughtered in the act of mercy and soon any attempt at this was abandoned. Instead any hint of life in an enemy on the ground was quickly snuffed, often at the pleading of the wounded fanatic himself.'

They were sensible enough to know when the game was up though. After Tamaii the defeated survivors were described as walking away from the battlefield,

'. . . as if sauntering down the Bazaar, with their arms folded or swinging them by their side. Often they were shot down as they thus withdrew, but that did not deter others following their example nor did it hasten their speed'.

There were cavalry units, the Baggara tribe being mainly concerned with this arm, but it did not feature widely in the Suakin campaigns. Artillery consisted of those guns captured from Baker's rabble but these were primitive and few, other than deserters, knew how to use them to any great effect.

These then were the enemy Graham and his men faced.

Warriors of the Mahdi. Young fanatics steeped in the teachings of the Koran and the wily promises of Osman Digna, they were proud and utterly without fear of death. Merciless to their opponents, they proved a formidable foe.

THE OLD FIRM

Britain assembled a small but well-chosen force to put a stop to the rot in the Eastern Soudan. Wolseley's stamp was put on it and a top-quality outfit resulted. To lead the force Maj-Gen Sir Gerald Graham was selected, a fairly natural choice backed by General Sir Frederick Stephenson, C-in-C of the British Army in Egypt, from where the bulk of the regiments were to come. He was a tall (6ft 4in), handsome man with blue eyes, well-versed in literature and with a slow, methodical and modest manner. Like most of this breed of Victorian generals, (Gordon, Kitchener, Bindon Blood, Roberts) Graham's talents lay in good organising and preparation rather than in personal brilliance in the field although, like them, his outstanding bravery was unquestioned. He married twice and had the typically Victorian large brood of children.

Graham, originally a Royal Engineer, was a close associate of Wolseley and both had been in the Crimea, where Graham had won the Victoria Cross. They also served together at the fall of the Taku Forts and of course their most recent association had been in the Egyptian campaign where Graham's brigade had distinguished itself both at Kassassin and the final battle. He was also a close friend of Maj-Gen Charles Gordon, former Governor-General of the Soudan and another former Royal Engineer, with whom he had also served in China. Some time *before* he actually took over his new command Graham accompanied Gordon for part of the way as far as Korosko, on what was to prove the latter's final journey up the Nile, to take up his fateful position at Khartoum. Gordon was armed solely with vague instructions from the British Government, tactfully dispensed second-hand via Sir Evelyn Baring (later Lord Cromer), British Agent and Consul-General in Egypt and the real dispenser of power there from 1883 onward. He was told to evacuate as many Egyptians as he could before the Mahdi took over.

We are left with some moving memoirs of the final days Graham spent with his old friend. While on that last trip Graham persuaded Gordon to adopt the *fez* as a symbol of his authority and so put heart into the fearful Egyptians at Khartoum by showing them that he meant to stay and share their troubles. On their final leave-taking Gordon presented Graham with a silver-mounted *kourbash*, '. . . as a token that the reign of the *kourbash* was over'.

With the subsequent defeat of Baker *Pasha's* army and Graham's own appointment to the force sent to clear the littorals of Suakin, it is little wonder that two old

Major-General Sir Gerald Graham, VC. Tall and distinquished he was a typical Victorian general in attitude and manner. A personal friend of Gordon, he fought hard in the hope of helping his old comrade in his hour of need.

comrades like Graham and Gordon were as one in interpreting this as but the beginning of a firmer policy by the British Government, which might result in Graham clearing the route to Berber and reinforcing Khartoum from there. Alas it was to be but wishful thinking on their part.

The bulk of Graham's forces were to come from Egypt but Britain's complete command of the sea made the switching of land forces about the globe easy in those days. By its very naturalness this ability to land troops anywhere that was required, emphasised just why Suakin was *not* allowed to fall to the Mahdi, while Khartoum and Berber were. Thus the 19th Hussars sailed from Cairo as did the 1st Battalion, The Black Watch, the Gordon Highlanders and the King's Royal Rifles. The Yorks and Lancasters were brought in from Aden while the Royal Irish Fusiliers were diverted to Trinkitat while *en route* to India. Finally the 10th (Prince of Wales's Own Royal) Hussars came out from home. Graham was able also to renew his acquaintance with the Royal Marines, who had fought very well in his Brigade in both the

Egyptian battles, as a strong force of these men was landed by Admiral Hewett as we have seen and they were reinforced with four Gardner machine-guns, heavy multi-barrelled .450 calibre weapons, manned by sailors of the fleet. Two batteries of artillery, 9pdrs and 7pdrs, were also sent out, along with about one hundred Abyssinian scouts.

Under Graham's overall command were other Tel-el-Kebir veterans. Lt-Col Herbert Stewart again had the cavalry, which included some mounted infantry, but these were not well handled by him in this campaign and did not feature largely in the battles that followed. The terrain of the Eastern Soudan, barren scrub-covered sand and rock, beset by hidden, dry water-courses and gulleys (*nullahs* or *khors*), did not lend itself for the dashing deployment of horses and nor did the climate. Moreover the enemy developed special tactics to hamstring mounted men by lying hidden in innumerable ambush points and killing the horses, cutting the throats of the dismounted men as they scrambled to their feet. As dismounted flankers, with their carbines protecting the infantry squares, the British Cavalry did however play a small, but vital role, but there was little chance for the usual dash and flourish that had so triumphantly led to the fall of Cairo two years earlier.

To command one of the two Infantry Brigades of his army, and also to act as his second-in-command, Graham had another member of 'The Ring', Brig-Gen Sir Redvers Buller, yet another old China War and Egyptian campaign man and another holder of the Victoria Cross, which he had won in the Zulu War. He was a stoutly-built, taciturn man of the old school; a grim no-nonsense soldier who detested politicians and their meddling with the army, and consequently had no great love of Gordon and his 'dabbling'. Maj-Gen J. Davis commanded the 2nd Brigade. As Senior Military Officer he was in charge of the troop disembarkations at Trinkitat and the subsequent re-deployment by sea to Suakin, both of which were carried out very smoothly. Graham commented that he did, '. . . his utmost to preserve steadiness and good discipline on all occasions,' but he did not endear himself to his men very much.

The first engagement fought was on 29 February at the wells of El Teb on the way to relieve Tokar. The British advanced in a solid square, despite the fact that the Dervish army used Egyptian Krupps cannon serviced by the former gunners 'chained' to their guns and subjected them to a hail of fire from captured rifles fresh from the Baker debacle on the same spot a few weeks earlier. Graham stolidly ignored all this, marched his square round to the enemy flank and, when the expected

wild charge came, mowed down the Arabs by the hundred with steady volley fire. Having killed about 2,000 of them and broken their attack, the British then moved in to capture the fort on the hill, release the prisoners and re-take the old guns. All this was good work and well done, but at one point in the otherwise perfect battle Davis ordered the Black Watch to charge to their front. As at the time the only enemy ahead were those concealing themselves in holes and gulleys, the officers of the Regiment saw this as a completely pointless exercise. Instead they placed themselves in front of their men but instructed them to hold firm and wait until the order came from Colonel Green. As no such order was given by him nobody moved and, as a result, Davis gave the Black Watch a bad report to Graham, and Graham passed it on, with interest, to the troops.

'Black Watch,' he later hectored them, 'I am a plain-spoken man and I must tell you I am not pleased with what you did at Teb the other day'.

More in the same vein followed, Graham ending his scolding by assuring the sullen and resentful Highlanders that he would give them the position of honour leading

The Black Watch advance with fixed bayonets at the battle of El Teb. Although a victory, some confusion in the direction of the battle was evident and earned this proud regiment a rebuke from Graham which they were eager to refute at the first opportunity.

the advance in the next battle so that they could retrieve their honour. This hurt and it led directly to what followed at Tamaii. Capt Andrew Scott Stevenson of the Black Watch observed that this speech lowered moral considerably, and put it down to, '. . . General Davis's stupidity'.

For the most part the regiments fought as they had done in the Zulu War, in square or line. They had the Martini-Henry .450 single-shot, breech-loading rifle and many, hearing in advance of the power of a Dervish charge, had nicked or cut off the head of their bullets making them into 'dum-dums' to open up on impact. Even this added stopping-power failed to hold the Arabs in many cases however. The most obvious difference was that British troops now all fought in drab brown (khaki) uniforms instead of splendid red tunics. (Although it was

179

not until 1885 that the khaki drill became worn for all purposes other than ceremonial.) The white pith helmet was also khaki-covered, (with the regimental flash on the side) as was its neck protective curtain. The officers still wore trousers tucked into black booting while the men had *puttees*, (which had first appeared in the Afghan War), and carried spare rounds bandolier-style. They wore Sam Browne belting, braces and large, flapped pouches. The one exception, Assistant-Commissary-General R. A. Nugent refused to abandon the scarlet for the brown despite the temperatures. Graham recalled that the sight of his red tunic busy about its duties was a re-assurance for him that the jobs were getting done. Officers still carried the old 1822 style swords with the curved steel three-bar hilt, but Scottish regiments were equipped with claymores, while drummers, bandsmen and buglers had the bladed short sword.

All water had to be carried from Suakin and there were no roads. Camel tanks were brought out and the Navy provided barrels. There was a strong medical team on hand under Surgeon-Major W. D. Wilson and Surgeon-Major B. B. Connolly. Surgeons could be as exposed as the men when the fighting began. Surgeon J. Prendergast for example was himself badly wounded while attending a wounded man at the Tamaii battle.

Suakin, on the Red Sea. On the route from the newly-opened Suez Canal to the Indian Empire, Suakin could not be allowed to fall into the hands of the Mahdi's followers.

THE INITIAL ADVANCE

General Graham moved his army out from Suakin again at 18:00 on the evening of 11 March thus avoiding the worst excesses of the heat. Their immediate objective was the established camp of Baker's *zereba* (an enclosed temporary camp) which lay some eight and a half miles distant. The force marched under a bright moon with the night air soft and pleasant and, for the majority of the force, the conditions were pleasant, although the Naval Brigade with their heavier equipment, found it hard work. They left behind at Camp Suakin a garrison under the command of Lt-Col R. W. T. Gordon of the Argyll and Sutherland Highlanders, (under the order of Admiral Hewett), which consisted of 100 Royal Marines with five guns mounted in defensive positions, as well as the sick and weak men left in charge of the camp whose tents were all left standing. The Cavalry Brigade and Mounted Infantry, under Brig-Gen Stewart, were also left behind overnight but had orders to join the Infantry early next day.

At dawn Stewart's Cavalry and Mounted Infantry watered at Suakin and joined the rest of the force at Baker's *zereba* around 07:00.

At about 10:00 Graham received word from the Mounted Infantry that the Dervish main forces were about six miles ahead and the men were sent to their dinners and, this done, the whole force prepared to move out by 13:00. The day was baking hot and frequent halts

General Graham's force for the march to Tamaii

Royal Artillery
6th Battalion, 1st Brigade Scottish Division, (Major F. T. Lloyd)
7pdr Camel Battery with 8 guns, seven officers and 100 NCO's and men, with 66 camels carrying 90 rounds of ammunition per gun.
'M' Battery, 1st Brigade, (Major E. H. Holley). 9pdr Battery with 4 guns 3 officers and 66 NCO's and men, with 52 mules carrying 86 rounds per gun.

First Brigade (Brigadier-General Sir Redvers Buller, VC, KCMG, CB, ADC)
Staff Officers: Capt W. F. Kelly (Sussex Regiment) Brigade Major. *Lt J. T. St Aubyn (Grenadier Guards)* Aide-de-Camp. *Colonel Ardagh,* Intelligence Officer
26th Company, Royal Engineers (Major K. R. Todd, RE) 5 officers and 57 NCO's and men.
3rd King's Royal Rifles—formerly the 60th Regiment of Foot—Colonel Sir Cromer Ashburnham, KCB, ADC), 19 officers, 546 NCO's and men
1st Gordon Highlanders—formerly 75th Regiment of Foot—(Lt-Col D. Hammill, CB) 23 officers, 689 NCO's and men
2nd Royal Irish Fusiliers—formerly 89th Regiment of Foot—(Lt-Col B. S. Robinson) 17 officers, 326 NCO's and men

Second Brigade **Maj-Gen J. Davis)**
Staff Officers: Capt T. B. Hitchcock, (Shropshire Light Infantry) Brigade Major. *Lt C. C. Douglas, (Scottish Rifles)* Aide-de-Camp
1st Royal Highlanders,—formerly 42 Regiment of Foot—(Lt-Col W. Green) 19 officers, 604 NCO's and men
1st York and Lancaster, (formerly 65th Regiment of Foot) (Lt-Col W. Byam) 14 officers, 421 NCO's and men
Royal Marine Artillery and Light Infantry (Colonel H. B. Tuson, CB, ADC, RMA) 14 officers, 464 NCO's and men.
Naval Brigade (Capt Rolfe, Royal Navy) 4 Gardner machine-guns.
Army Medical Department (Deputy Surgeon—General E. G. M'Dowell)
The Abyssinian Scouts.

Cavalry (Brigadier-General Herbert Stewart)
Staff Officers: Lt-Col A. M. Taylor (19th Hussars) Brigade Major. *Lt. F. W. Rhodes (1st Dragoon Guards)* Aide-de-Camp
10th Hussars (Brevet-Colonel Evelyn A. Wood) 16 officers, 235 NCO's and men.
19th Hussars (Lt-Col A. G. Webster) 19 officers, 343 NCO's and men.
Mounted Infantry (Lt (Local captain) H. Humphreys, Welsh Regiment) 6 officers, 118 NCO's and men.
Giving total horse troops as 41 officers and 696 NCO's and men.

---

were necessary as the men marched across the burning scrubland. Sgt Danby described such a halt:

'The journey was most difficult . . . . we were served out with ship's biscuits and half a pint of water.'

After which the column moved on again. At about 17:00 the cavalry scouts came in to report that the enemy were advancing in force to attack. On the nearest piece of suitable ground which gave a clear field of fire for some distance ahead, Graham therefore deployed his force in a defensive position. Dusk was drawing on fast and there was clearly no point in advancing further that day. Accordingly the Royal Engineers and Battalion pioneers were sent to cut down the spiky mimosa bushes which covered most of the desert in this region and construct

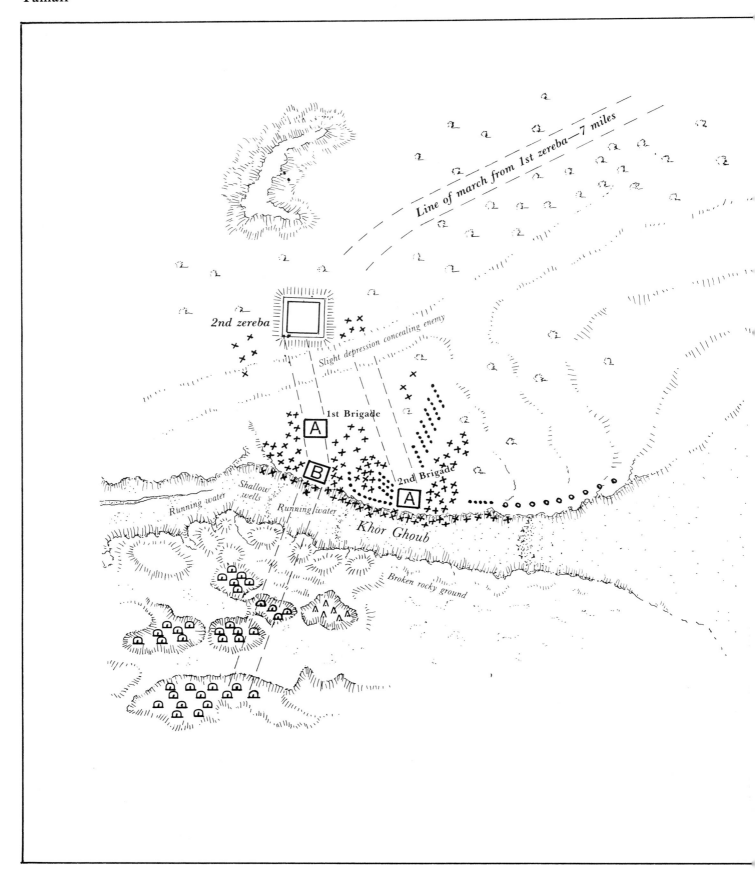

Line of march from 1st zereba—7 miles

2nd zereba

Slight depression concealing enemy

1st Brigade

A

B

2nd Brigade

A

Shallow wells

Running water

Running water

Khor Ghoub

Broken rocky ground

a *zereba* around the force.

At 18:00 the Mounted Infantry were sent back to Baker's camp to provide protection for the convoy of 245 camels carrying two days' supply of water, 4400 rations for the men, forage for 1,200 horses and reserve ammunition that was coming up from the coast in support in case any of the Dervishes worked their way round to the rear of the main force. Isolated shots penetrated gathering gloom from a ridge some 1,500 yards ahead, heralding the arrival of the advanced units of Digna's men. To keep this sniping to a minimum and to show the enemy what he was dealing with, Graham ordered out a pair of Major Holley's 9pdrs and they quickly fired two rounds apiece at these worthies, two of them exploding with great accuracy. Capt Rolfe also took one of his Gardners forward and after a few bursts no more was heard from the enemy. Not content with this, Rolfe undertook his own scouting mission in the darkness to see the effects of the fire. He reported that he found one or two dead bodies and also some Dervish sentries sound asleep! Further down the ridge he saw fires, and much shouting and dancing could be made out in the distance as the Dervishes worked themselves up into their customary frenzy for the day's work ahead. Meanwhile the convoy had duly arrived half-an-hour after these events. They had been attacked and thrown into a panic by just one Arab until a sergeant with the convoy grabbed his rifle and dropped the enemy with a single shot.

This was not the end of the night disturbances however. At 00:45 there was an alarm and long-range firing commenced from out of the blackness and continued at intervals for the rest of the night. The range was so great that the bulk of the shot was exhausted and merely dropped into the camp. It caused a few casualties, four men, two camel drivers and some horses were struck and one soldier of the York and Lancaster Regiment was killed, but it was chiefly instrumental in disturbing the men's rest, which no doubt was precisely its purpose. Capt Andrew Scott Stevenson recalled:

'It was moonlight and a shower of bullets were going over the square. It was lucky the ground we were on sloped as it did: our men behaved very well. They were not allowed to return the fire and it is very jumpy work being fired at for four hours. The ping, and purr, and whistle of the bullets was awful. The Colonel was sleeping near me on the top of the hill

The Battle of Tamaii

A	1st position of Brigades
B	2nd position of Brigades
	Cavalry to cover advance of 2nd Brigade
o o o o o	Position of Mounted Infantry
	Dervish encampment
	Heaps of enemy dead

The battlefield at Tamaii, showing the British night encampment and the route taken by the two brigades.

and the bullets were whizzing very near our heads and one struck a water tin between us and another went thud into a folded blanket close to us. The Brigadier's horse was shot and one or two men killed and wounded. I hated that night and was glad to see the dawn.'

Although the Naval Brigade again ran out two of its machine-guns they held their fire. The range of the enemy was calculated by the interval between the flash of their rifles and the sound of the bullets and estimated to be about 1,400 to 1,500 yards, nor could any of the enemy be seen so Graham decided to refrain from any response rather than make ineffective noises in return.

With the dawn the camp was early astir and the Cavalry arrived from Baker's *zereba* at 07:00. Half-an-hour later Stewart sent the Mounted Infantry out to gauge the strength of the enemy. However the most precise intelligence was freely given by a deserter from Osman Digna's army. This worthy volunteered the information that the bulk of the Dervish force would be hidden in a deep *nullah*, or dry water-course, known as the Khor Ghoub which ran through broken, rocky ground the complete length in front of Tamaii camp and wells before petering out in the smooth sand and gravel

Throughout the night preceding the battle the Dervish tribesmen kept up harrassing fire at long range, causing little damage but disturbing the men's slumbers.

of the plain. The steep sides of this wide gorge would serve perfectly as entrenchments for the defenders and mask any approach by way of Tesela Hill, a slightly rocky outcrop projecting from the otherwise featureless desert due north of the Dervish position. It was described as being about 60ft deep and 200-300ft wide, with steep sides almost impassable for cavalry.

Graham decided to make his advance to the left of this strong position and therefore approach it from where the frontal ground rose a little. From here the gulley could be swept by artillery and machine-gun fire and cleared to facilitate the general attack. In order to cross the open plain between the gorge and Tesela outcrop the British were to deploy their two Brigades, in separate squares in direct *echelon* to the left in order to give each other mutual support and covering fire, with the Mounted Infantry serving as an advance screen and flank support for the leading (2nd Brigade) square and the main cavalry force acting in the same role for the 1st Brigade in readiness to complete the rout.

THE BATTLE COMMENCES

The 2nd Brigade commenced the advance at 08:00 with their Abyssinian scouts to the fore and two squadrons of Mounted Infantry from the left rear, sent forward to skirmish. The left flank of the square comprised four companies of the 1st Royal Highlanders in open column of companies, the front face three more companies of the Black Watch and, with an interval of 30 yards, three companies of the 1st York and Lancasters. On the right flank of the square were three further companies of the York and Lancs, while a portion of the Royal Marines formed the rear face of the square. Inside, the Gatling and Gardner guns of the Naval Brigade moved forward ready to be run out when needed and the 9pdr Battery, together with its transport, also moved in rear of the right front of the square. As it moved out this square was joined by General Graham himself along with his staff officers. Now occurred a hitch which contributed a little to the course of the battle. As Davis's square moved out over the slight ridge, down the small depression and then across the plain, Buller's square was somewhat tardy in forming up and following it. Therefore the gap between the two, at first about 1,000 yards, although later closed to half that distance, was somewhat greater than Graham

had originally intended.

The advance had been in progress across the dry water-courses of the plain for only half-an-hour when the first Dervish counter-attack came boiling up out of the ravine directly ahead of the 2nd Brigade's square. One eyewitness recalled how:

'We could plainly see the enemy ranged all along the hills on our front and right. Their black forms stood out boldly against the glare of day. Some were within 1,200 yards. The main body however, appeared to be about a mile away.'

The Abyssinian Scouts were soon heavily engaged and began to fall back on the flanks to clear the field of fire of the square, wisely dragging their wounded with them. They were well aware of the fate of any man left behind. The 9pdr battery, under Major Holley, had also been ordered out of the square on the right flank in readiness to give supporting fire and was in a very exposed position should the line fail to hold. This first enemy onslaught began at 09:00. The Black Watch were steadily advancing, not firing a shot, expecting at any moment to be halted to await the charge of the enemy. However, when within about a hundred yards from the edge of the *khor*, Graham ordered Colonel Green to charge. The Colonel accordingly ordered the the Black Watch to

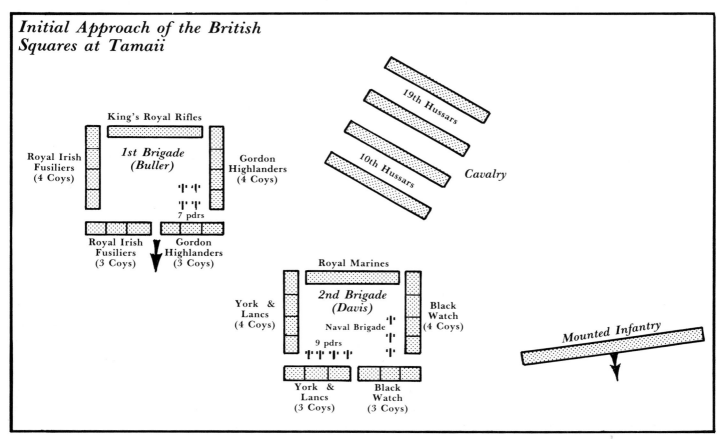

Initial Approach of the British Squares at Tamaii

comply, whereupon, '. . . with a terrific yell of delight . . .' 1, 2 and 3 Companies charged, followed by 4, 5, 6 and 7 in column of companies behind 3 Company. The mood of the regiment after their 'ticking off' by Graham the day before was described by Colonel Green as 'sticky'. What is certain is that there was a burning resentment of a false charge and they were not to be called laggardly a second time! However the other half of the front and right face of the square, the Yorks and Lancs, initially received no such command and in consequence the square became opened up as shown in the diagram below.

After a wild charge across some 700 yards of sloping desert the Black Watch reached the edge of the gorge where the front companies halted and the rear companies were ordered by their commanders to wheel into line. Thus dressed at the edge of the gully the Black Watch was fully deployed in advance of the rest of the 2nd Brigade's square. Although the enemy ahead were put to flight an even greater force, held in reserve, now appeared from out of the *Khor* and charged the great gap in the square, '. . . with reckless determination, utterly regardless of all loss . . .'. The weight of their attack burst upon the right-hand corner of the square where the Yorks and Lancs were struggling to close the space between

them and the Black Watch, and into which the Naval Brigade had been bringing its Gardners forward to hold the gap.

Burleigh related that:

'As we gained the edge of the *nullah* the fire became very hot on our front, the enemy mostly contenting themselves by attempting to rush at us with their spears and swords. The gaps in the square were meanwhile closed. Our men could not easily be got, despite trumpet calls and officer's shouts, to reserve their fire and aim carefully. In a few minutes our line was obscured by dense smoke from our own rifles, and under cover of this the enemy crept up the sides of the *nullah*, and a succession of rushes by our brave and resolute foes was made at the troops.

The 65th, who were on the right, and 42nd on the extreme left, were nearest the brink of the *nullah* which, on 65th's front, made a bend inwards towards them. Marines were in the rear. The enemy appeared to have gathered there 1,000 strong. Creeping up under cover of the smoke and sloping ground they dashed at the Marines and 65th. A hundred swarthy Arabs came bounding over the rocks up the plain, spear and sword in hand. Half were instantly shot down, but thirty or forty were able to throw themselves upon our

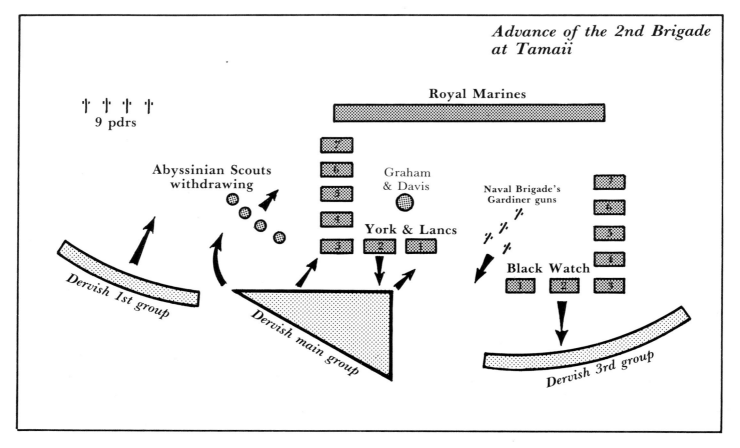

Advance of the 2nd Brigade at Tamaii

The Black Watch at Tamaii. Their eagerness to wipe away an earlier undeserved slur on their fighting qualities guaranteed their prompt compliance with the order to advance.

bayonets, giving and receiving fearful wounds.

Quick as lightning the rush increased, and in less time than it takes to tell the 65th gave way, falling back upon the Marines. To their credit be it ever said many men disdained to run, but went back with their faces to the foe, firing and striking with the bayonet. The bulk of the regiment crowded in upon the Marines, throwing them into disorder, and back everybody was born in a confused mass, men and regiments being inextricably mixed up.'

Capt Scott Stevenson recalled these ferocious moments vividly:

'During the charge the machine guns drawn by the Naval Brigade were left a little behind and were unable to get into their place on the right corner of my company. The Colonel ordered me to right wheel my right half-company. The Colonel then saw the Arabs were going to our right, so he ordered me to wheel up my left half and give them a flank fire.

Two Gatlings (*sic*) then came up and unlimbered among the left half of my company and I gave the word "protect the Gatlings". A perfectly terrific fire was now going on and I could not see to my front for smoke; the Gatlings near me never came into action. To my horror on looking round I saw crowds of Arabs at the Gatlings. One was on top of the gun and threw himself on me with a spear but it passed over my left shoulder and I hit him in the jaw with my right hand and sent him flying. Another came at me from under the gun and I just had time to kick him in the mouth. I had no time to draw my revolver and never fired it. I then drew my claymore. My brave Colour-Sergeant, Michael Johnstone, was hard at work with his bayonet beside me and he and my two Sergeants, J. E. Reid and William Anderson, were killed bravely fighting. We fell back crushed as it were by a weight and then my trusty claymore found its way to the hilt into several black devils. I clove a slice out of one of their heads just as one does an egg for breakfast and saw his white brain exposed. I was mad with rage and fury and had I not been a strong man I must have been thrown down and killed. I think God must have put a coat of armour on me that day. I received never a scratch and I killed five Arabs and assisted in the

As always the Naval Brigade strove to get into the thick of the action. At Tamaii they succeeded only too well. When the corner of the square opened out the brave sailors were cruelly exposed and hacked down at their guns.

The desperate fight 'midst scrub, sand and rock that was the battle of Tamaii. Hard-pressed the men of the 2nd Brigade fight to stem the Dervish onrush. It was typical of the hand-to-hand and close-quarters fighting.

slaughter of many others.'

Instantly the sailors were overwhelmed by the ferocious enemy hacking and stabbing in a black tide. Many officers and men were cut down as they stood by the guns, but fortunately had the sense to lock their weapons and remove their sights at the last instant so they could not be used. It was at this time, when bravely defending their charges, that Naval Lieutenants Almack, Houston Stewart, and Montresor, with seven seamen, were killed; Lt Conybeare and seven others being wounded. The survivors fell back fighting and thus, in a few terrible moments, the Arabs captured the machine-guns, by which, says Graham later, the men 'stood to the last'. Here too Pte Edwards, an Englishman serving with the Black Watch, and acting as a muleteer to the Navy machine-gunners, earned himself his Victoria Cross in trying to defend one of the Gardners.

The 2nd Brigade gave way some 800 yards gradually, moving in an easterly direction as they did so and fighting and dying fiercely as they withdrew in a no-quarter,

hand-to-hand scramble. Colonel Green, '. . . a splendid man . . .', shot two warriors dead and then his service revolver misfired. He was narrowly missed by a thrown spear and hit on the head by a thrown stone, which left him helmetless and wounded under the blazing sun until Capt Norman McLeod gave him his helmet and wrapped a cloth around his own head. Stevenson's subaltern also lost his helmet but fought on wearing a dead bluejacket's hat instead! Other Highlanders had their kilts pulled off them by the enemy, while a young officer, MacRae, who only joined the battalion the previous day, armed himself with an enemy spear and fought with it as ferociously as any Fuzzy-Wuzzy. In his choice of weapon he was probably well advised, as the very observant Burleigh again recorded:

'I again noticed the poor quality of the steel wrought into cutlasses and bayonets for the soldiers. If these weapons touched a bone, they bent like hoop iron without piercing the body of the Arabs. Their spears and swords, sharp as razors, cut, as I saw scores of

The advance resumes. Re-organised in line the 2nd Brigade advanced once more to the edge of the khor to re-capture their guns. The tribesmen resisted but steadily their masses were pressed back over the edge of the ravine.

them do, through bone, sinews, and every obstacle without turning the edge of the weapon. Another matter worth notice was that the savages made better use of their weapons than the troops. When they made a thrust it was invariably for a vital part, about the head, throat, or chest.

Tommy Atkins (the name the British soldier is always known by), after missing his man at short ranges, too often struck in such a way as to make grazing or slight flesh wounds. Two officers of the Black Watch, on the other hand, killed several of the enemy with their claymores, running the blades up to the hilt every time.'

Stevenson was later to write:

'After the action was over we found that when Graham ordered the 42nd to charge, he did not order the 65th on our right to do the same and therefore when we got to the gully there was no square and the Arabs came in on our right. Thus we lost 65 men and nearly all our sergeants. *Who is to blame for this?'*

The General himself provided the answer:

'For this disorder I am to some extent personally responsible, as the charge took place under my eyes, and with my approval. My own observations of the attack were made from the right front angle, formed by the two half-battalions of the 1st York and Lancaster, where I posted myself as soon as I saw the enemy's attack, and it was here that the first rush came. It is the habit of these Arabs to attack the angles of squares, as they know the least fire can be brought to bear on them from these points.

As the 9lb Battery was on the right, the sailors' guns were on the left, but I at once sent for them to meet this attack from the right. The Arabs, however, gave no time for further arrangements, but, throwing themselves with desperate determination upon the angle of the square, broke it, carrying all before them. There were many attempted rallies among the York and Lancaster, and at one time I was almost surrounded by the enemy, one of whom got over my horse's quarter.

In rear of the square were the Royal Marines, than whom there can be no finer troops, on whom I had calculated as a reserve in the last emergency. Such, however, was the sudden nature of the disorder, and the impetuosity of the rush, that the Royal Marines were for a few minutes swept back, and mixed up in the general confusion

And yet, I submit, there was no panic among the men; they had been surprised, attacked suddenly, and driven back by a fanatical and determined enemy, who came on utterly regardless of loss, and who were, as I have since learned, led by their bravest chiefs. As soon as the men had had time to think they rallied and re-formed.'

A little further back, the officers and gunners of the 9pdrs stood firm, although unprotected by infantry, and reversed the shells in the guns so that they burst just in front of the enemy. Thus raked with inverted shrapnel as an improvised form of case the advancing crowds of tribesmen had great swathes hewn out of chanting and shouting ranks and here they were stopped cold.

Meanwhile the 2nd Brigade was regaining its composure. From the rear came the cry of Major Colwell of the Royal Marine Light Infantry, 'Men of the Portsmouth Division, rally'. Some 150 Royal Marines did and formed their own small square. Soon other groups were similarly engaged, fighting back-to-back, thrusting and stabbing. The ranks held firm and the deadly onrush was halted all along the line. Thus the crisis of the battle passed.

THE BATTLE WON

The cost of stemming the attack had been heavy, some 35 bodies of the 65th and a similar number of the 42nd were counted within a fifty yard radius, '. . . all shockingly mangled and hewn with sword-cuts and spear-wounds . . .' Around them the corpses of the Arabs lay in mounds of hundreds.

One eyewitness emphasised the point made by Graham that, although thrown back, the men did not panic:

'I must revert to the way in which several hundreds of Marines and Highlanders fought back-to-back, firing and retiring in excellent order. They were over 200 yards to the Brigade front when it was halted and reformed, and to their great coolness and steadiness is largely due the final success of the day. Ten minutes after the rally was effected four Marines brought in a wounded comrade on a stretcher, and a private of the Black Watch came limping up to the square out of the jaws of death.'

One officer and fifteen men of the York and Lancs stood their ground as the onrush overwhelmed their corner of the square. They deserve to be remembered

The climax of the battle of Tamaii. The difficult nature of the terrain, and the tenacity of the Dervish wounded, is apparent in this sketch.

in that they saved a greater calamity. Capt C. W. Ford, Corporal W. Maynard, Lance-Corporal R. Mayors and Ptes J. Brophy, R. Cripps, G. Higginson, I. Hope, S. Le Blancq, P. Molloy, J. Pilbeam, C. Read, J. Richards, C. Rookyard, J. Roy, W. Webb and W. West. They, it was reported, '. . . stood their ground and would not be forced back'. Their mutilated bodies were later found strewn on the edge of the *nullah* in the positions they fought and died to hold the tide.

Likewise the artillery fought their position with vigour, Gunner W. Hanson of 'M' battery distinguished himself when, in a rush of Dervishes on his gun, a companion was overwhelmed. Nothing daunted, Hanson clubbed the fierce assailant with his rammer and drove him off thus saving his friend's life.

Meanwhile the 1st Brigade's square some 500 yards over to the right had been similarly assaulted. Here however the enemy wave had a greater distance to cover

with the 160 survivors from the Naval Brigade in the immediate rear of the line. Thirty rounds of ammunition having been fired off in repulsing the first attack fresh rounds were issued to each man, but they were strictly instructed to hold their fire this time until the enemy came within close range. All the time the 'Fuzzy-Wuzzy'warriors kept up a long-range hail of dropping fire which did little damage. Meantime the 1st Brigade, having broken its own onslaught, moved up on the right while some of the cavalry also moved into position here and the 100 Abyssinian Scouts, led by Mr Wyld of the Suakin police, again began individual combats with the Dervishes. They, following the usual practice, were infiltrating to the rear by crawling and creeping through the gullys, bushes and shrubs and behind the litter of red boulders, almost invisible.

To clear these and once more move forward to the lip of the gorge, the Line was advanced, with the Marines soon reaching the edge of the *kohr*, the whole British line firing steady volleys as they advanced, re-capturing all the lost machine-guns in the process and thus enabling the eager sailors to get them back into working order and turn them on their former captors. Despite the short time between their loss and re-capture the enemy had already managed to man-handle one of them down to the lip of the *nullah* and set fire to one of the ammunition limbers which burnt, hissed and sent off random shots for half-an-hour afterwards. As the steady advance proceeded, a flanking fire was maintained by the 1st Brigade's square which prevented any new envelopment by the enemy.

Once the edge of the gully was reached the remaining warriors hiding in it were quickly and simply picked off and it was soon cleared completely of the enemy. The 2nd Brigade held its position and then it was the 1st Brigade's turn to advance in their square, now commanded by General Graham, into the *nullah*, across it, and up and out the other side. This square moved at 11:00. Their immediate objective was to gain the further red granite ridge some 800 yards away. Beyond nestled Osman Digna's camp. As they crested this first ridge in blistering heat the bulk of the Dervish army could be seen massed atop the second ridge. The 1st Brigade opened a steady fire to which the Arabs replied with a wild and ineffectual volley and soon they began to trot off to the rear in obvious defeat, heading for the shelter of the distant mountains beyond.

The defeated warriors made off, 'slowly and sullenly', acting it was said, 'like men defeated but not routed'.

Thus the second ridge was taken almost without opposition and, a mere forty minutes or so after the final

in the open and suffered accordingly. Graham praised the ' great coolness and steadiness' of the 3rd King's Royal Rifles.

War correspondent Wylde watched the Dervish wave break against Buller's square:

> 'He commenced firing volleys at them. The Arabs who were in irregular formation, and from three to ten deep, came along at a run, and it was just like a big black wave running up a beach. It began to break on the crest, the white foam being represented by the men that fell simultaneously with every volley, and the way it began to grow less the more it approached the square. With 250 yards left it had nearly ceased, and not one man could get near enough to use his spear. It was an awful sight and as an exhibition of pluck, or rather, fanaticism, it could not be equalled.'

The 2nd Brigade finally reformed at 09:00, being dressed in line and then advancing once more for 100 paces before halting for fifteen minutes. In this formation the Royal Marines were placed on the right, the Yorks and Lancs in the centre and the Black Watch on the far left,

Admiral Sir William Hewett. This energetic officer was C-in-C on the East Indies station and also nominally the Governor of Suakin.

advance had commenced the British soldiers were looking down into the valley some 180 feet below. Here lay Tamaii, some hundred empty and deserted huts and Arab tents, numerous enough to hold some 7,000 natives, from which now only a few fanatics were firing. These last-ditch defenders were quickly despatched and the only occupant to greet the conquerors was a solitary woman with a bullet hole in her shoulder, which was immediately tended to. There was ample running water in the camp and in the huts and tents were found piles of stores and ammunition along with trophies and loot from their earlier massacres. Also taken were two of Osman Digna's personal battle flags.

There was no point in advancing any further. The country beyond was wild and broken which made cavalry pursuit out of the question other than a few probes to keep the enemy moving on. Graham therefore ordered bivouac at the village. Graham despatched a signal to Admiral Hewett giving the first news of the victory.

'Camp taken, after hard fighting since eight o'clock. Killed, over 79, among whom Montresor, Almack, H. Stewart, Naval Brigade; Aitken, Royal Highlanders; Ford, York and Lancaster. About 100 wounded.'

This brought considerable relief to the Governor for earlier heliographed messages seem to have magnified the 2nd Brigade's setback into a massive repulse, even the possible defeat of the whole army! Fortunately Hewett had the sense to prevent any such alarming signals being despatched to London until the true facts were known.

It was time to take stock. In fact the British dead totalled about 100, while among the wounded were Major Dalgetty and Dr Prendergast of the 65th, and Major MacDonald of the 42nd. However the surgeons were soon busy about their work. Colonel Barrow owed his life to the bravery of Quartermaster-Sergeant Marshall of the 19th Hussars, who stood over his body when he was wounded and brought him safely out of the mêlée. For his courage Marshall became the second winner of the Victoria Cross that day. In view of their known reluctance to die without taking as many of their enemies with them as possible the Dervish wounded were despatched without hesitation, as Capt Stevenson related:

'I took a splendid spear and killed a great many wounded men with it; it went into them like lightning and their blood flowed out on the sand. I had a

marvellous escape from a half-dead Arab. He sent his spear close to my leg and I stabbed him in the heart.'

Lest hands be raised in horror at this it should be remembered how the same Arabs responded to any of their British foes foolish enough to try to tend the enemy wounded though several men were speared and hacked by men they sought to aid before the lesson was again bitterly re-learnt.

The fighting over the men took a well-deserved rest that night. This time their sleep was undisturbed and, in the morning the camp was put to the torch and all munitions and stores destroyed. By 13:00, they were all in flames, the smoke rising in immense black volumes, broken here and there by the white vapour of exploding gunpowder. The effect of this spectacle must have been more telling upon Osman Digna and his followers than any number of proclamations. Then the whole British force marched back to the northern *zereba* and the cavalry returned to Baker's camp beyond and by the 15th the whole force was back at Suakin.

General Graham puts both the Dervish village and encampment to the torch, following the victory at Tamaii.

A WASTED VICTORY

As so often in Britain's long history, that which her soldiers' and sailors' fortitude and courage had accomplished was now immediately negated by political vacillation and weakness.

After the thrashing he had received and the melting away of his disillusioned survivors, Osman Digna had no choice but to retreat and for a brief period the road from Suakin to Berber lay open. The feeble flutterings of the lethargic Gladstone administration soon threw this chance to the wind.

On 12 March the tribes about the village of Halfiyeh, ten miles along the river below Khartoum, went over to the Mahdi and cut the telegraph wires connecting Gordon with Berber thus giving clear indication that these people had, after a long period of indecision, concluded that the Mahdi was more resolute than the British and that the threatened British army was never coming. This not only cut off Khartoum but placed Berber itself in the front line, thus effectively moving the prospect of war much closer to Cairo as Sir Garnet had foreseen. It also ended any hopes that Gordon might still be able to establish a credible Soudanese government in opposition to the Mahdi. Moreover even the prospect of being able to evacuate Khartoum was rendered almost impossible unless the British Government changed its mind on the use of force.

All links were cut south from Berber, save for nine armed steamers, these vessels available being insufficient to take out all the Egyptians, even if that had been practicable in the face of hostile warriors assembled on either bank for hundreds of miles. The rapids below Berber prevented the vessels' going further north so any such attempt would merely result in shifting the problem from Khartoum to that town and, with the withdrawal of Graham, Osman Digna's chastised army began regaining its confidence once more. The Berber-Suakin road was closed again, as was now the Berber-Korosko road as far as Abu Hamed. Baring was to write to Granville that he regretted allowing Gordon to go to Khartoum but now that he was there and cut off, 'I do not think we can leave him stranded if from a military point of view it is at all possible to help him'. He also wrote to the Government in England that, other than hoping Khartoum could hold until the autumn, 'the only other plan is to send a proportion of General Graham's army to Berber with instructions to open up communications with Khartoum . . . we all consider that, however difficult the operations from Suakin may be, they are more practicable than any operations from

Korosko and along the Nile'.

Graham was all for an attempt to fight his way through to Berber and had the full support of Admiral Hewett for such a policy, despite the acknowleged difficulties that would be encountered in crossing the 300 mile route from Suakin to Berber through the hell of the Nubian Desert. That white men could accomplish this was later to be postulated by Major De Cosson, who had wide experience of travelling in the remote areas of the Soudan and it was to be fully proven by a British sergeant who marched with a group of Egyptian reinforcements without any difficulty.

Graham wrote earnestly in favour of such an operation. 'Present position of affairs is that two heavy blows have been dealt at rebels and followers of the Mahdi, who are profoundly discouraged. They say, however, that the English troops can do no more, must re-embark, and leave the country to them. To follow up these victories, and bring waverers to our side, we should not proclaim our intention of leaving, but rather make a demonstration of an advance towards Berber, and induce a belief that we can march anywhere we please. I propose, therefore, making as great a show as possible without harassing troops. A strong battalion, with a regiment of cavalry, advances tomorrow to Handoub, and thence a reconnaissance will be made along the Berber road.'

Clearly he would have made the greater effort, indeed badly wanted to, despite the climate and lack of water. But he would not have suggested it had he not thought it feasible. To Gordon, a military man lacking political deviousness, such a move seemed the only logical course to take. He was frustrated by the time the Government were taking to authorise Graham to get on with it, but he hardly doubted that, in the end, word to proceed would come from London.

Naively he had earlier written to Baring. 'In the event of sending an expedition, the greatest importance is speed. A small advanced guard at Berber might keep the riparian tribes between this and Berber quiet, and would be an assurance to the populations of the towns'. Once the worst had come to pass he naturally expected the situation to be quickly retrieved. He warned what would happen otherwise. 'You must remember that when the evacuation is carried out, the Mahdi will come down here and, by agents, will not let Egypt be quiet. Of course my duty is evacuation and the best I can do for establishing a quiet government.' He added, 'Remember that once Khartoum belongs to the Mahdi, the task will be far more difficult'. He stressed that this was not due to Imperial ambition: 'I maintain fully the

policy of eventual evacuation, but I tell you plainly it is impossible to get Cairo employees out of Khartoum unless the government helps.'

So confident was he that Graham would be given the go ahead within a short period that he issued a proclamation in Khartoum that, 'British troops are now on their way, and in a few days will reach Khartoum'.

Both he and Graham had reckoned without the Cabinet's attitude. They had made a reluctant military gesture to hold Suakin, for Suakin lay athwart the vital sea route to India. No such consideration weighed in their commercial hearts with regard to Khartoum and it had no economic or stategic importance. As for Gordon and his aides, they seemed entirely expendable and not Gladstone's reponsibility. Granville spoke to the House of Lords expressing this view. There was absolutely no intention of the Government's despatching a costly military expedition at great risk just to save a man, 'who had volunteered for a forlorn hope'. The Foreign Secretary repeated this message even more clearly,

Death of a Victorian Hero. General Gordon is depicted fearlessly facing his final moments at the hands of the Mahdi's fanatical followers at the fall of Khartoum.

stating that, 'Her Majesty's Government are not prepared to send troops to Berber'.

On 25 March Granville amplified this attitude to Baring informing him that due to, 'the extraordinary risk from a military point of view, HMG do not think it justifiable to send a British expedition to Berber'. He added that Gordon was to be told that the Government gave him full discretion, 'to remain in Khartoum if he thinks it necessary or to retire by southern or any other route which may be found available'. In case there was any doubt the Government also curtly informed Graham that they had not the slightest intention of sending his force, or any other British troops, to Berber. On the contrary, they informed him, any further military operations by his force should be ended as quickly as possible and, 'must be limited to the pacification of the districts around Suakin'.

Even that which Graham and his men had so bravely and honourably achieved in following out his precise orders, was disparaged by the Prime Minister who sneered that these hard-fought victories had been nothing but the 'frightful slaughter of most gallant Arabs in two bloody battles'. Even Lord Cromer joined in the belittlement: 'It had been shown, not for the first time in history, that a small body of well-disciplined British troops could defeat a horde of courageous savages. But no other important object had been obtained'.

But the route lay open. In the reconnaissance made by Stewart on 22 March which penetrated as far as Tambok, there were no armed Arabs to be seen anywhere. The country along the route lay perfectly peaceful, so much so that a caravan of unarmed pilgrims from Central Africa arrived at Handoub after a fourteen day journey from Berber, entirely unmolested! Graham had achieved an important objective but the Government did not want to know it!

General Graham's reasoning failed to turn the Government from the policy on which it had embarked. He was ordered home and left for Egypt. Ever afterwards he was to regret bitterly not having turned his face away from the spineless posturings of Whitehall and taken the initiative without waiting for permission. It might have broken him but his old friend might have been saved and indeed the whole Soudan spared more than a decade of suffering and slaughter. But it was not to be.

The Queen had showed grave concern for events in the Eastern Soudan and had applauded the initial despatch of Graham's army. How did she feel at such craven behaviour by her Ministers? There was no doubt that she agreed with the General. On 25 March she wrote to the Secretary of State for War, Lord Hartington;

'Gordon is in danger: you are bound to try and save him'. She confided to her Private Secretary that the effort should be made, if not only for humanity's sake, but for the honour of the Government and the nation itself. In vain did she agonise, there was no moving such men. On the contrary, there was even talk of holding peace talks with Osman Digna and making this former slaver the Governor of the Province! This the two British commanders could not stomach and instead on 24 March, another column was despatched to try to force conclusions on him at Tamanieb, but, although they again burnt his stores and supplies, the elusive leader had slipped away.

But time proved that the wily Digna had read the situation clearly. The British were forced to leave the country, other than the immediate area around Suakin to him, and, with their departure his broken power slowly waxed fulsome again.

It was the beginning of the end and although the martyrdom of the gallant Gordon was still far ahead, and a last-minute change of heart resulted in a desperate rescue attempt mounted far too late, British politicians had already sealed his fate. Meanwhile, with the departure of Graham the whole British force in the Eastern Soudan withdrew to Suakin, and the bulk trans-shipped to Cairo. A holding force was left to keep the vital ports secure. The Royal Marines spent the rest of the year as part of that small garrison holding Suakin, based in makeshift forts and seeing little of the enemy. Graham returned the following year, and fought further battles with the same military outcome, but the political torpidity remained the same.

And so the victors departed the field of battle and abandoned it to the Dervishes. The fate of General Gordon was thus sealed.

As for the wild tribesmen, their place in military history is as secure as all those other courageous, tough opponents that Victoria's soldiers had met and defeated throughout the 19th century. Like the Sikhs, the Zulus and the Cossacks they had been beaten but they had earned the grudging, but sincerely felt, respect of the British soldier in the process. The words of Rudyard Kipling's eulogy to the Dervish warriors reflected this perfectly:

> Then here's *to* you Fuzzy-Wuzzy, an' the missus an' the kid,
> Our orders were to break you, an' of course we went and did.
> We sloshed with Martini's, an' 'twan't hardly fair,
> But for all the odds agin you, Fuzzy-Wuzzy, you broke the square.

Select Bibliography

Apart from the many Regimental and Official Histories, herewith are listed some of the more accessible sources which I have consulted. This list is by no means comprehensive.

Armytage, Fennella	Wars of Queen Victoria's Reign	1887
Barker, A. J.	The Vainglorious War 1854-56	1970
Benson, A. C. and Asher, Viscount	The Letters of Queen Victoria	1907
Blood, General Sir Bindon	Four Score Years and Ten	1933
Bond, Brian	Victorian Military Campaigns	1967
Burleigh, B.	Desert Warfare 1884-5	1885
Butler, Sir William	Campaign of the Cataracts	1887
Butler, Sir William	Sir Charles Napier	1890
Callwell, C. E.	Small Wars. Their principles and practice	1906
Churchill, Winston S.	The River War	1899
Clarke, Sonia	Zululand at War 1879	1984
Clay, Dr William	Battle of Gujrat (*Soldiers of the Queen*)	
Colenso, John William and Frere, H. Bartle	The Zulu War	1879
Colville, H. E.	History of the Sudan Campaign	1889
Department of Archives, National Army Museum	Sketch Plan of British Square at Ulundi, (Army Museum MSS 7612/82)	
Farmer, J. S.	The Regimental Records of the British Army 1660-1901	1901
Farwell, Brian	Queen Victoria's Little Wars	1973
Field, Colonel C.	Britain's Sea Soldiers	1924
Fitzgibbon, Andrew, VC	Letters and Documents, relating to Taku Forts, (Army Museum MSS 5910/284)	
Fortescue, Sir John	A History of the British Army	1930
French, Gerald	Lord Chelmsford and the Zulu War	1939
Gough, General Sir Charles and Innes, Arthur D.	The Sikhs and the Sikh Wars	1897
Gowing, Thomas	A Soldier's Experience	1896
Graham, General Sir G.	Papers and Report relating to the First Sudan Campaign and Battle of Tamaii (Army Museum MSS 7312/4)	

Harris, Henry	The Alma	1971
Herbert, Lieutenant General Hon Sir Percy	Letters to General Farren relating to the Brave Conduct of two soldiers of 47th Foot at The Alma, (Army Museum MSS 6112/479)	
James, Captain	(Letters to his mother relating to Magdala, March/April, 1868, Army Museum MSS 5910/87)	
Kinglake, Alexander William	The Invasion of the Crimea	1863
Lehmann, Joseph	All Sir Garnet	1964
Lovett, Major A. C. and MacMunn, Major G. F.	The Armies of India	1911
Low, Charles Rathbone	Her Majesty's Navy	1895
McCourt, Edward	Remember Butler	1967
Morris, Donald R.	The Washing of the Spears	1966
Myatt, F.	March to Magdala	1970
Napier, H. D.	Napier of Magdala	1927
Napier, Sir Robert	Papers, Report and Maps relating to Admiral Hope on the Capture of Taku Forts, (Army Museum MSS 7303/75)	
Pemberton, W Baring	The Battles of the Crimean War	1962
Russell, William Howard	Russell's Despatches from the Crimea 1854-1856	1966
Ryder, John	Four Years Service in India	1853
Sangster, William	Pictorial Records of the English in Egypt	1890
	Second Sikh War 1848-49 (USI of India Journal)	1899
Shadwell, Lawrence	The Life of Colin Campbell, Lord Clyde	1881
Simkin	Our Soldiers and Sailors in Egypt	1888
Spiers, Edward M.	The Army and Society	1980
Stevenson-Hamilton, V. E. O.	Action at Tamai, *(Red Hackle)*	1970
Stothead, Lieutenant E A, 93rd Highlanders	Letter to his brother Richard, relating to The Alma, dated 21 September, 1854, (Army Museum MSS 6905/25)	
Stokes, F L	Letters to his nephew relating to the Battle of Googerat (1849), March/April, 1849 (Army Museum MSS 6710/1)	
Strachan, Hew	European Armies and the Conduct of War	1983
Tuck, Private M. M., 58th Foot	Diary relating to Ulundi, (Army Museum MSS 7005/21)	
Vetch, Colonel R. H.	The Life and Letters of Sir Gerald Graham	1891
Vine, P. A. L.	By Elephant to War in Abyssinia (*Country Life*)	1977
Wilkinson-Laltham, Christopher	Uniforms and Weapons of the Zulu War	1978
Wilmot, A.	History of the Zulu War	1880
Wolseley, Sir G.	The Story of a Soldier's Life	1903
Wood, Evelyn	From Midshipman to Field Marshal	1906
Wyle, I.	'83-'87 in the Soudan	1888
Young, Peter & Lawford, J. P.	The History of the British Army	1970

Index

Illustration Credits

BBC Hulton Picture Library: p8-9, 140, 141, 173.

Mary Evans Picture Library: p194.

Philip Haythornthwaite: p31, 32, 40-45 (top), 48-49, 58 (top), 60, 62-63, 71 (top), 82 (bottom), 94, 97, 98, 103, 104, 110, 116, 119, 142, 146, 169 (right).

Military Archive & Research Services: p2-3, 10-11, 12, 14, 15, 16, 18-20, 22-26, 36-39, 61, 64-69, 71 (bottom), 73, 76-77, 78, 79, 85-87, 95, 111-113, 118 (bottom), 122, 125 (bottom)-128, 130-131, 134-136, 143-145, 147-151, 155-162, 163 (bottom), 164, 167, 169, 172, 174, 176, 179-187, 190-193.

National Army Museum: p13, 21, 33, 34, 35, 45 (bottom), 47, 52-57, 58 (bottom), 59, 70, 76, 80, 82 (top), 83, 84, 88-89, 90 (bottom), 96, 97, 98, 101, 102, 104, 105, 107-109, 115, 117, 118 (top), 120, 121, 125 (top), 129, 133, 137, 153, 154, 163 (top), 165, 166, 170-171, 175, 178, 188 (left), 189.

P Smith: p91 (top).